A Prescriptive Behavioral Checklist for the Severely and Profoundly Retarded

A PRESCRIPTIVE

BEHAVIORAL CHECKLIST FOR THE SEVERELY AND PROFOUNDLY RETARDED

BY **Dorothy Popovich, M.A.**

Instructor, Department of Educational Psychology
College of Human Resources
West Virginia University

University Park Press Baltimore • London • Tokyo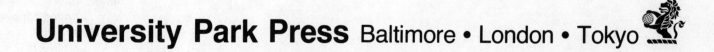

UNIVERSITY PARK PRESS
International Publishers in Science and Medicine
Chamber of Commerce Building
Baltimore, Maryland 21202

Typeset by The Composing Room of Michigan, Inc.
Manufactured in the United States of America by Collins Lithographing and Printing Co., Inc.

Library of Congress Cataloging in Publication Data
Popovich, Dorothy.
A prescriptive behavioral checklist for the severely
and profoundly retarded.

Bibliography: p.
1. Mentally handicapped children. 2. Mentally
handicapped children—Education. 3. Mentally
handicapped—Rehabilitation. I. Title.
HV891.P66   362.7'8'2   77-3614
ISBN 0-8391-1100-2

Contents

SECTION III APPENDICES

Preface

Before 1974 there were few provisions for educating severely and profoundly retarded persons. Retardates kept at home were sometimes fortunate enough to find a community center that was day-care oriented; those who were institutionalized were often relegated to "back wards" for custodial care.

The general inability to meet the educational needs of retarded persons was detailed in hearings before an ad hoc subcommittee of the Education and Labor Committee of 1966. At that time it was reported that only one-third of approximately 5.5 million children were being provided with an appropriate specialized education (*US Congressional and Administrative News,* 1974, p. 4257). Severely and profoundly retarded persons were, for the most part, not among the third receiving an education.

Nine years after the above statistics were reported there was little call for optimism; census data again demonstrated a continued deficit in programs designed for this population: only 40 percent of mentally retarded persons were receiving training appropriate to their special needs (*US Congressional and Administrative News,* 1974, p. 4138). In 1974, Public Law 93-380 was passed, admonishing the individual states to identify and evaluate their retarded citizens. Promise became the catch-word.

The task of identifying and evaluating these persons has been a laborious one. Tests initially designed for normally developing children have been adapted for this purpose, often failing to assess the lower functioning levels in detail.

Recent instruments designed specifically for assessing and training this population have taken a more global approach to the retarded person. AAMD's Adaptive Behavior Scale for Children and Adults (Nihira et al., 1975) assesses eating, toilet use, social language development, numbers and time, perseverence, and numerous other behaviors. The Primary Progress Assessment Chart (PAC) of Social Development (Gunzburg, 1966) has been used to provide an assessment for parents and teachers in the areas of self-help, socialization, communication, and occupation. Similarly, the Vulpe (Vulpe, 1970) assessment battery for home care and management of the mentally retarded assesses areas such as basic senses and function, play, body concepts, gross motor skills, and behavior and work habits. Included in the Vulpe were many of the skills needed for assessment of the lower functioning persons. The Camelot Behavioral Checklist (Foster, 1974) is unique in providing an extensive bibliography for use in creating a prescription for the deficit skill areas.

Through the use of these and other instruments, an analysis of both the positive and the negative aspects of each assessment was initiated. These analyses provided direction for the writing of this book. All of the instruments, though positive contributions, had the same deficits to varying degrees: they did not include the areas involving early infant development (i.e., head control, grasping) and, more importantly, lacked a prescription for remediation.

This book was written to fulfill the requirements of evaluating severely and profoundly retarded children as well as prescribing an individualized method of teaching the needed skills. The Prescriptive Behavioral Checklists cover the following areas: eye-hand coordination, language development, physical eating problems, and motor development.

The Checklists are prescriptive in that each Objective on the Checklist has a corresponding Task Analysis, which breaks down the Objective into easy-to-teach Steps. Principles of operant psychology are used in the design of the Checklists and Task Analyses, as well as in the actual teaching of the Objectives.

The activities in each area are prerequisites for developing communication and self-care skills. The motor coordination objectives prepare the student to walk, the eye-hand coordination objectives facilitate hand function, and the language development objectives build early receptive language.

EFFECTIVENESS

This curriculum in its present form has been used for two years in Macomb County, Michigan, and an HEW Hospital Improvement Grant No. 51-P-15511/3-01 has been received to demonstrate the efficacy of the program. The graphs beginning on page 422 indicate the progress made by the first seven profoundly retarded students in the West Virginia program. These students were nonambulatory residents of a West Virginia institution for the retarded. All of the students were residents of a crib ward and were grouped together for instruction. The graphs indicate their progress over a period of nine months.

A multiple baseline was taken before intervention began. Training was conducted by the ward aides with a ratio of one ward aide to 5½ students. Two fifteen-minute maintenance sessions occurred each afternoon for each student. At this time the student was required to perform the learned task in the appropriate area outside the training center.

The use of this text is not limited to the institutional setting. It was implemented by the author in a day care center in Mt. Clemens, Michigan, and in a community and parent program in West Virginia. For optimal success the program should be implemented at home as well as in school, or, if being conducted in an institution, training should transpire seven days a week with an aide to student ratio of 1/4.

CHECKLIST RELIABILITY

Thirty-one samples of inter-rater reliability were taken on the Checklists. A percentage of agreement was computed for each Checklist area. The percentages were as follows:

Eye-Hand Coordination	99%
Attending	90%
Auditory Training	90%
Physical Imitation	97%
Sound Imitation	98%
Concept Development	96%
Object Discrimination	96%

Motor development and physical eating problems were trained through the physical therapy department, and reliability checks were not taken in those areas. Although the percentages were high, criteria for each Objective are listed in Chapter 9 for further explanation.

USE

The use of the Checklists and the prescriptions for remediation are detailed in Chapters 2, 3, 4, 5, and 6. These chapters follow a programmed instruction format. The user should first read the chapter then answer the questions, which test chapter comprehension. The correct answers can be found in Appendix Two. The user is advised to check the questions as soon as they are answered.

A series of stories and questions also follow each chapter. These stories give the user an opportunity to apply the principles learned. Answers to these stories can be found in Appendix Three and should be checked immediately after writing out the answer. Re-read any subject area that was missed in the question-answer section before continuing to the next chapter.

The actual presentation of this book has, wherever possible, sought to minimize the use of jargon with the hope that such an approach will facilitate communication and understanding among parents, aides, teachers, and nurses.

SUGGESTED READINGS

Barro, S. M. 1970. An approach to developing accountability measures for the public schools. Phi Delta Kappan 52:196–205.

Bijou, S. W. 1968. The mentally retarded child. Psychology Today 2:47–50.

Skinner, B. F. 1968. The Technology of Teaching. Appleton-Century-Crofts, New York.

Travers, R. M. W., Van Wagenen, R. K., Haygood, D. H., and McCormick, M. 1964. Learning as a consequence of the learner's task involvement under different conditions of feedback. J. Educ. Psych. 55:167–173.

Travers, R. M. W. 1967. Essentials of Learning. 2nd Ed. MacMillan, New York.

Wallen, N. E., and Travers, R. M. W. 1963. Analysis and investigation of teaching methods. In: N. L. Gage (ed.), Handbook of Research on Teaching. Rand-McNally, Chicago.

Acknowledgments

A Prescriptive Behavioral Checklist for the Severely and Profoundly Retarded has been developed over a period of six years. It would not have been possible without the assistance of Don Thomas, Director of Special Education, Macomb County, Michigan, and the following training aides who implemented the Task Analyses as they were being written: Sherry Kohrs, Theresa Kulikowski, Denise Groves, Lorraine Totske, Doris Ivory, and Sherry Hathcock. I would also like to thank Anna Brown, P.T., for her assistance in developing the Motor Coordination Checklists.

Finally, I should like to thank Dick Walls, without whose assistance and encouragement this publication would not have been possible, Rogers McAvoy and Julie Vargas for their assistance, Rodney Katich for his editing, and Richard Kulics for his unending patience and understanding.

TO MY FATHER

A Prescriptive Behavioral Checklist for the Severely and Profoundly Retarded

SECTION I

USING THE CHECKLISTS AND THEIR ELEMENTS

CHAPTER ONE

An Instructional Cycle

Operant psychology is a behavioral science that develops practical techniques for producing changes in socially significant behaviors (Baer, Wolf, and Risley, 1968). It has been used to eliminate disruptive behaviors (Ayllon and Roberts, 1974), eliminate inappropriate speech of the severely retarded (Barton, 1970), train correct utensil use in retarded children (Nelson, Cone, and Christopher, 1975), and control chronic self-injurious behavior (Tate, 1972). The list of undesirable behaviors eliminated and those desirable behaviors added to the repertoire of the retarded are extensive. The techniques of operant psychology have become a major tool in teaching the retarded population. The use of this behavioral science begins as Behavioral Objectives are written. Behavioral Objectives are the central element of the Prescriptive Behavioral Checklists presented in the second section of this text, but before discussing their importance in the instructional cycle, a brief outline of the Checklists and their elements is given here.

The flow chart shows each element and its internal relationship to the Checklist. Each *Area,* such as Motor Development or Eye-Hand Coordination, has its own *Checklist,* which lists Behavioral Objectives in an ascending order of complexity. Each *Objective* has a corresponding *Criterion,* which explains in fuller terms what behavior the Objective is teaching. Each Objective also has a list of *Task Analyses,* which break the behavior down into small, easy-to-follow *Steps* as an aid in teaching the Objective. Added to each Objective is an *Implementation* section listing the various materials to be used, any prerequisite skills needed, and any problems the teacher may encounter with that particular Objective. Each of the chapters in this section discusses these elements as they are used for understanding the instructional cycle, assessing students, prescribing a curriculum, training aides, and collecting behavior data.

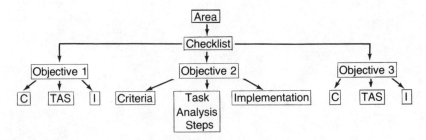

When assessing a student, the Behavioral Objectives listed in the Checklists state specifically what behavior is to be observed. Use of these Objectives helps to make communication clear to everyone involved in the behavior change process as well as to provide a consistent description for everyone observing the student. The Checklists provide a direct observation for the assessor.

Deficit areas are apparent after the student has been assessed on the Behavioral Checklists. For example:

BEHAVIORAL CHECKLIST FOR EYE-HAND COORDINATION
Objectives

The student will:

1. make random patterns in shaving cream
2. make random patterns in finger paint
3. grasp a sound tube

If the student can do Objectives 1 and 2 but not 3, the teacher now knows what behavior the student does not possess in his repertoire of skills, and she can now train the student on Objective 3, "... grasp a sound tube."

Once the Behavioral Objective to be taught has been determined, the cycle of instruction begins. The instructional cycle comprises four variables: the *Behavioral Objective, stimulus, response,* and *reinforcer.*

The *Behavioral Objective* states specifically what behavior is to be observed. The *stimulus* is the event that precedes and sets the occasion for the response. The stimulus can be a toy, a demonstration, a command, or a combination of these elements. The *response* is the activity the student performs. It is the actual performance, such as sitting, walking, grasping a ball, or stacking a stacking ring. *Reinforcers* are the things or events following a behavior that will increase the possibility of the behavior occurring again.

INSTRUCTIONAL CYCLE

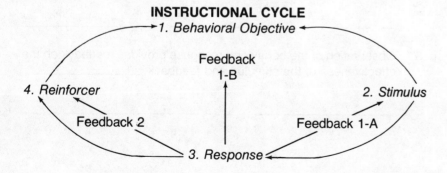

There is also a component *within* the instructional cycle, *feedback.* Feedback segments of the instructional cycle provide the following:

1-A. Observation of the behavioral response provides feedback on the effectiveness of the stimulus. For example, Johnny, a student, is being trained to press the button on the busy box, but he is not responding to this activity. The stimulus should then be changed. Another toy can be used that has only one button present, or the extraneous objects on the busy box can be "masked" by .covering the extraneous object with colored tape that corresponds to the color of the toy.

1-B. Observation of the behavioral response provides feedback on the choice of Objectives. An Objective that is too easy or too difficult may have been selected. For example, Johnny was not capable of pushing a button on the busy box. The teacher manipulated the stimulus in the following way:
 1. She masked out extraneous objects on the busy box.
 2. She provided him with a toy that had only one button on it.
 3. She provided him with a toy that had many buttons placed close together, hoping he would press one of them.
 It was now obvious that the Objective was too difficult for Johnny. The teacher went back to the Eye-Hand Coordination Checklist to select a manipulative task that would be easier for Johnny.

2. Observation of the reinforcer provides information on its effectiveness. If the student is not progressing as expected, the reinforcer may be inadequate for the Objective to be completed. This would necessitate selecting a more appropriate reinforcer. For example, Ms. Smith, a teacher, may give John, a student, a piece of her favorite chocolate every time he places a stacking ring on a spindle. As the teacher places the chocolate in the student's mouth, he tries to turn his face away. After one and a half months of training, the student is still placing only one stacking ring on the spindle and will not place a second one on. In this instance, if the teacher were aware of what the feedback is telling her, she would know that chocolate candy is not a reinforcer for this particular student.

Teachers should be sensitive to the feedback the instructional cycle provides. Instruction should be manipulated to facilitate individual needs. This can be accomplished only by being aware of what the student is communicating through feedback.

CHAPTER ONE/Questions

All of the questions below must be completed with 100-percent accuracy before going on to the Chapter One stories.

1. What is operant psychology?

   _____

   _____

2. Draw a flow chart of a Behavioral Checklist and its elements.

3. A B_____ O_____ specifies exactly what behavior is to be observed.

4. Behavioral Objectives help to:

   a._____

   b._____

5. Draw and label the diagram of the "instructional cycle."

6. Write out a definition for each of the four labels on the circle of the diagram.

   _____

   _____

   _____

   _____

   _____

   _____

7. Observation of the behavioral response provides feedback on the effectiveness of the stimulus and feedback_____

   _____

   _____

8. What type of feedback does the observation of the reinforcer provide?

_____

9. How does the student indicate that there are problems with instruction?

_____

10. Identify the stimulus, response, and reinforcer in this unit of instruction.

_____

_____

_____

Story 1-A

Sammy, a student, has completed the first two Objectives on the Eye-Hand Coordination Checklist. He now begins Objective 5, " . . . release a sound tube in a box."

The teacher sits directly across from the student and gains his attention by calling his name. Then, as she drops the sound tube into the box, she commands, "Sammy, do this." The teacher then immediately puts a sound tube in the student's hand, and he drops it into the box. She then squirts cherry Kool-Aid into his mouth and he immediately spits it out.

1. Identify the following components of the instructional cycle:

Objective

Stimulus

Response

Reinforcer

2. What feedback did you receive from the response? Explain in detail.

3. What feedback did you receive from the reinforcer?

Story 1-B

Miss Terry, a teacher, has counted 10 gray hairs on her head since she began training Bradley. Bradley is two years old, and he cannot sit. He was assessed on the Motor Development Checklist and completed Head and Trunk Control and Sitting; he is now on Objective 4, " . . . sit without support." Miss Terry has worked with Bradley on this Objective for two months. When he did not respond she used all the suggestions in the implementation to change the stimulus provided. Miss Terry also asked the ward aides to refrain from giving Bradley his favorite juice so it could be used only during training sessions. Miss Terry knew that she was long overdue for an assessment of her situation. Help her by filling in the questions below.

1. Identify the following components of the instructional cycle:

   Objective

   Stimulus

   Response

   Reinforcer

2. What type of feedback did you receive from the response? Explain in detail.

3. What feedback did you receive from the reinforcer?

Story 1-C

Susan, an aide, feels as though her job has lost its importance because of the following situation:

Linda had completed the first 13 Objectives on the Eye-Hand Coordination Checklist and has been responding well to her reinforcer, lemonade. Susan has been training Linda on Objective 14, ". . . slide the knob on the busy surprise box." Susan sits across from Linda and gains her attention by calling her name, "Linda," and giving the command, "Do this," as she slides the knob on the busy surprise box. Linda immediately reaches up and pushes the button and laughs hysterically. She has done this for the entire training session five days in a row. Susan realizes that she should have analyzed the situation a few days ago. See what she found out by answering the following question.

1. Identify the following components of the instructional cycle:

   Objective

   Stimulus

   Response

   Reinforcer

Suggested Readings

Ackerman, J. M. 1969. Operant Conditioning Techniques for the Classroom Teacher. 6th Ed. Linn County Mental Health Clinic, Albany, Oregon.

Anderson, R. C., Faust, G. W., Roderick, M. C., Cunningham, D. J., and Andre, T. (eds.). 1969. Section V, Reinforcement and feedback. In: Current Research on Instruction. Prentice-Hall, Englewood Cliffs, N.J.

Giradeau, F. L. 1971. The systematic use of behavior principles in training and teaching developmentally young children: In: B. Stevens (ed.), Training the Developmentally Young. John Day, New York.

Hall, R. V., and Broden, M. 1967. Behavior changes in brain-injured children through social reinforcement. J. Exper. Child Psych. 5:463–479.

Kuhlen, R. G. (ed.). 1968. Section 9, Methods of Providing Reinforcement in the Schools. Studies in Educational Psychology. Blaisdell, Waltham, Mass.

Wittrock, M. C., and Twelker, P. A. 1964. Prompting and feedback in the learning retention and transfer of concepts. Bri. J. Ed. Psych. 34:10–18.

CHAPTER TWO

Use OF THE Prescriptive Checklists

Five hundred thousand teachers with special education certification would be needed if the nation's seven million retarded children were to receive an adequate special education. There are currently 175,000 teachers with these qualifications and there is little hope that the shortage will be overcome (Smith, 1971).

Not only is there a shortage of teachers for the retarded, there is also a limited amount of diagnostic services for this population as well. Yet these problems are not insurmountable if a teacher possesses a tool to assess the whole person and a prescription to direct the student's instructional needs.

After reading this chapter, you will be able to assess students through the use of the Behavioral Checklists. Student assessment is the first step toward providing the adequate education the handicapped person is entitled to receive.

METHOD OF ASSESSMENT

Equipment or materials and environment are prepared before the assessment is begun, whether it occurs in the home, hospital, institution, or school. The Materials Lists at the end of this book are categorized according to individual areas such as Motor Development and Language Development (see pages 407–409). It is recommended that only one area be assessed each day when you are assessing institutionalized students or hospitalized patients.

The ideal setting is a quiet room with a small table and chair, a cerebral palsy or relaxation chair for extremely active students, and a mat on the floor for the gross motor activities. A small cabinet to store the necessary materials is also helpful to minimize extraneous stimulation. Only one toy should be in view during assessment.

All of the equipment used in the Behavioral Checklists can be purchased or ordered from your local toy or discount store. Be certain that the toys you are using are those specified in the Materials List.

Assessment area, name, and date should be recorded on a cover sheet and attached to the appropriate Checklist. A final spot-check in the equipment cabinet should be made to ensure the presence of appropriate materials and selection of the first toy to be used.

After the room is ready and the correct toy has been selected, the student should be brought to the room. If you have never interacted with this student before, you will want to talk to him in his own environment. Often, it is helpful to have a ward aide, nurse, or parent present if the student appears frightened or overly anxious. This support person can leave the assessment room after the student has become accustomed to you.

ASSESSMENT RATING SYSTEM

Direct observation is used to assess the student on the Behavioral Checklists. It is recorded by indicating a check mark (√) for a positive response and a no mark (—) for a negative response after each Objective.

Criteria for each Objective are listed in Chapter 9. The criterion for each Objective on the Checklist being used for assessment must be kept within the rater's view during assessment. This will provide a cue to the rater as to the behavior she should observe for a positive (√) rating. It will also ensure reliability among raters if the criterion is consistent. For example:

A teacher is assessing Sammy, a student, on the Eye-Hand Coordination Checklist. The student is to perform Objective 6, " . . . pick up a clutch ball."

The teacher picks up the ball and says, "Sammy, do this," as she holds the ball. She then holds the ball, awaiting the student's response.

The criterion for this Objective (p. 80) states, "The student will pick up and hold a clutch ball for five seconds upon command after it has been placed on the table." The teacher obviously was not reading the criterion for the correct response and, as a consequence, the student does not receive credit for a behavior which may well be a part of his repertoire.

The assessment chain's four variables are:

1. *Behavioral Objective*
   ↓
2. *Stimulus*
   ↓
3. *Response*
   ↓
4. *Rating*

The *Behavioral Objective* states specifically what behavior is to be observed. The *stimulus* is the event that precedes and sets the occasion for the response. The stimulus can be a toy, a demonstration, a command, or a combination of these variables. The *response* is the activity the student performs. The *rating* is a (√) if the response is positive as stated in the criterion for that Objective; the rating is left blank if the response is negative. For example:

The teacher rereads the instruction and reassesses Sammy on Eye-Hand Coordination Objective 6.

1. Behavioral Objective—The student will pick up a clutch ball.
2. Stimulus—The teacher says, "Sammy, do this," as the teacher picks up and holds the clutch ball, then places the clutch ball on the table.
3. Response—Sammy picks up and holds the clutch ball.
4. Rating—The teacher checks off the Objective on Sammy's Checklist to indicate he has completed Objective 4.

In the preceding example it is apparent that the rater engages in three behaviors. She 1) selects the Objective and reads through the criterion, 2) presents the stimulus, and 3) rates the student's response. The second behavior, presenting the stimulus, must be implemented in very precise, consistent steps. It sets the occasion for the response and must give the student every opportunity to respond correctly.

In the above example, three elements have been combined to present the stimulus: 1) a command, "Sammy, do this"; 2) a demonstration, "The teacher picks up and holds the clutch ball"; and 3) a toy, the clutch ball. The stimulus, a combination of toy, command, and demonstration, may be presented each time to give the student every opportunity to respond. The response will be compared to the criterion set for that specific Objective, and if it is correct or incorrect the appropriate mark will be given and the assessment chain will be completed for the Objective.

CHAPTER TWO/Questions

All of the questions below must be completed with 100-percent accuracy before going on to the Chapter Two stories.

1. There is a tremendous shortage of teachers for the retarded. List two ways a teacher can overcome the problems of too many students and too few diagnostic services.

   a._____

   b._____

2. E_____ and e_____ are prepared before the assessment is begun.

3. A nurse would like to assess the 20 patients on her ward. Give her advice on the number of Checklists to be assessed in one day with each patient.

   _____

4. The ideal setting for assessment is a small room. List the five things this room should contain.

   t_____

   c_____

   c_____ _____ _____

   m_____

   c_____

5. Why should the rater have all toys put away except for the one she is using?

   _____

6. True or False (circle one)
   Toys of your choice can be used in assessing your students.

7. When should the student be brought to the assessment room?

   _____

8. List the information needed for the Behavioral Checklist cover sheets.

   1._____

   2._____

   3._____

9. D_____ o_____ is used to assess students on the Behavioral Checklists.

10. How is the direct observation recorded on the Checklist?

    _____

11. Select one Objective and write out the criterion for it.

    _____

    _____

12. The criterion for a Behavioral Objective will provide a cue to the rater as to the behavior she should observe for a positive rating (√).

It will also _____

_____

_____

13. Draw and label the assessment chain.

14. Write out a definition for each label on the assessment chain.

_____

_____

_____

_____

_____

_____

15. What combination of elements have been used to present the stimulus?

_____

16. What elements does the assessment chain have that the instructional cycle lacks? Why?

_____

_____

_____

17. What is the difference between the instructional cycle and the assessment chain?

_____

_____

_____

_____

18. When a stimulus is presented it should take the form of a toy, command, demonstration. Give two illustrations of this procedure.

_____

_____

19. When is the assessment chain completed?

_____

20. Write a story that illustrates the Behavioral Objective, stimulus, response, and rating. Label each segment of the story appropriately.

Story 2-A

A principal is using the Behavioral Checklist to determine its effectiveness with the profoundly retarded students in his day-care center. He came to the conclusion that it was a useless tool because the students did not respond. After reading a sample of his method of assessment, analyze the techniques in reference to the assessment chain.

Using the Behavioral Checklist for Sound Imitation, the principal selects the first Objective, " . . . clap hands upon command." He turns to Sonya, a student, who is seated across from him, and says, "Sonya, clap your hands," Sonya does not respond, so the principal takes her hands and claps them for her. He places her hands on the table and says, "Sonya, clap your hands." Again, Sonya does not respond and the principal is reassured that no one ever responds to the Checklist.

1. What is the:

   a. Objective

   b. Stimulus

   c. Response

   d. Rating

2. Why isn't the assessment working for this principal?

Story 2-B

In this scenario, a teacher is assessing Sally, a student, on the Object Discrimination Checklist. The teacher selects the Objective, "... give spoon." She sits opposite the student and says, "Sally, give spoon." The student looks at her T-shirt and laughs.

1. What is the:

   a. Objective

   b. Stimulus

   c. Response

   d. Rating

Story 2-C

In this example a teacher is hesitant to assess a student using the assessment chain. She feels the student needs more help during the assessment. She has taken ten days to assess a student on the Attending Checklist.

The teacher holds a large doll in front of the student as she says, "look." The student turns her head away. The teacher gives the command again and holds the student's head in place so that she will look at the doll. The teacher immediately tells the student she is a good girl for looking at the doll and gives the student a big hug.

1. What is the Objective?

2. What is the stimulus? Is there an element in the stimulus that should not be there during assessment?

3. What is the response? Is there a real student response?

4. Is there an element from the instructional cycle? If so, what is it?

CHAPTER THREE

Prescribing
THE
Curriculum

Upon completing the assessment in each area, record the date of assessment next to each check mark to provide a record for each student. A series of check marks indicates behaviors that are a part of the student's repertoire. The blank spaces represent those behaviors needing training.

Prescribing the appropriate curriculum begins with viewing the entire Checklist, first within subject areas (i.e., Language Development/Attending, Motor Development/Sitting) and then across subject areas (i.e., Motor Development, Eye-Hand Coordination).

The first blank space encountered in each Checklist should be the behavior targeted for training. For example:

LANGUAGE DEVELOPMENT/Attending
Objectives

The student will:
1. fixate on an object upon the command, "Look"   *1/26/76*
2. follow a moving object in a horizontal pattern   *1/26/76*
3. follow a moving object in a vertical pattern   *1/26/76*
4. follow a moving object in a diagonal pattern   *1/26/76*
5. follow a moving object in a circular pattern   *1/26/76*

In the above example, Attending, Objective 5, "... follow a moving object in a circular pattern," should be the first Objective prescribed for training in the Language Development area. Training may occur simultaneously on an Eye-Hand Coordination activity requiring minimal visual attention as well as on a Motor Development Objective. The Objectives for Eye-Hand Coordination and Motor Development will be prescribed in the same fashion. For example:

MOTOR DEVELOPMENT/Standing
Objectives

The student will:
1. tolerate weight bearing on his feet while supported   *1/26/76*

15

2. support part of his body weight and actively bend and straighten his legs _____

EYE-HAND COORDINATION

Objectives

The student will:
1. make random patterns in shaving cream
2. make random patterns in finger paint
3. grasp a sound tube
4. release a sound tube

1/86/76
1/26/76
1/26/76
_____

The prescribed Objectives for the areas of Attending, Motor Coordination, and Eye-Hand Coordination would be the following:

Attending—Objective 5 " . . . follow a moving object in a circular pattern"
Standing—Objective 2 " . . . support part of his body weight and actively bend and straighten his legs"
Eye-Hand Coordination—Objective 4 " . . . release a sound tube"

These Objectives can be prescribed vertically within each area and horizontally across all areas.

Objectives have been prescribed and training has occurred for one month. Assessing the assigned Objectives, all have been completed except for Attending, Objective 5, ". . . follow a moving object in a circular pattern." During the training of the Eye-Hand Coordination Objective 4, " . . . release a sound tube," the teacher has discovered difficulties in attending to circular motions only. The student had no problems when attending to items directly in front of him. This information would discourage placement of mobiles above his line of vision, but it would also encourage the teacher to begin training on other Language Development areas (i.e., Auditory Training, Physical Imitation) while continuing to train on Attending Objectives.

The number of Objectives prescribed for training will depend upon the amount of training time. Three training sessions lasting 15 minutes each have proved to be successful in the past. During this time three Objectives can be trained per day. This will vary with the attention span of the student as well as the training time available.

SUMMARY

The first rule for prescribing Objectives for remediation is to target the first deficit behavior within a Checklist area. Second, list those Objec-

tives and select three that are most similar and present the least amount of conflict in training. For example, a student would not be trained to dress if he were not capable of grasping, or a student would not be trained to sit if he had poor trunk control.

Never prescribe Objectives across a group of students. Each student should have an individual assessment that outlines his specific problems.

CHAPTER THREE/Questions

All of the questions below must be completed with 100-percent accuracy before going on to the Chapter Three stories.

1. True or False (circle one)
   Immediately after assessment, the prescription for remediation is made.

2. Prescribing the appropriate curriculum begins with

   _____

3. The blank spaces on a Checklist indicate:
   A. Those behaviors that have not been assessed
   B. Those behaviors not included in the student's repertoire
   C. Those behaviors needed for immediate training
   D. Those behaviors unclear to the assessor

4. Give an example of vertically prescribing an Objective.

   _____

5. Give an example of horizontally prescribing an Objective.

   _____

6. Why would the information on Attending, Objective 5 (p. 20) discourage a teacher from placing a mobile above the student and then training him to manipulate it?

   _____

   _____

   _____

7. The number of Objectives prescribed for training will depend upon

   t_____ t_____

8. A reasonable number of Objectives to train on at one time is

   _____

9. List the two rules in prescribing Objectives for remediation:

   a._____

   b._____

10. Can Objectives be prescribed across a group of students? Why, or why not?

    _____

    _____

Story 3-A

Sally, a student, was assessed on all Checklists. She was capable of mastering all Objectives in Motor Development, and she did not have problems with Feeding. From her Language Development and Eye-Hand Coordination Checklists on the next pages prescribe three Objectives for remediation. Follow the two steps as outlined in this chapter.

BEHAVIORAL CHECKLIST
FOR EYE-HAND COORDINATION

OBJECTIVES

The student will:

1. make random patterns in shaving cream   ✓ 1-12-76
2. make random patterns in finger paint   ✓ 1-12-76
3. grasp a sound tube   ✓ 1-12-76
4. release a sound tube   ✓ 1-12-76
5. release a sound tube in a box   ✓ 1-12-76
6. pick up a clutch ball   ✓ 1-12-76
7. punch a balloon   ✓ 1-12-76
8. reach for a soap bubble   ✓ 1-12-76
9. spin the bubble on the mobile   ✓ 1-12-76
10. spin the handle on the mobile   ✓ 1-12-76
11. squeak the ball on the mobile   _____
12. pull the handle on the merry-go-round   _____
13. turn the knob on the busy box   _____
14. turn the crank on the busy box   _____
15. press the button on the busy box   _____
16. push the car on the busy box   _____
17. slide the door on the busy box   _____
18. turn the telephone dial on the busy box   _____
19. spin the wheel on the busy box   _____
20. open the door on the busy box   _____
21. open the drawer on the busy box   _____
22. press the button on the surprise busy box   _____
23. slide the knob on the surprise busy box   _____
24. turn the knob on the surprise busy box   _____
25. turn the dial on the surprise busy box   _____
26. flip the switch on the surprise busy box   _____

27. place three pegs in a peg board   _____
28. remove stacking rings   _____
29. randomly stack stacking rings   _____
30. stack two stacking rings in order   _____
31. nest nesting blocks   _____
32. stack nesting blocks   _____
33. nest nesting cups   _____
34. stack nesting cups   _____
35. place a circle in the form board   _____
36. place a square in the form board   _____
37. place a triangle in the form board   _____
38. place a circle in the shape sorting box   _____
39. place a square in the shape sorting box   _____
40. place a triangle in the shape sorting box   _____
41. assemble a three-piece puzzle   _____
42. assemble a four-piece puzzle   _____
43. assemble a five-piece puzzle   _____
44. assemble a six-piece puzzle   _____
45. trace a horizontal line with his finger   _____
46. trace a vertical line with his finger   _____
47. trace a horizontal curved line with his finger   _____
48. trace an up and down curve with his finger   _____
49. trace a circle, using a template   _____
50. trace a square, using a template   _____
51. trace a triangle, using a template   _____

BEHAVIORAL CHECKLIST FOR LANGUAGE DEVELOPMENT/Attending

OBJECTIVES

The student will:

1. fixate on an object upon the command, "Look"   ✓ 1-10-76
2. follow a moving object in a horizontal pattern   ✓ 1-10-76
3. follow a moving object in a vertical pattern   ✓ 1-10-76
4. follow a moving object in a diagonal pattern   ✓ 1-10-76
5. follow a moving object in a circular pattern   ✓ 1-10-76
6. converge   ✓ 1-10-76

BEHAVIORAL CHECKLIST FOR LANGUAGE DEVELOPMENT/Physical Imitation

OBJECTIVES

The student will:

1. slap the table   ✓ 1-13-76
2. clap hands   ✓ 1-13-76
3. imitate ringing a bell   ✓ 1-13-76
4. imitate pounding a mallet   _____
5. ring a bell and pound a mallet   _____
6a. *blow a feather *or*   _____
6b. *blow out a candle *or*   _____
6c. *blow a whistle   _____

---

*No. 6a, b, and c are interchangeable. If the student can do one, he can receive credit for all.

BEHAVIORAL CHECKLIST FOR LANGUAGE DEVELOPMENT/Auditory Training

OBJECTIVES

The student will:

1. look to the left to a sound   ✓1-13-76
2. look to the right to a sound   ✓1-13-76
3. follow a sound from left to right   ✓1-13-76
4. locate a sound behind him   ✓1-13-76
5. follow graduated sounds   ✓1-13-76
6. imitate pounding a mallet   _____
7. imitate ringing a bell   _____
8. ring a bell and pound a mallet   _____
9. imitate the sound of a bell   _____
10. imitate the sound of a mallet   _____
11. physically imitate the sound of a bell and the sound of a mallet when both are present   _____

BEHAVIORAL CHECKLIST FOR LANGUAGE DEVELOPMENT/Object Discrimination

OBJECTIVES

The student will:

1. give spoon   _____
2. give spoon when spoon and fork are present   _____
3. give fork   _____
4. give fork and give spoon when both are present   _____
5. give fork and give spoon when an extraneous object is present   _____
6. give comb   _____
7. give comb when both comb and toothbrush are present   _____
8. give toothbrush   _____
9. give toothbrush when both toothbrush and comb are present   _____
10. give spoon and give toothbrush when both are present   _____
11. give spoon and give toothbrush when an extraneous object is present   _____
12. give cup   _____
13. give cup when an extraneous object is present   _____
14. give ball   _____
15. give ball when both ball and cup are present   _____
16. give ball and give cup when both are present   _____

BEHAVIORAL CHECKLIST FOR LANGUAGE DEVELOPMENT/Concept Development

OBJECTIVES

The student will:

1. sit down _____
2. stand up _____
3. look _____
4. stop _____
5. come _____
6. open the door _____
7. close the door _____
8. *go to the _____ _____
9. *give the _____ _____
10. *put the _____ on the _____ _____
11. *take the _____ off the _____ _____
12. *pick up the _____ _____

_____

*For Objectives 8 to 12, use nouns with which the student is familiar.

BEHAVIORAL CHECKLIST FOR LANGUAGE DEVELOPMENT/Sound Imitation

OBJECTIVES

The student can imitate:

1. clapping hands ✓1-13-76
2. stamping feet ✓1-13-76
3. blowing on your hand _____
5. blowing a whistle _____
5. opening his mouth _____
6. closing his mouth _____
7. sticking out his tongue _____
8. the "ah" sound _____
9. the "oo" sound _____

Story 3-B

Jody is a six-year-old, profoundly retarded girl. She has been on a soft diet for six years because of her inability to swallow. She lies in bed and remains motionless. Prescribe Objectives for remediation after assessing her Checklists on the following pages. Follow the two steps as outlined in this chapter.

BEHAVIORAL CHECKLIST FOR MOTOR DEVELOPMENT/Head and Trunk Control

OBJECTIVES

The student will:

1. hold his head erect without support when on his stomach or held over your shoulder   ✓ 1-1-76
2. left his head and upper chest when lying down   ✓ 1-1-76
3. raise his head up and forward from a back-lying position   _____
4. hold his head up when supported in a sitting position   _____
5. hold his head in proper alignment when pulled to a sitting position   _____

BEHAVIORAL CHECKLIST FOR MOTOR DEVELOPMENT/Sitting

OBJECTIVES

The student will:

1. go from a back-lying to a side-lying position   _____
2. go from a front-lying to a side-lying position   _____
3. sit with support   _____
4. sit without support   _____

BEHAVIORAL CHECKLIST FOR MOTOR DEVELOPMENT/Hand-Knee Position

OBJECTIVES

The student will:

1. go from a front-lying to a hand-knee position with assistance _____
2. go from a front-lying to a hand-knee position without assistance _____
3. maintain a hand-knee position with assistance _____
4. maintain a hand-knee position without assistance _____

BEHAVIORAL CHECKLIST FOR MOTOR DEVELOPMENT/Standing

OBJECTIVES

The student will:

1. tolerate weight bearing on his feet while supported _____
2. support part of his body weight and actively bend and straighten legs _____
3. balance trunk _____
4. pull self to a standing position from a squatting position _____
5. pull self to a standing position from a hand-knee position _____
6. stand independently _____

BEHAVIORAL CHECKLIST FOR PHYSICAL EATING PROBLEMS

OBJECTIVES

The student will:

1. keep his tongue in his mouth _____
2. keep his lips closed _____
3. open his mouth _____
4. close his mouth _____
5. swallow ✓1-1-76
6. chew _____
7. bite with strength and chew _____

BEHAVIORAL CHECKLIST FOR LANGUAGE DEVELOPMENT/Attending

OBJECTIVES

The student will:

1. fixate on an object upon the command, "Look" _____
2. follow a moving object in a horizontal pattern _____
3. follow a moving object in a vertical pattern _____
4. follow a moving object in a diagonal pattern _____
5. follow a moving object in a circular pattern _____
6. converge _____

BEHAVIORAL CHECKLIST FOR LANGUAGE DEVELOPMENT/Physical Imitation

OBJECTIVES

The student will:

1. slap the table
2. clap hands
3. imitate ringing a bell
4. imitate pounding a mallet
5. ring a bell and pound a mallet
6a. *blow a feather *or*
6b. *blow out a candle *or*
6c. *blow a whistle

---

*No. 6a, b, and c are interchangeable. If the student can do one, he can receive credit for all.

BEHAVIORAL CHECKLIST FOR LANGUAGE DEVELOPMENT/Auditory Training

OBJECTIVES

The student will:

1. look to the left to a sound ✓ I-1-76
2. look to the right to a sound ✓ I-1-76
3. follow a sound from left to right
4. locate a sound behind him
5. follow graduated sounds
6. imitate pounding a mallet
7. imitate ringing a bell
8. ring a bell and pound a mallet
9. imitate the sound of a bell
10. imitate the sound of a mallet
11. physically imitate the sound of a bell and the sound of a mallet when both are present

BEHAVIORAL CHECKLIST FOR LANGUAGE DEVELOPMENT/Object Discrimination

OBJECTIVES

The student will:

1. give spoon _____
2. give spoon when spoon and fork are present _____
3. give fork _____
4. give fork and give spoon when both are present _____
5. give fork and give spoon when an extraneous object is present _____
6. give comb _____
7. give comb when both comb and toothbrush are present _____
8. give toothbrush _____
9. give toothbrush when both toothbrush and comb are present _____
10. give spoon and give toothbrush when both are present _____
11. give spoon and give toothbrush when an extraneous object is present _____
12. give cup _____
13. give cup when an extraneous object is present _____
14. give ball _____
15. give ball when both ball and cup are present _____
16. give ball and give cup when both are present _____

BEHAVIORAL CHECKLIST FOR LANGUAGE DEVELOPMENT/Concept Development

OBJECTIVES

The student will:

1. sit down _____
2. stand up _____
3. look _____
4. stop _____
5. come _____
6. open the door _____
7. close the door _____
8. *go to the _____ _____
9. *give the _____ _____
10. *put the _____ on the _____ _____
11. *take the _____ off the _____ _____
12. *pick up the _____ _____

_____

For Objectives 8 to 12, use nouns with which the student is familiar.

BEHAVIORAL CHECKLIST FOR LANGUAGE DEVELOPMENT/Sound Imitation

OBJECTIVES

The student will imitate:

1. clapping hands   ✓1-1-74
2. stamping feet
3. blowing on your hand
4. blowing a whistle
5. opening his mouth
6. closing his mouth
7. sticking out his tongue
8. the "ah" sound
9. the "oo" sound

Story 3-C

John has been assessed for training in the out-patient clinic at General Hospital. Using the attached Checklists, prescribe three Objectives for remediation that the hospital personnel will train and one Objective for his mother to train at home. Refer to the text for procedures on prescribing Objectives. Generally, it is a good idea to give the parents the least complex Objective to begin home training.

BEHAVIORAL CHECKLIST
FOR EYE-HAND COORDINATION

OBJECTIVES

The student will:

1. make random patterns in shaving cream   ✓ 3-3-76
2. make random patterns in finger paint   ✓ 3-3-76
3. grasp a sound tube   ✓ 3-3-76
4. release a sound tube   ✓ 3-3-76
5. release a sound tube in a box   ✓ 3-3-76
6. pick up a clutch ball   ✓ 3-3-76
7. punch a balloon   ✓ 3-3-76
8. reach for a soap bubble   ✓ 3-3-76
9. spin the bubble on the mobile   ✓ 3-3-76
10. spin the handle on the mobile   ✓ 3-3-76
11. squeak the ball on the mobile   ✓ 3-3-76
12. pull the handle on the merry-go-round   ✓ 3-3-76
13. turn the knob on the busy box   ✓ 3-3-76
14. turn the crank on the busy box   ✓ 3-3-76
15. press the button on the busy box   ✓ 3-3-76
16. push the car on the busy box   ✓ 3-3-76
17. slide the door on the busy box   ✓ 3-3-76
18. turn the telephone dial on the busy box   ✓ 3-3-76
19. spin the wheel on the busy box   ✓ 3-3-76
20. open the door on the busy box   ✓ 3-3-76
21. open the drawer on the busy box   ✓ 3-3-76
22. press the button on the surprise busy box   ✓ 3-3-76
23. slide the knob on the surprise busy box   ✓ 3-3-76
24. turn the knob on the surprise busy box   ✓ 3-3-76
25. turn the dial on the surprise busy box   ✓ 3-3-76
26. flip the switch on the surprise busy box   ✓ 3-3-76

27. place three pegs in a peg board   ✓ 3-3-76
28. remove stacking rings   ✓ 3-3-76
29. randomly stack stacking rings   ✓ 3-3-76
30. stack two stacking rings in order   ✓ 3-3-76
31. nest nesting blocks   _____
32. stack nesting blocks   _____
33. nest nesting cups   _____
34. stacking nesting cups   _____
35. place a circle in the form board   _____
36. place a square in the form board   _____
37. place a triangle in the form board   _____
38. place a circle in the shape sorting box   _____
39. place a square in the shape sorting box   _____
40. place a triangle in the shape sorting box   _____
41. assemble a three-piece puzzle   _____
42. assemble a four-piece puzzle   _____
43. assemble a five-piece puzzle   _____
44. assemble a six-piece puzzle   _____
45. trace a horizontal line with his finger   _____
46. trace a vertical line with his finger   _____
47. trace a horizontal curved line with his finger   _____
48. trace an up and down curve with his finger   _____
49. trace a circle, using a template   _____
50. trace a square, using a template   _____
51. trace a triangle, using a template   _____

BEHAVIORAL CHECKLIST FOR LANGUAGE DEVELOPMENT/Attending

OBJECTIVES

The student will:

1. fixate on an object upon the command, "Look" ✓3-1-76
2. follow a moving object in a horizontal pattern ✓3-1-76
3. follow a moving object in a vertical pattern ✓3-1-76
4. follow a moving object in a diagonal pattern ✓3-1-76
5. follow a moving object in a circular pattern ✓3-1-76
6. converge ✓3-1-76

BEHAVIORAL CHECKLIST FOR LANGUAGE DEVELOPMENT/Physical Imitation

OBJECTIVES

The student will:

1. slap the table ✓3-1-76
2. clap hands ✓3-1-76
3. imitate ringing a bell ✓3-1-76
4. imitate pounding a mallet ✓3-1-76
5. ring a bell and pound a mallet
6a. *blow a feather *or* ✓3-1-76
6b. *blow out a candle *or* ✓3-1-76
6c. *blow a whistle ✓3-1-76

---

*No. 6a, b, and c are interchangeable. If the student can do one, he can receive credit for all.

BEHAVIORAL CHECKLIST FOR LANGUAGE DEVELOPMENT/Auditory Training

OBJECTIVES

The student will:

1. look to the left to a sound   ✓ 3-1-76
2. look to the right to a sound   ✓ 3-1-76
3. follow a sound from left to right   ✓ 3-1-76
4. locate a sound behind him   ✓ 3-1-76
5. follow graduated sounds   ✓ 3-1-76
6. imitate pounding a mallet   ✓ 3-1-76
7. imitate ringing a bell   ✓ 3-1-76
8. ring a bell and pound a mallet   ✓ 3-1-76
9. imitate the sound of a bell   ✓ 3-1-76
10. imitate the sound of a mallet   ✓ 3-1-76
11. physically imitate the sound of a bell and the sound of a mallet when both are present   _____

BEHAVIORAL CHECKLIST FOR LANGUAGE DEVELOPMENT/Object Discrimination

OBJECTIVES

The student will:

1. give spoon   _____
2. give spoon when spoon and fork are present   _____
3. give fork   _____
4. give fork and give spoon when both are present   _____
5. give fork and give spoon when an extraneous object is present   _____
6. give comb   _____
7. give comb when both comb and toothbrush are present   _____
8. give toothbrush   _____
9. give toothbrush when both toothbrush and comb are present   _____
10. give spoon and give toothbrush when both are present   _____
11. give spoon and give toothbrush when an extraneous object is present   _____
12. give cup   _____
13. give cup when an extraneous object is present   _____
14. give ball   _____
15. give ball when both ball and cup are present   _____
16. give ball and give cup when both are present   _____

BEHAVIORAL CHECKLIST FOR LANGUAGE DEVELOPMENT/Concept Development

OBJECTIVES

The student will:

1. sit down _____
2. stand up _____
3. look _____
4. stop _____
5. come _____
6. open the door _____
7. close the door _____
8. *go to the _____ _____
9. *give the _____ _____
10. *put the _____ on the
    _____ _____
11. *take the _____ off the
    _____ _____
12. *pick up the _____ _____

---

*For Objectives 8 to 12, use nouns with which the student is familiar.

BEHAVIORAL CHECKLIST FOR LANGUAGE DEVELOPMENT/Sound Imitation

OBJECTIVES

The student will imitate:

1. clapping hands ✓ 3-4-76
2. stamping feet ✓ 3-4-76
3. blowing on your hand ✓ 3-4-76
4. blowing a whistle ✓ 3-4-76
5. opening his mouth ✓ 3-4-76
6. closing his mouth ✓ 3-4-76
7. sticking out his tongue ✓ 3-4-76
8. the "ah" sound ✓ 3-4-76
9. the "oo" sound ✓ 3-4-76

BEHAVIORAL CHECKLIST FOR MOTOR DEVELOPMENT/Head and Trunk Control

OBJECTIVES

The student will:

1. hold his head erect without support when on his stomach or held over your shoulder   ✓ 3-1-76
2. lift his head and upper chest when lying down   ✓ 3-1-76
3. raise his head up and forward from a back-lying position   ✓ 3-1-76
4. hold his head up when supported in a sitting position   ✓ 3-1-76
5. hold his head in proper alignment when pulled to a sitting position   ✓ 3-1-76

BEHAVIORAL CHECKLIST FOR MOTOR DEVELOPMENT/Sitting

OBJECTIVES

The student will:

1. go from a back-lying to a side-lying position   ✓ 3-1-76
2. go from a front-lying to a side-lying position   ✓ 3-1-76
3. sit with support   ✓ 3-1-76
4. sit without support   ✓ 3-1-76

BEHAVIORAL CHECKLIST FOR MOTOR DEVELOPMENT/Hand-Knee Position

OBJECTIVES

The student will:

1. go from a front-lying to a hand-knee position with assistance   ✓ 3-1-76
2. go from a front-lying to a hand-knee position without assistance   ✓ 3-1-76
3. maintain a hand-knee position with assistance   ✓ 3-1-76
4. maintain a hand-knee position without assistance   ✓ 3-1-76

BEHAVIORAL CHECKLIST FOR MOTOR DEVELOPMENT/Standing

OBJECTIVES

The student will:

1. tolerate weight bearing on his feet while supported   ✓ 3-1-76
2. support part of his body weight and actively bend and straighten his legs   ✓ 3-1-76
3. balance his trunk   ✓ 3-1-76
4. pull himself to a standing position from a squatting position   ✓ 3-1-76
5. pull himself to a standing position from a hand-knee position   ✓ 3-1-76
6. stand independently   ✓ 3-1-76

BEHAVIORAL CHECKLIST FOR PHYSICAL EATING PROBLEMS

OBJECTIVES

The student will:

1. keep his tongue in his mouth   ✓ 3-3-76
2. keep his lips closed   ✓ 3-3-76
3. open his mouth   ✓ 3-3-76
4. close his mouth   ✓ 3-3-76
5. swallow   ✓ 3-3-76
6. chew   ✓ 3-3-76
7. bite with strength and chew   ✓ 3-3-76

CHAPTER FOUR

Training Methods

After the Objective has been prescribed, the corresponding *Task Analysis* provides a detailed description of *Steps* to teach the task. For example, Objective 6 of Eye-Hand Coordination is, "The student will pick up a clutch ball." To teach this Objective you would follow this Task Analysis:

The student will:
1. let you put his hand on the clutch ball upon the command, "Do this"
2. let you hold the clutch ball with his hands upon the command, "Do this"
3. hold the clutch ball upon the command, "Do this"
4. let you use his arms to reach for the clutch ball; he will hold it upon command
5. let you position his arms next to the clutch ball; he will pick it up and hold it upon command
6. pick up the clutch ball upon the command, "Do this"

The Task Analysis is the set of skills the student is to accomplish to perform the target response. It lists, in order, the Steps the student will take to reach his Objective.

DETERMINING THE OPERANT LEVEL

With the prescribed Objective and the Task Analysis, the trainer is ready to begin. First, the operant level within the Task Analysis must be determined. The operant level is the last Step within the Task Analysis that the student can perform accurately. Using Eye-Hand Coordination Objective 6 as an example, determining the operant level would follow this pattern:

Step 1   The student will let you put his hand on the clutch ball upon the command, "Do this."

Aida, an aide, sits across from Sally and says, "Sally, do this," as Aida puts her hands on the clutch ball. Aida immediately takes Sally's hands and puts them on the ball. Sally responds with a smile and Aida continues.

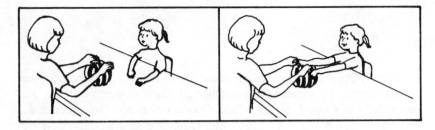

Step 2   The student will let you hold the clutch ball with his hands upon the command, "Do this."

Aida sits across from Sally and says, "Sally, do this," as Aida holds the clutch ball. Aida immediately takes Sally's hands and holds the clutch ball with them.

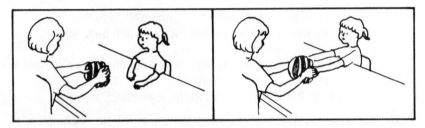

Step 3   The student will hold the clutch ball upon the command, "Do this."

Aida sits across from Sally and says, "Sally, do this," as Aida holds the clutch ball. Aida immediately places the clutch ball in Sally's hands, and Sally smiles as she holds it.

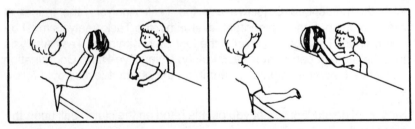

Step 4   The student will let you use his arms to reach for the clutch ball; he will hold it upon command.

Aida sits across from Sally and says, "Sally, do this," as Aida reaches out to the clutch ball on the table and then holds it. Aida

immediately takes Sally's hands to reach for the clutch ball, but Sally will not extend her arms.

Sally is operating at Step 3 in this Task Analysis, and the new training will begin on Step 4. The operant level must be determined each time an Objective is prescribed. It is a relatively fast procedure that saves time and effort during the actual training.

REINFORCEMENT PREFERENCE

Reinforcement preference should also be determined before the actual training begins. Remember that a reinforcer is the thing or event following a behavior that will increase the possibility of the behavior occurring again. Any behavior that is followed by a reinforcer is likely to increase in frequency. The purpose of training is to increase the occurrence of the desired responses and eventually to reach the target response.

To determine what is reinforcing to a particular student, a survey can be taken by the ward aides, parents, siblings, etc. They will record what toys, activities, foods, or juices the student enjoys. A variety of candy, crackers, fruit, Kool-Aide, or juices can be available for a cafeteria-like selection. After a reinforcer is found, the training can begin.

Aida has discovered that Sally's reinforcement preference is grape juice. Aida pours a small amount of grape juice into an old plastic hair-coloring bottle. She uses the hair-coloring bottle because a small amount of the grape juice can be squeezed into Sally's mouth with little or no mess. Aida also has control over how much juice is given to Sally by the pressure of her hand on the bottle. Aida sits across from Sally and goes back to Step 3, Sally's operant level. Aida wants Sally to be successful at the beginning of training so she can be reinforced with her favorite beverage. Sally performs Step 3 correctly on five consecutive trials, and Sally smiles each time after reinforcement. Aida goes to Step 4. She says, "Sally, do this," as she reaches for the clutch ball and holds it. Aida immediately takes Sally's hands and reaches out to the clutch ball but Sally will not hold it. Aida removes the ball from the table and waits approximately five seconds before presenting the ball again. This time, Aida provides an extra physical prompt. She says, "Sally, do this," as she reaches for the ball and holds it. Aida immediately takes Sally's hands to the ball and uses Sally's hands to hold it. Aida says, "Good girl," as soon as Sally's hands are on the ball. She then sets Sally's hands free as she reinforces Sally with grape juice.

The above example illustrates the necessity of starting with the operant level, assuring five successful trials for the student before beginning a new training step.

Each time, Sally was reinforced immediately. The longer the reinforcer is withheld, the less effective it will be. In situations where the trainer is providing physical assistance, it is often impossible to deliver the reinforcer immediately. Here, the bridging technique comes to the rescue.

BRIDGING

Bridging can be a verbal "Good girl" or "Good boy," or a combination of a verbal praise and a pat on the back with one hand while the other is reaching for the edible reward. Attention or praise is reinforcing for some students, and the pairing of these with an edible reinforcer provides stronger reinforcement. For example, Mrs. Thomas is training her son Jimmy to stack the stacking rings. She is using ice cream as a reinforcer. The ice cream is in a cup and she must bend down, dip a spoon into the cup, and bring the spoon back up to Jimmy's mouth. This activity makes immediate reinforcement an impossibility, so Mrs. Thomas uses the bridging technique. Jimmy puts the last ring on the spindle and Mrs. Thomas immediately says, "Good boy, Jimmy" as she simultaneously pats Jimmy on the back with her left hand and reaches for the ice cream with her right hand. The pat on the back and verbal praise serve as a bridge between Jimmy's appropriate response and his reinforcer, ice cream.

SCHEDULES OF REINFORCEMENT

Learning new behaviors can be a tedious task for a student, so continuous reinforcement is used. Continuous reinforcement is rewarding the student every time he performs the desired response. Once the student has learned the desired response, continuous reinforcement is no longer necessary.

Intermittent reinforcement is used to maintain behavior. During intermittent reinforcement the frequency of the reinforcer is decreased. This is done very gradually to ensure the continued high frequency of behavior. Although there is no rule for intermittent reinforcement, it is safe to drop from 100 percent reinforcement to 85, to 70, to 45, to 25, and eventually, you will be reinforcing the correct response only occasionally.

PROMPTS AND FADING

There are three types of prompts: physical, gestural, and verbal. A physical prompt is a movement made by the trainer using the student's hand or other body part appropriate for accomplishing the task. A gestural prompt is a gesture made by the trainer to the student to indicate what is to be done. The gestures used most often are pointing and nodding.

During the second trial on Step 4, Aida provides a physical prompt for Sally. Aida says, "Sally, do this," as she reaches for the ball and picks it up. Aida immediately takes Sally's hands to the ball and uses Sally's hands to pick it up. Aida says, "Good girl" and reinforces Sally. Five consecutive training periods pass and Sally continues to respond positively to the above training. Aida now alters her technique of assistance; she fades out the physical prompt and replaces it with a gestural prompt. Aida says, "Sally, do this," as she reaches for the ball and holds it. Aida immediately takes Sally's hands to the ball and then gestures for Sally to pick it up. Sally picks up the ball and Aida says, "Good girl," as she reinforces her. Sally continues to respond positively to this Step for five consecutive training periods. Aida can now fade out the gestural prompt. Aida says, "Sally, do this," as she reaches for the ball and picks it up. Aida immediately takes Sally's hands to the ball and Sally picks it up. Aida says, "Good girl" and reinforces Sally. After Sally has responded positively to this Step for five consecutive periods, she moves on to Step 5.

In the preceding examples, the trainer needed special help to accomplish Step 4. This help was provided in the form of physical, gestural, and verbal prompts; it is assistance given by the teacher to the student to help him perform the response.

CHAPTER FOUR/Questions

All of the questions below must be completed with 100-percent accuracy before going on to the Chapter Four stories.

1. The T_____ A_____ will provide a detailed description of Steps to teach the task.

2. What is a Task Analysis?

   _____

   _____

3. What is the operant level?

   _____

   _____

4. The operant level must be determined each time _____

   _____

5. What is a reinforcer?

   _____

   _____

6. Is a reinforcer the same for everyone? Why, or why not?

   _____

7. How can the reinforcement preference be determined?

   _____

   _____

8. Reinforcement should be i_____

9. The longer the reward is withheld, the _____

   _____

   _____

10. Give an example of a bridging technique.

    _____

    _____

11. C_____ reinforcement is rewarding the student every time he performs the desired behavior.

12. When is continuous reinforcement no longer necessary?

    _____

13. I_____ reinforcement is used to maintain behavior.

14. True or False (circle one)
    During intermittent reinforcement, the frequency of the reward is decreased.

15. What is a prompt? _____

16. What are the three types of prompts? _____

_____

17. Give an example of a physical prompt.

_____

_____

18. Give an example of a gestural prompt.

_____

_____

19. Give an example of a verbal prompt.

_____

_____

20. Gradual withdrawal of prompts is called _____.

Story 4-A

Jaime was a new student on the ward. After she was on the ward for two weeks, the special education teacher assessed her in all areas of the Prescriptive Behavioral Checklists. Objectives were prescribed, and her operant level was determined for all areas. A note was written to the aide telling her to use a continuous reinforcement schedule and that grape juice would be the most effective reinforcer.

Susan, an aide, had been training for several years and recognized the need for the appropriate training prompt. She looked at the operant level the teacher had assessed and found that Jaime should be on Step 3 of Eye-Hand Coordination Objective 29 and Susan should be using a gestural prompt (use the review sheet for Story 4-A):

1. What type of prompt will Susan be using?

2. Susan will want to fade her gestural prompt to a _____ prompt.

3. What techniques might Susan use during reinforcement?

4. When will Susan want to reinforce?

5. When will Susan continue to the next Step?

TEACHER AND AIDE REVIEW/Story 4-A

The teacher will:

1. _____ prescribe an Objective for each student based on his individual needs.
2. _____ determine the operant level within that Objective.
3. _____ assign the Task Analysis Step for each Objective based on the student's operant level.
4. _____ determine the student's reinforcement preference.
5. _____ assign the appropriate reinforcement schedule (continuous to teach a new behavior and intermittent to maintain the behavior).

The aide will:

1. _____ use physical, gestural, and verbal prompts appropriately.
2. _____ fade prompts from physical to gestural to verbal.
3. _____ use a bridging technique during reinforcement.
4. _____ reinforce immediately after the appropriate behavior occurs.
5. _____ go on to the next Step after the student has responded with five consecutive appropriate responses to a verbal command.

Story 4-B

Miss Stevens, a teacher, has assessed 40 students on the Eye-Hand Coordination Checklist and she is assigning Objective 5 to all of the students. She has instructed Melanie, an aide, to begin working with ten of these students (selected randomly) on Step 1 of the Task Analysis. They will be on a continuous reinforcement schedule because it will be a new behavior for most of them.

Melanie begins training on Objective 5, " . . . release a sound tube in a box." The first student is Sarah. Melanie sits across from Sarah and says, "Sarah, do this," as she puts the sound tube in the box and releases it. Melanie gives Sarah the sound tube and puts Sarah's hand in the box. Sarah releases the sound tube and Melanie says, "Good girl" and gives her a hug, while she reaches for a piece of cookie and puts it in Sarah's mouth.

Assess this situation using the review sheet for Story 4-B. For each behavior that the teacher was deficient in, tell how the behavior can be remediated.

TEACHER AND AIDE REVIEW/Story 4-B

The teacher will:

1. _____ prescribe an Objective for each student based on his individual needs.
2. _____ determine the operant level within that Objective.
3. _____ assign the Task Analysis Step for each Objective based on the student's operant level.
4. _____ determine the student's reinforcement preference.
5. _____ assign the appropriate reinforcement schedule (continuous to teach a new behavior and intermittent to maintain the behavior).

The aide will:

1. _____ use physical, gestural, and verbal prompts appropriately.
2. _____ fade prompts from physical to gestural to verbal.
3. _____ use a bridging technique during reinforcement.
4. _____ reinforce immediately after the appropriate behavior occurs.
5. _____ go on to the next Step after the student has responded with five consecutive appropriate responses to a verbal command.

Story 4-C

Natalie assessed each student on her ward. After assessment, she prescribed an individualized curriculum for each student and selected the Task Analysis Step for each Objective. Natalie talked to aides and foster grandparents about the foods and toys each student was fond of; she also introduced many new foods and toys to each student and kept a record of their preferences. All students were on a continuous reinforcement schedule because they were all learning new behaviors.

Natalie began training by calling each student's name to gain his attention and then giving the verbal command, "Do this." Some of the students responded to the verbal command, while others did not. When a student responded, he was reinforced. A few of the students immediately attained five consecutive appropriate responses to a verbal command and then moved on to the next Step.

Not all of the students were receiving appropriate training. Use the review sheet for Story 4-C to diagnose their problems.

TEACHER AND AIDE REVIEW/Story 4-C

The teacher will:

1. _____ prescribe an Objective for each student based on his individual needs.
2. _____ determine the operant level within that Objective.
3. _____ assign the Task Analysis Step for each Objective based on the student's operant level.
4. _____ determine the student's reinforcement preference.
5. _____ assign the approximate reinforcement schedule (continuous to teach a new behavior and intermittent to maintain the behavior).

The aide will:

1. _____ use physical, gestural, and verbal prompts appropriately.
2. _____ fade prompts from physical to gestural to verbal.
3. _____ use a bridging technique during reinforcement.
4. _____ reinforce immediately after the appropriate behavior occurs.
5. _____ go on to the next Step after the student has responded with five consecutive appropriate responses to a verbal command.

Suggested Readings

Bandura, A. 1965. Behavioral Modification through modeling procedures. In: L. Krasner and L. P. Ullman, eds., Research in Behavior Modification. New York: Holt, Rinehart & Winston.

Homne, L. E., de Baca, C., Devine, J. V., Steinhorst, R., and Rickert, E. J. 1963. Use of the premack principle in controlling the behavior of nursery school children. J. Exper. Anal. Behav., 6:544.

CHAPTER FIVE

Aide and Parent Training

While in most cases training aides will be the direct agents of behavior change, one need not teach all the principles of operant psychology if the Objectives of the program are outlined and a Task Analysis is used to guide the aide in training each Objective.

Role playing is an excellent alternative to the pencil-paper type of ongoing in-service training. It provides program-specific tasks which train the aide in the use of the program while simultaneously introducing the principles in an easy-to-understand format.

Before the role playing can began, a model is provided. The teacher, nurse, or psychologist trains a student on one Step of an Objective. During this modeling, one aspect of behavior modification is stressed and a question-answer session follows.

The first question-answer session should pertain to the concept of reinforcement. The following questions and answers could transpire after each modeling session.

Q. *What was the teacher trying to get the student to do?*
A. Some Observable behavior.

Q. *What did the teacher do after the student's desirable behavior?*
A. Reinforce.

Q. *What is a reinforcer?*
A. Something good.

Q. *Are the same things reinforcing for everyone?*
A. No.

Q. *Once something is a reinforcer for someone, is it always a reinforcer for that person?*
A. No, reinforcement preferences change.

Q. *How can you find out what a reinforcer is for a specific student?*
A. Watch and see what he likes and then try it.

Q. *What happens to a behavior when it is followed by a reinforcer?*
A. It increases; the student does it more often.

Q. *When did the teacher present the reinforcement?*
A. Immediately after the behavior.

Q. *Why is it important to reinforce immediately after the behavior occurs?*
A. If you wait, you may be reinforcing some other behavior and that will increase in frequency.

Q. *What did the teacher do when the student did not perform the behavior or task?*
A. He ignored him.

Q. *Why did the teacher do this?*
A. So that the behavior would not be strengthened or weakened. (When you ignore a behavior it is very important to be reinforcing some other behavior at the same time so the student has a chance to earn some reinforcement.)

Q. *You should reinforce only when* _____, *and never reinforce when* _____.
A. The desired behavior occurs; it does not occur.

Q. *What would happen if the model gave the whole reinforcer (or too much of it) at once?*
A. It would quickly lose its effectiveness—satiation.

Q. *What would happen if just a very small part of the reinforcer were given?*
A. It may not work because the reinforcer must be worthwhile.

Q. *What things could we do so that the student will work best with a reinforcer; for example, what would happen if the student just had a lot of the reward for lunch?*
A. The reward would not work and the behavior would not be strengthened.

Q. *How could we solve this problem?*
A. Make sure the student has not received the reinforcer recently.

The teacher, nurse, or psychologist should provide a minimum of five modeling demonstrations before the aides begin role playing. When the role playing begins, only the concept of reinforcement should be stressed.

Reinforcement is the component of the instructional cycle which the aide will use to have direct control over the student's behavior.

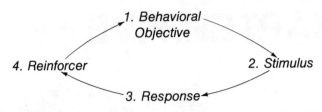

If the response is rewarded, the behavior will increase; if it is not rewarded, the behavior will decrease.

Not only will it be necesary for the aide to have a model and an opportunity for role playing but it will also be beneficial to have questions and answers available for any aide who may have difficulty with the concept of reinforcement. The following questions may be used for remediation.

REINFORCEMENT QUESTIONS I

1. Harry was just transferred from unit 5 to unit 1. With him came a note:
   "Twice a day Harry has a tantrum; he cries, kicks, and screams for Oreo cookies. As soon as a cookie is given to Harry, he calms down."
   a. Was a reinforcer given for behavior that is appropriate?
   b. Was a reinforcer given for a behavior you did not want Harry to display? What was this behavior?
   c. What was the reinforcer?
   d. When should the reinforcer be given to Harry?

2. In training Jimmy to play with a puzzle, Hazel would give him one potato chip immediately after the desired behavior occurred. This was the only time during the week he was able to earn potato chips.
   a. Which items on the Checklist were included in this training?

3. Emily was just married and enjoyed cooking for her husband. One night she made fried chicken and had dinner ready when her husband came home from work. He sat down and took one bite of the chicken and screamed, "This is the worst chicken I've ever eaten. I wouldn't feed it to our dog." He then threw all the chicken in the garbage.
   a. Was throwing the chicken into the garbage a reinforcer for Emily's hard work?

b. What could her husband have said to make her effort more reinforcing?

c. Do you think Emily will make chicken for her husband again?

4. Petie loves to drive his big wheel down the sidewalk. In the morning he eats breakfast and yells, "I wanna go out and drive my big wheel." His mother ignores him and he comes back to her, saying quietly, "Mom, can I go outside and drive my big wheel?" His mother gets his jacket and gives him a kiss as she tells him to have fun.

a. What is the behavior Petie's Mom is reinforcing?

b. What is the reinforcer?

5. Irma made herself a new dress and wore it to church. Everyone of her friends told Irma that the dress was pretty. Irma made another dress a month later and wore it to a dance. People were telling Irma what a beautiful dress she was wearing. One month later, Irma went Christmas shopping and was able to buy beautiful gifts for her grandchildren because she saved money by making her own clothes.

a. List the reinforcers that Irma experiences in the above situation.

6. Write a story about a training session and include all the items on the reinforcement review, below.

7. A new aide began training on unit 1. She was trying to discover a reinforcer for Clyde. She watched the nurses and grandparents giving juice to Clyde every time they played with him. She decided to try to use the same reinforcer during training but it did not work.

a. Why didn't juice serve as a reinforcer for Clyde?

8. Debbie was toilet trained when she was 2 years old. When she was 4, her mother had another baby. Debbie started having accidents and screaming each time they happened. Her mother thought she would have to start toilet training her all over again.

a. Why was Debbie doing this?

b. What would happen every time her mother gave her attention when the accidents occurred?

c. When should Debbie get the attention?

d. What is the reinforcer in this situation?

9. Before Louie started in the training program everyone gave him love, attention, and treats just for being a "cute little guy." Now you want to teach him to feed himself.

a. What will you use as a reinforcer?

b. What will you have to tell the other people who see Louie each day?

c. What will happen to your training program if others keep reinforcing Louie just for being a "cute little guy?"

REINFORCEMENT REVIEW

_____ Was a reinforcement given?
_____ Was it given immediately after the desired behavior?
_____ Was the reinforcer given only when the behavior occurred and not at any other time?
_____ Was the size of the reinforcer appropriate?
_____ Was there an appropriate state of deprivation?
_____ Was there an increase in behavior?

REINFORCEMENT EXERCISE

Now, design your own example of the use of a reinforcer in your setting.

1. Choose a desirable behavior of a specific student.
2. Choose a reward that you are fairly certain is effective with that student.
3. Describe how you would design the procedure (or use the reward).
4. Make sure your example contains all of the features listed in the "Reinforcement Checklist."
5. Be prepared to role play this example with a partner.

REINFORCEMENT QUESTIONS II

If the aide or parent experiences difficulty with the reinforcement questions, the following examples can be provided for additional remediation. After the examples have been completed, the aide or parent can return to the reinforcement questions and then demonstrate their ability to answer the questions correctly.

1. You have observed that one of your favorite children likes to be hugged. You want to teach this child to play with a new teddy bear more often. Every time the child touches the teddy bear, you immediately give the child a big hug. Soon the child begins playing with the teddy bear more often. Is this an example of reinforcement?

2. Wanda is working on language with one of her children. The child can say "da" but does not say it very often. Every time the child says "da," Wanda immediately gives her a sip of her favorite grape juice. The child receives the grape juice only when she says "da." The child begins to say "da" more often. Is this an example of reinforcement?

3. Mary wants to teach one of her children, Kristy, to touch a ball. Each time Kristy touches the ball, Mary immediately pats her on the head and says, "Good girl." Mary ignores Kristy until she touches the ball. Soon Kristy is touching the ball more often. Is this an example of reinforcement?

4. Martha wanted little Jimmy to reach toward his mobile when it was moving. She set the mobile in motion and as soon as Jimmy raised his arm toward the mobile, she tickled him for ten seconds. (Jimmy loved to be tickled.) Gradually, Jimmy reached toward the mobile more often. Is this an example of reinforcement?

5. After a large dessert of five cookies, Sandy went to her training session, where Danella was teaching her to ring a bell. Sandy saw the bell and eventually picked it up and rang it. Knowing that she should reinforce immediately, Danella gave Sandy a cookie right away. Sandy only took one bite of the cookie and did not pick up the bell again. Is this an example of reinforcement?

PARENT TRAINING

Prompting and fading are questionable training areas. If the program is used properly, the teacher, nurse, or psychologist would provide the appropriate prompt. However, the parent implementing this program would need to demonstrate a basic understanding of these concepts. For this group alone, the following section is introduced.

Prompting

Prompting means giving the students cues that help them to learn the behavior you are trying to teach them. The three types of prompts used in this program are physical, gestural, and verbal. The *physical prompt* is physical manipulation of the student's body; the *gestural prompt* is a gesture made toward the activity to be accomplished; and a *verbal prompt* consists of verbal instructions.

When you begin to teach a new behavior, first give verbal instructions. For example, say, "Look at the ball." If an appropriate response does not occur, repeat the command and also gesture toward the ball. If an appropriate response still does not occur, repeat the command and the gesture and use physical prompts. Physically turn the student's head toward the ball and immediately reinforce the student.

If an appropriate response occurs to a verbal command, then it is not necessary to use gestural or physical prompts. Likewise, if any appropriate response occurs when gestures are used with the verbal command, there is no reason to use physical prompts. Whenever a correct response occurs to a specific prompt level, begin training with that prompt level. Remember, the verbal prompt is always given at the beginning of a trial even when gestural and/or physical prompts are used.

When criterion is reached with one level of prompts (five consecutive correct responses), then it is time to move on to the next level of prompts for the same behavior. For example, if you began with physical prompts to teach the student to look at the ball, you would move on to gestural prompts only after the student had five consecutive correct responses with the physical prompt. (This should not take many more than five trials, because you are manually guiding the student to do the behavior.) When the student makes five consecutive correct responses while using the gestural prompt, you should move on to the verbal command alone. When criterion is reached using only the verbal command, you have successfully taught the behavior.

The goal is to get the student to perform the behavior upon verbal command. Gestural and physical prompts can help to meet that goal, but they must be eliminated before we can say that the student can perform the behavior upon command.

Fading

The most successful method for eliminating gestural and physical prompts is called fading. Fading simply means that the prompts are removed gradually. The following is an example where it was necessary to begin by using physical prompts. Note the gradual fading (removal) of the physical and gestural prompts.

1. Make sure the student is properly seated.
2. Say, "Look at the ball." Point to the ball (and touch it) while turning the student's head toward the ball.
3. Reinforce immediately after the response. Say, "Good" or give a hug or use some other appropriate reinforcer.
4. Repeat this five times.
5. Now begin fading the physical prompts by saying, "Look at the ball," while pointing to the ball and turning the student's head only three-fourths of the way toward the ball, letting the student complete the rest of the response. Reinforce immediately.
6. Gradually reduce the amount of the response that you physically help the student to complete, until you are just touching the student's head. At this point, you are still using the verbal and gestural prompts.
7. After five consecutive correct responses using physical prompts and fading (even when you just touch the student's face, it is a physical prompt), begin fading the gestural prompts. Say, "Look at the ball," and point to the ball. If the student looks at the ball, reinforce immediately.
8. Say, "Look at the ball," and move your arm only three-fourths of the way toward the ball.
9. On each trial, move your arm less and less close to the ball until you are just pointing, without moving your arm.
10. When five consecutive correct responses are made with the gestural prompt, begin using only verbal prompts (commands).
11. When five consecutive correct responses occur to the verbal prompt, you have taught the behavior successfully.
12. Remember to continue to reinforce each correct response at every Step.

One important warning is to be careful to fade the prompts *gradually.* If they are faded too quickly, the student will begin making mistakes (not making the correct response). If this happens, you should move back one Step to the amount of prompting that aided the last correct response.

Physical prompts, when combined with verbal commands and gestures, allow the student to *feel,* as well as *hear* and *see,* what he is to do. Remember, fade physical prompts first, then gestures. Be sure to fade the prompts in small steps. Do not fade prompts too quickly, or the student may not be able to perform the behavior. If the student does not respond to the new prompt, go back to the previous Step and start again. Every student is different and learns at a different rate.

Now, design a procedure using the three prompt levels and fading to teach a student to pick up a spoon. Write your example in a series of Steps and be very specific.

CHAPTER FIVE/Questions

All of the questions below must be completed with 100-percent accuracy before going on to the Chapter Five stories.

1. Aide training begins by providing a m_____

2. A minimum of f_____ modeling demonstrations should be provided before the aide begins role playing.

3. Reinforcement is the _____ component of the instructional cycle. a. first; b. second; c. third; d. fourth

4. If a response is reinforced it will _____

5. If a response is not reinforced it will _____

6. True or False (circle one).
   All aides must be able to explain the principles of fading and prompting.

7. What are the three types of prompts?

   1. _____

   2. _____

   3. _____

8. True or False (circle one).
   Prompts must be faded quickly.

9. True or False (circle one).
   Aide training should consist of a two-week in-service program where all aides are required to read "Principles of Behavior Modifications."

10. Why is it the responsibility of the teacher, nurse, or psychologist to provide the appropriate prompts for the aides?

_____

_____

_____

QUESTIONS FOR PARENTS ON PROMPTING AND FADING

1. P_____ means giving the students cues that help them to learn the behavior you are trying to teach them.

2. When you begin to teach a new behavior, you first use a _____ prompt. If an appropriate response does not occur, repeat the command and provide a _____ prompt. If an appropriate response still does not occur, repeat the _____ and the _____ and use _____ prompts.

3. Do you continue to use gestural and physical prompts if an appropriate response occurs to a verbal prompt? _____

4. True or False (circle one).
   A verbal prompt is always given at the beginning of a trial.

5. How many consecutive correct responses are needed to reach criterion with one level of prompts? _____

6. After a student has made five consecutive correct responses to a gestural command, you should move on to the _____.

7. What is the most successful method of eliminating gestural and physical prompts? _____

8. What should you do if the student does not respond to the new prompt?

   _____

9. Does every student learn at a different rate? _____

10. Prompts should be faded _____.

Suggested Readings

Patterson, G. R., Ebner, M., and Shaw, D. 1969. Teachers, peers, and parents as agents of change. In: A. Benson (ed.), Behavior Modification in the Schools. University of Oregon Press, Eugene.

Rettig, E. B. 1973. A.B.C.'s For Parents. Associates for Behavior Change, Van Nuys, Calif.

Salzinger, K., Feldman, R. S., and Portnoy, S. 1970. Training parents of brain-injured children in the use of operant conditioning procedures. Behav. Ther. 1:4–32.

CHAPTER SIX

Data
Collection

Data must be collected daily on each student. These data determine when the student should progress to the next Step within a Task Analysis, or the next Objective. Data collection is completed after the following steps are implemented:

Filling out data sheets (daily)—use a new sheet for each Objective:

1. Write student's name next to "Name."
2. Write area of the curriculum (i.e., Language, Eye-Hand Coordination, etc.) next to "Area."
3. Write the Objective number next to "Objective _____"
4. Write in "Step _____"
5. Write in the reinforcer used next to "Reinforcers."
6. Write your name under the first set of empty blocks next to "Trainer Signature."
7. Write the day of the week and the date next to "Day and Date."
8. Write the type of prompt used (physical, gestural, or verbal) next to "Prompt."
9. Begin the training session. For each trial, mark a (√) if the response is correct and satisfactory. If the response is incorrect, mark a (0). Each block corresponds with one trial. Begin marking in the first block and continue through the blocks in consecutive order until the student gives five consecutive correct responses in one session with one type of prompt (i.e., physical).

   A training session is ended:
   a. after a student makes five consecutive correct responses to one prompt
   b. after five consecutive incorrect responses
   c. after ten incorrect responses
   d. after twenty trials

10. Count all the check (√) marks and enter that number on line 1, "Correct response."
11. Count all responses (√ and 0) and enter that number on line 2, "Total responses."
12. Count the consecutive correct responses and enter that number on line 3, "Highest total number of consecutive responses."

DATA SHEET

Name _____ Objective _____

Area _____ Reinforcers _____

TRIAL ___

1	2	3	4	5	6	7	8	9	10
11	12	13	14	15	16	17	18	19	20

Step ___

Trainer signature _____

Day and Date _____

Prompt _____

1. Correct responses _____
2. Total responses _____
3. Highest number consecutive responses _____

TRIAL ___

1	2	3	4	5	6	7	8	9	10
11	12	13	14	15	16	17	18	19	20

Step ___

Trainer signature _____

Day and Date _____

Prompt _____

1. Correct responses _____
2. Total responses _____
3. Highest number consecutive responses _____

TRIAL ___

1	2	3	4	5	6	7	8	9	10
11	12	13	14	15	16	17	18	19	20

Step ___

Trainer signature _____

Day and Date _____

Prompt _____

1. Correct responses _____
2. Total responses _____
3. Highest number consecutive responses _____

TRIAL ___

1	2	3	4	5	6	7	8	9	10
11	12	13	14	15	16	17	18	19	20

Step ___

Trainer signature _____

Day and Date _____

Prompt _____

1. Correct responses _____
2. Total responses _____
3. Highest number consecutive responses _____

TRIAL ___

1	2	3	4	5	6	7	8	9	10
11	12	13	14	15	16	17	18	19	20

Step ___

Trainer signature _____

Day and Date _____

Prompt _____

1. Correct responses _____
2. Total responses _____
3. Highest number consecutive responses _____

CHAPTER SIX/Questions

All of the questions below must be completed with 100-percent accuracy before going on to the Chapter Six stories.

Answer these questions, using the following data sheet.

1. What is the student's name? _____

2. What area in the curriculum is the student training on?

   _____

3. The student is training on Objective _____.

4. The Step within that Objective is _____.

5. What reinforcer is being used? _____

6. What is the trainer's name? _____

7. What prompt is being used? _____

8. What does a (√) indicate? _____

9. What does a (0) indicate? _____

10. When is a training session terminated?

    a. _____

    b. _____

    c. _____

    d. _____

11. What is the total number of correct responses?

    _____

12. What is the total number of responses?

    _____

13. What is the highest number of total consecutive responses?

    _____

DATA SHEET

Name _Ivan_ Objective _3_

Area _Auditory Training_ Reinforcers _cheese bits_

TRIAL _1_

1	2	3	4	5	6	7	8	9	10
✓	✓	✓	0	0	✓	0	0	0	0
✓	✓	✓	✓	✓					
11	12	13	14	15	16	17	18	19	20

Step _2_

Trainer signature _Terry_

Day and Date _3-12-76_

Prompt _gestural_

1. Correct responses _9_
2. Total responses _15_
3. Highest number consecutive responses _5_

TRIAL ___

1	2	3	4	5	6	7	8	9	10
11	12	13	14	15	16	17	18	19	20

Step ___

Trainer signature ___

Day and Date ___

Prompt ___

1. Correct responses ___
2. Total responses ___
3. Highest number consecutive responses ___

TRIAL ___

1	2	3	4	5	6	7	8	9	10
11	12	13	14	15	16	17	18	19	20

Step ___

Trainer signature ___

Day and Date ___

Prompt ___

1. Correct responses ___
2. Total responses ___
3. Highest number consecutive responses ___

TRIAL ___

1	2	3	4	5	6	7	8	9	10
11	12	13	14	15	16	17	18	19	20

Step ___

Trainer signature ___

Day and Date ___

Prompt ___

1. Correct responses ___
2. Total responses ___
3. Highest number consecutive responses ___

TRIAL ___

1	2	3	4	5	6	7	8	9	10
11	12	13	14	15	16	17	18	19	20

Step ___

Trainer signature ___

Day and Date ___

Prompt ___

1. Correct responses ___
2. Total responses ___
3. Highest number consecutive responses ___

Story 6-A

Sally, a student, was assessed by Harry, a training aide. The aide prescribed the area of Eye-Hand Coordination and found Sally to be on Objective 7. After determining the operant level, the aide knew that Sally would need a gestural prompt if she were to complete Step 2. The aide is on his way to the market to buy peppermint patties to use as Sally's reinforcer. While he is gone, fill in the following daily data sheet.

DATA SHEET

Name _____ Objective _____

Area _____ Reinforcers _____

TRIAL ___

	1	2	3	4	5	6	7	8	9	10

Step ___   11 12 13 14 15 16 17 18 19 20

Trainer signature _____

Day and Date _____

Prompt _____

1. Correct responses _____
2. Total responses _____
3. Highest number consecutive responses _____

TRIAL ___

	1	2	3	4	5	6	7	8	9	10

Step ___   11 12 13 14 15 16 17 18 19 20

Trainer signature _____

Day and Date _____

Prompt _____

1. Correct responses _____
2. Total responses _____
3. Highest number consecutive responses _____

TRIAL ___

	1	2	3	4	5	6	7	8	9	10

Step ___   11 12 13 14 15 16 17 18 19 20

Trainer signature _____

Day and Date _____

Prompt _____

1. Correct responses _____
2. Total responses _____
3. Highest number consecutive responses _____

TRIAL ___

	1	2	3	4	5	6	7	8	9	10

Step ___   11 12 13 14 15 16 17 18 19 20

Trainer signature _____

Day and Date _____

Prompt _____

1. Correct responses _____
2. Total responses _____
3. Highest number consecutive responses _____

TRIAL ___

	1	2	3	4	5	6	7	8	9	10

Step ___   11 12 13 14 15 16 17 18 19 20

Trainer signature _____

Day and Date _____

Prompt _____

1. Correct responses _____
2. Total responses _____
3. Highest number consecutive responses _____

Story 6-B

Constance has just completed her first trial on Step 2 of Attending, Objective 1. What information is supplied for the second trial? Fill in the following information for Trial 2:

Trial: _____

Step: _____

Trainer Signature: _____

Day and Date: _____

Prompt: _____

DATA SHEET

Name __Constance Smith__   Objective __1__

Area __Attending__   Reinforcers __Kool-Aid__

TRIAL __1__

1	2	3	4	5	6	7	8	9	10
0	0	0	0	✓	✓	✓	✓	✓	0
✓	✓	✓	✓	✓					
11	12	13	14	15	16	17	18	19	20

Step __2__

Trainer signature __Jenny__

Day and Date __12-1-76__

Prompt __physical__

1. Correct responses __10__
2. Total responses __15__
3. Highest number consecutive responses __5__

TRIAL ____

1	2	3	4	5	6	7	8	9	10
11	12	13	14	15	16	17	18	19	20

Step ____

Trainer signature ____

Day and Date ____

Prompt ____

1. Correct responses ____
2. Total responses ____
3. Highest number consecutive responses ____

TRIAL ____

1	2	3	4	5	6	7	8	9	10
11	12	13	14	15	16	17	18	19	20

Step ____

Trainer signature ____

Day and Date ____

Prompt ____

1. Correct responses ____
2. Total responses ____
3. Highest number consecutive responses ____

TRIAL ____

1	2	3	4	5	6	7	8	9	10
11	12	13	14	15	16	17	18	19	20

Step ____

Trainer signature ____

Day and Date ____

Prompt ____

1. Correct responses ____
2. Total responses ____
3. Highest number consecutive responses ____

TRIAL ____

1	2	3	4	5	6	7	8	9	10
11	12	13	14	15	16	17	18	19	20

Step ____

Trainer signature ____

Day and Date ____

Prompt ____

1. Correct responses ____
2. Total responses ____
3. Highest number consecutive responses ____

Story 6-C

Myrtle filled out the following data sheet while training Nicky on Attending, Objective 2. She made five mistakes on this sheet. Find them and list them below.

1. _____

2. _____

3. _____

4. _____

5. _____

DATA SHEET

Name __Nicky Jones__   Objective __2__
Area __Attending__   Reinforcers __Froot Loops__

TRIAL 1

1	2	3	4	5	6	7	8	9	10
0	✓	✓	✓	✓	✓	✓	✓	✓	✓
✓	✓	✓	0	✓	✓	✓	✓	✓	✓
11	12	13	14	15	16	17	18	19	20

Step __2__

Trainer signature __Myrtle__
Day and Date __2-20-76__
Prompt __physical__

1. Correct responses __18__
2. Total responses __20__
3. Highest number consecutive responses __12__

TRIAL 2

1	2	3	4	5	6	7	8	9	10
0	0	0	0	✓	✓	✓	✓	0	0
✓	0	✓	✓	✓	✓	✓	✓	✓	✓
11	12	13	14	15	16	17	18	19	20

Step __2__

Trainer signature __Myrtle__
Day and Date __2-21-76__
Prompt __Gestural__

1. Correct responses __13__
2. Total responses __20__
3. Highest number consecutive responses __8__

TRIAL 3

1	2	3	4	5	6	7	8	9	10
0	0	0	0	0	0	0	0	0	0
0	0	0	0	0	0	0	0	0	0
11	12	13	14	15	16	17	18	19	20

Step __2__

Trainer signature __Myrtle__
Day and Date __2-22-76__
Prompt __verbal__

1. Correct responses __0__
2. Total responses __20__
3. Highest number consecutive responses __20__

TRIAL 1

1	2	3	4	5	6	7	8	9	10
✓	✓	0	✓	✓	0	0	0	✓	✓
✓	0	0	0	0	0	✓	✓	✓	0
11	12	13	14	15	16	17	18	19	20

Step __3__

Trainer signature __Myrtle__
Day and Date __2-23-76__
Prompt __physical__

1. Correct responses __10__
2. Total responses __20__
3. Highest number consecutive responses __5__

TRIAL 4

1	2	3	4	5	6	7	8	9	10
0	0	0	0	0	0	✓	0	0	0
11	12	13	14	15	16	17	18	19	20

Step __2__

Trainer signature __Myrtle__
Day and Date __2-24-76__
Prompt __verbal__

1. Correct responses __1__
2. Total responses __10__
3. Highest number consecutive responses __6__

CHAPTER SEVEN

Writing Behavioral Objectives AND Task Analyses

BEHAVIORAL OBJECTIVES

Behavioral Objectives describe what the student will be doing. This description provides a basis for establishing criterion as well as a consistent understanding of the terminal goal. An Objective is behavioral only if it describes an observable act. The following phrases are not behavioral. An Objective containing these phrases would be a general Objective, not a Behavioral Objective.

General Objective Phrases

to think
to value
to be responsible
to integrate
to be socialized
to contribute
to distinguish
to acquire
to enjoy
to imagine
to understand

Observable acts are the distinguishing feature of Behavioral Objectives. Behavioral Objectives make selection of learning activities easier because one knows the behavior to be produced. The following list of phrases are behavioral, any Objective containing these or other active phrases would be Behavioral Objectives.

Behavioral Objective Phrases

to name
to write
to list
to construct
to classify
to demonstrate
to sequence
to outline
to compute

to describe orally
to read orally

An alternative to selecting the various phrases is to construct a form for all Behavioral Objectives. A form was constructed to be used in this program and it can continue to be used for any new behaviors you would like to train. Fill in the form with an observable behavior:

The student will _____ after attaining five consecutive positive responses to a verbal command on each Step of the Task Analysis.

This form for Objectives contains the criterion (five consecutive positive responses to a verbal command), it states who will perform the activity (the student) and one need only insert the desired observable behavior.

Task Analyses

The Task Analyses break the behavior down into small, easy-to-teach Steps. Task Analyses can be written only after the observable behavior has been stated. As you begin to write a Task Analysis, there are three questions that must be asked:

1. What is your goal?
2. What are the entering behaviors?
3. What steps lie between the goal and the entering behaviors?
   a. list the skills for that behavior
   b. sequence the skills

The following is an example of teaching a student to insert a circle in a shape sorting box.

Behavioral Objective—The student will insert the circle in the shape sorting box after attaining five consecutive positive responses to a verbal command on each Step of the Task Analysis.

Task Analysis Step 1—What is your goal?
The student will insert the circle in the shape sorting box.
Task Analysis Step 2—What are the entering behaviors?
Give the student an opportunity to perform the action to determine the entering behaviors. If the action is being written for general use, assume that the entering behaviors are at Step 1 and write all the Steps for the entire action.

Task Analysis Step 3—What steps lie between the goal and the entering behavior?
In this example, assume that the entering behavior will begin at zero, therefore all Steps lie in between.
Task Analysis Step 3a—List Steps.
If the student is to insert the circle in the shape sorting box, he must:
1. be able to pick up the circle
2. be able to take the circle to the box
3. find the appropriate inset
4. insert the circle into the shape sorting box
Task Analysis Step 3b—Sequence Steps.
Steps should be sequenced so that easy Steps occur before the more difficult ones. The Steps should be small, and prompts can be used throughout. For example:
1. The student will let you pick up the circle and put it in the box using his hand.
2. The student will let you pick up the circle using his hand and position it by the inset, and he will put it in the box after a gestural prompt is given.
3. The student will let you pick up the circle using his hand and position it by the inset, and he will put it in the box.
4. The student will let you pick up the circle and take it to the box using his hand, and he will put it in the box after a gestural prompt is given.
5. The student will let you pick up the circle and take it to the box using his hand, and he will put it in the box.
6. The student will let you pick up the circle using his hand, and he will put it in the box after a gestural prompt is given.
7. The student will let you pick up the circle using his hand, and he will put it in the box.
8. The student will pick up the circle and put it in the box after a gestural prompt is given.
9. The student will pick up the circle and put it in the box.

IMPLEMENTATIONS

All prompts are faded gradually, but problems may still occur. Implementations are constructed for those unexpected problems. For example, a student may have difficulty with the various shapes on the shape sorting box. These shapes can be masked, leaving only the circle for the student to see. The tape can be faded gradually as the student becomes proficient in the behavior.

The implementation would contain the following information: 1) materials to be used, 2) prerequisite skills, 3) procedures, and 4) problems encountered in the past. Together, the Behavioral Objectives, Task Analysis Steps, and Implementations provide a full training program that is designed for individual needs.

CHAPTER SEVEN/Questions

All of the questions below must be completed with 100-percent accuracy before going on to the Chapter Eight stories.

1. Behavioral Objectives describe _____

2. Which of the following Objectives are behavioral?
    a. John will think of three states he visited within the last ten years.
    b. The student will enjoy the ring tossing game after attaining five consecutive positive responses on each Step of the Task Analysis.
    c. Becky will write three spelling words correctly on a sheet of 9″ × 12″ paper.
    d. John will correctly recite the poem, "The Highwayman."
    e. Students will imagine themselves to be barnyard animals.

3. What is the distinguishing feature of a Behavioral Objective?

    _____

4. List four behavioral phrases:

    1. _____

    2. _____

    3. _____

    4. _____

5. Write the form constructed for writing Behavioral Objectives.

    _____

6. What function does a Task Analysis serve?

_____

7. What three questions must be asked when you begin to write a Task Analysis?

1. _____

2. _____

3. _____

8. After the Steps have been determined, what should be done next?

3a. _____

3b. _____

9. On a separate sheet of paper, write a Task Analysis for assembling a three-piece puzzle.

10. On a separate sheet of paper, write a Task Analysis for turning the dial on a busy surprise box or telephone.

Suggested Readings

Anderson, R. C., Faust, G. W., Roderick, M. C., Cunningham, D. J., and Andre, T. (eds.). 1969. Section II, Instructional Objectives, Current Research on Instruction. Prentice-Hall, Englewood Cliffs, N.J.

Bivens, L. W., 1964. Feedback complexity and self-direction in programmed instruction. Psych. Repts. 14:155–160.

Bloom, B. S. 1956. Taxonomy of Educational Objectives. Longmans, Green, New York.

Cronbach, L. J. 1967. How can Instruction be adapted to individual differences? In: R. M. Gagné, ed., Learning and Individual Differences. Charles E. Merrill, Columbus, Ohio.

Della-Piana, G. 1962. An experimental evaluation of programmed learning. J. Ed. Res., 55:495–501.

Ebel, R. L. 1970. Behavioral objectives, a close look. Ed. Tech. 10: 171–173.

Gagné, R. M. 1969. The acquisition of knowledge. In: R. C. Anderson et al., Current Research in Instruction. Prentice-Hall, Englewood Cliffs, N.J.

Kapfer, P. G. 1970. Behavioral objectives and the curriculum process. Ed. Tech. 5:14–17.

Mechner, F. 1965. Science education and behavioral technology. In: R. Glaser, ed., Teaching Machine and Programmed Learning II. National Education Association, Washington, D.C.

Popham, W. J. 1970. The instructional objectives exchange: New support for criterion—referenced instruction. Ed. Tech. 10:174–175.

CHAPTER EIGHT

A System
OF
Maintenance
FOR THE
Prescriptive
Checklist

Prescriptions for remediation have been assigned, and the students are now being trained. The supervisor is writing new Objectives and Task Analyses, and the many components of the program are operating with little difficulty. The next question one would naturally ask is: How are these behaviors maintained?

To maintain student behaviors, one should institute a maintenance program. For example, a typical day would consist of two fifteen-minute training sessions and a fifteen-minute maintenance session at the end of each day. During this maintenance session, a stimulus (i.e., toy) would be provided in the appropriate environment. If the student had been trained to manipulate a busy box in the training area, the student would now have the opportunity to play with the busy box on the floor or in his bed. This enables the newly trained behavior to generalize from the training area to the general ward environment.

The chart on page 71 is used to assess the students on the Checklist every four weeks. This will determine which behaviors have generalized. For example, the student may have completed Eye-Hand Coordination Objectives 1 through 6 and is being trained on Objective 7. Assessment one week later indicates that the student now has assimilated Objectives 9 and 10 into his repertoire. These Objectives were mastered, but they were not trained on. One can now say that generalization has occurred.

This monthly assessment will also depict those behaviors in need of maintenance. For example, an assessment was made in June, and Keith had completed Eye-Hand Coordination Objectives 1 through 10. One month later the assessment revealed that he had mastered Eye-Hand Coordination Objectives 1 through 5 and 8 through 12. Although he learned two new Objectives, he is in need of a maintenance program for Objectives 6 and 7.

Just as the student behaviors must be maintained, so should the staff behaviors. The aides should be assessed weekly in a random fashion. The Therapy Evaluation Form on page 72 provides an instant evaluation. Feedback can be given to the aides immediately, and it provides an observable record of staff effectiveness. These forms can also be used by the aides to monitor each other as well as to provide guidelines for role playing.

The high quality of instruction can be maintained only if the program supervisor works within the program. Being physically removed from the ward or classroom, one cannot maintain an objective assessment of the problems encountered with the instructional materials or the needs of the students. Maintenance of an effective program requires full participation by all persons involved.

STUDENT ASSESSMENT CHART

Objective Number

AREA	1 2 3 4 5 6 7 8 9 10 11 12 13 14 15 16 17 18 19 20 21 22 23 24 25 26 27 28 29 30 31 32 33 34 35 36 37 38 39 40 41 42 43 44 45 46 47 48 49 50 51
Motor Development Head & Trunk	
Sitting	
Hand-knee	
Standing	
Eye-Hand	
Language Attending	
Auditory	
Physical Imitation	
Object Discrimination	
Concept Development	
Sound Imitation	
Eating	

Baseline ▉

Completed Objectives ▥

Comments:

THERAPY EVALUATION FORM

Prescriptive Checklist for the Severely Retarded

Therapist _____ Evaluator _____ Date _____

Student _____ Curriculum Area _____

Objective _____ Step _____

Good	Needs work (see comments)		

General

1. Cooperates in following any general rules for the student specified by staff.

2. Uses reinforcers appropriate to the student.

3. Begins and ends session on time (+ or — five minutes).

4. Has materials (toys, reinforcers) ready at the beginning of the session and puts them away at the end of the session.

5. Teaching behavior appropriate for the student, i.e., student has prerequisite behaviors to complete the objective.

6. Asks for suggesions for changing a procedure that is not working.

Procedure

7. Follows procedure as specified in the curriculum unless another procedure has been written and approved.

8. Uses the appropriate physical, gestural, or verbal prompts at the right times according to the curriculum and the shaping and fading procedures.

9. Gives the student the same command or instructions consistently at the beginning of each trial.

10. Presents the command or instruction when the student is sitting quietly and looking at the therapist or equipment.

11. Delivers the reinforcers for appropriate behaviors immediately, enthusiastically, consistently.

12. Consequates inappropriate social behavior with extinction or verbal reprimand correctly and consistently.

13. Consequates inappropriate task-related behavior with extinction and consistently.

14. Records all data correctly according to the hand-out data sheet.

CHAPTER EIGHT/Questions

All of the questions below must be completed with 100-percent accuracy before going on to the Chapter Eight stories.

1. How are behaviors maintained?

   _____

2. How many maintenance sessions should a student experience in one day? _____

3. What transpires during a student maintenance session?

   _____

4. Cathy completed all seven Attending Objectives in July. An assessment was made in August, and it was discovered that Cathy could no longer master Objective 4. What should be done to help Cathy?

   _____

   _____

5. What areas are included in the Student Assessment Form?

   _____

6. How do you know if a behavior has generalized?

   _____

   _____

7. What information does the Student Assessment Form provide?

   a. _____

   b. _____

8. The aides should be assessed _____
   a. weekly
   b. bi-weekly
   c. daily
   d. monthly

9. The therapy evaluation form provides instant _____ for the aides and an _____ of staff effectiveness.

10. The supervisor of the program must _____
    a. visit the program daily
    b. be available for aide consultation
    c. work within the program
    d. dress well so that everyone will know who the supervisor is.

Story 8-A

Elaine, an aide, loved to work with her students. She took pride in the fact that they completed many Objectives when the program began. For the last month, Elaine has felt badly because her training has lost its effectiveness. She has asked her friends who are also aides for advice, but nothing seems to help.

Elaine has lost some of her appropriate training behaviors. Give at least one suggestion for remediation.

Story 8-B

Willy has completed all of the Objectives in every area of the program. He can complete each Objective upon command, but only when in the training area.

1. What did the teacher or aide forget to do after Willy learned each Objective?

2. Is it too late for the teacher or aide to alleviate the problem they created? If not, what can be done?

3. If time is allotted to working with Willy three times a day, how should this time be spent?

CHAPTER NINE

Criteria FOR Checklist Objectives

MOTOR DEVELOPMENT/Head and Trunk Control

Date_____ Name_____

OBJECTIVES

The student will:

1. hold his head erect without support when on his stomach or held over your shoulder

2. lift his head and upper chest when lying down

3. raise his head up and forward from a back-lying position

4. hold his head up when supported in a sitting position

5. hold his head in proper alignment when pulled to a sitting position

CRITERIA

The student will hold his head up when he is lying across your lap or held over your shoulder.

The student will lift his head and upper chest when a toy is dangled in front of him and he is lying on his stomach.

The student will lift his head and maintain a head-erect position for at least thirty seconds while watching a visual stimulus such as a mobile.

The student will hold his head up while you support him in a sitting position.

The student will hold his head in alignment with his arms as you pull him by his arms to a sitting position.

MOTOR DEVELOPMENT/Sitting

Date_____ Name_____

OBJECTIVES

The student will:

1. go from a back-lying to a side-lying position

2. go from a front-lying to a side-lying position

3. sit with support

4. sit without support

CRITERIA

The student will be lying on his back while you provide a stimulus to the side of him. He must roll over to his side for full credit.

The student will be lying on his stomach while you provide a stimulus to the side of him. He must roll over to his side for full credit.

The student will sit while you provide support with your hands or prop him in a corner.

The student will sit without any type of physical support.

MOTOR DEVELOPMENT/Hand-Knee Position

Date_____ Name_____

OBJECTIVES

The student will:

1. go from a front-lying to a hand-knee position with assistance

2. go from a front-lying to a hand-knee position without assistance

3. maintain a hand-knee position with assistance

4. maintain a hand-knee position without assistance

CRITERIA

The student will be lying on his stomach with his hands palm-down next to his shoulders and you will push his knees under his chest to help him attain this position.

Try to encourage the student to assume this position by using a great deal of verbal praise and by dangling a toy in front of him.

The student will maintain a hand-knee position as you support his elbows and legs.

The student will maintain this position without assistance.

MOTOR DEVELOPMENT/Standing

Date_____ Name_____

OBJECTIVES

The student will:

1. tolerate weight bearing on his feet while supported

2. support part of his body weight and actively bend and straighten his legs

3. balance his trunk

4. pull himself to a standing position from a squatting position

5. pull himself to a standing position from a hand-knee position

6. stand independently

CRITERIA

The student will keep his legs extended and feet flat on the floor as you support him under his arms.

The student will support part of his body weight as you provide partial support by holding him under his arms and encourage a bouncing movement.

The student will demonstrate trunk balance by regaining his position when tilted in any direction. He should be seated for this exercise.

The student will pull himself to a standing position from a squat as you hold his hands or position him by a table.

The student will pull himself to a standing position from a hand-knee position as you provide your hands or a table for assistance.

The student will stand without any type of assistance.

EYE-HAND COORDINATION

Date_____ Name_____

OBJECTIVES

The student will:

1. make random patterns in shaving cream

2. make random patterns in finger paint

3. grasp a sound tube

4. release a sound tube

5. release a sound tube in a box

6. pick up a clutch ball

7. punch a balloon

8. reach for a soap bubble

9. spin the bubble on the mobile

10. spin the handle on the mobile

11. squeak the ball on the mobile

12. pull the handle on the merry-go-round

CRITERIA

You will spread shaving cream on paper, and the student will make movements in it with his hands or fingers.

You will spread paint on paper, and the student will make movements in it with his hands or fingers.

The student will hold a sound tube for five seconds upon command.

The student will open his hand and release the sound tube upon command.

The student will release the sound tube in a box upon command.

The student will pick up and hold a clutch ball for five seconds upon command after it has been placed on the table.

The student will reach out and punch a balloon.

The student will reach for bubbles as they pass by or break a bubble that is held stationary in front of him.

The student will spin the bubble upon command. If the bubble moves enough to create a noise, credit should be given.

The student will touch or grasp the handle to make it move upon command.

The student will make the ball squeak upon command.

The student will pull the handle upon command, making the merry-go-round rotate.

(continued)

EYE-HAND COORDINATION, continued

Date_____ Name_____

OBJECTIVES

The student will:

13. turn the knob on the busy box

14. turn the crank on the busy box

15. press the button on the busy box

16. push the car on the busy box

17. slide the door on the busy box

18. turn the telephone dial on the busy box

19. spin the wheel on the busy box

20. open the door on the busy box

21. open the drawer on the busy box

22. press the button on the surprise busy box

23. slide the knob on the surprise busy box

24. turn the knob on the surprise busy box

CRITERIA

The student will turn the knob upon command, making the hands of the clock move.

The student will turn the crank upon command, enough to make the windmill rotate.

The student will press the button upon command so that a squeaky sound will be emitted.

The student will move the car from one end of the slot to the other upon command. Full credit will be given if it is moved half way or more.

The student will slide the door open upon command.

The student will turn the dial upon command. He can use a finger or his entire hand.

The student will make the wheel turn upon command. He can use his hand or finger.

The student will open the door upon command.

The student will slide the drawer open upon command.

The student will press the button upon command, making the door open.

The student will slide the knob upon command, making the door open.

The student will turn the knob upon command, making the door open.

(continued)

EYE-HAND COORDINATION, continued

Date_____ Name_____

OBJECTIVES

The student will:

25. turn the dial on the surprise busy box

26. flip the switch on the surprise busy box

27. place three pegs in a peg board

28. remove stacking rings

29. randomly stack stacking rings

30. stack two stacking rings in order

31. nest nesting blocks

32. stack nesting blocks

33. nest nesting cups

34. stack nesting cups

35. place a circle in the form board

36. place a square in the form board

CRITERIA

The student will turn the dial upon command, making the door open.

The student will flip the switch upon command, making the door open.

The student will place three pegs in a board upon command as they are handed to him, one by one.

The student will remove the stacking rings upon command.

The student will randomly stack three stacking rings (one large, one medium, one small) upon command.

The student will stack two rings in order upon command.

The student will nest one large, one medium, and one small nesting block upon command.

The student will stack one large, one medium, and one small nesting block upon command.

The student will nest one large, one medium, and one small nesting cup upon command.

The student will stack one large, one medium, and one small nesting cup upon command.

The student will place a circle in the inset upon command after the circle is handed to him.

The student will place a square in the inset upon command after the square is handed to him.

(continued)

EYE-HAND COORDINATION, continued

Date_____ Name_____

OBJECTIVES

The student will:

37. place a triangle in the form board

38. place a circle in the shape sorting box

39. place a square in the shape sorting box

40. place a triangle in the shape sorting box

41. assemble a three-piece puzzle

42. assemble a four-piece puzzle

43. assemble a five-piece puzzle

44. assemble a six-piece puzzle

45. trace a horizontal line with his finger

46. trace a vertical line with his finger

47. trace a horizontal curved line with his finger

CRITERIA

The student will place a triangle in the proper inset upon command after the triangle is handed to him.

The student will place a circle in the proper inset upon command after the circle is handed to him.

The student will place a square in the proper inset upon command after the square is handed to him.

The student will place a triangle in the proper inset upon command after the triangle is handed to him.

The student will put each puzzle piece in the proper inset upon command after they are handed to him, one by one.

The student will put each puzzle piece in the proper inset upon command after they are handed to him, one by one.

The student will put each puzzle piece in the proper inset upon command after they are handed to him, one by one.

The student will put each puzzle piece in the proper inset upon command after they are handed to him, one by one.

The student will trace the line upon command, using one or two fingers only.

The student will trace the line upon command, using one or two fingers only.

The student will trace the line upon command, using one or two fingers only.

(continued)

EYE-HAND COORDINATION, continued

Date_____ Name_____

OBJECTIVES

The student will:

48. trace an up and down curve with his finger

49. trace a circle, using a template

50. trace a square, using a template

51. trace a triangle, using a template

CRITERIA

The student will trace the line upon command, using one or two fingers only.

The student will trace a circle upon command, using his finger or a pencil.

The student will trace a square upon command, using his finger or a pencil.

The student will trace a triangle upon command, using his finger or a pencil.

LANGUAGE DEVELOPMENT/Attending

Date_____ Name_____

OBJECTIVES

The student will:

1. fixate on an object upon the command, "Look"

2. follow a moving object in a horizontal pattern

3. follow a moving object in a vertical pattern

4. follow a moving object in a diagonal pattern

5. follow a moving object in a circular pattern

6. converge

CRITERIA

The student will look at an object upon command as you hold it in front of him.

The student will look at an object upon command as you move it in a horizontal pattern.

The student will look at an object upon command as you move it in a vertical pattern.

The student will look at an object upon command as you move it in a diagonal pattern.

The student will look at an object upon command as you move it in a circular pattern.

The student will look at an object with both eyes upon command as you hold it in front of him.

LANGUAGE DEVELOPMENT/Physical Imitation

Date_____ Name_____

OBJECTIVES

The student will:

1. slap the table

2. clap hands

3. imitate ringing a bell

4. imitate pounding a mallet

5. ring a bell and pound a mallet

6a. *blow a feather *or*

6b. *blow out a candle *or*

6c. *blow a whistle

CRITERIA

The student will slap the table upon command after you have provided a model.

The student will clap hands upon command after you have provided a model.

The student will imitate ringing a bell upon command after you have provided the model.

The student will imitate pounding a mallet upon command after you have provided the model.

The student will ring a bell upon command and pound a mallet upon command when both are present.

The student will blow a feather upon command after you have provided a model.

The student will blow a candle out upon command after you have provided a model.

The student will blow a whistle upon command after you have provided a model.

_____

*No. 6a, b, and c are interchangeable. If the student can do one, he can receive credit for all.

LANGUAGE DEVELOPMENT/Auditory Training

Date_____ Name_____

OBJECTIVES

The student will:

1. look to the left to a sound

2. look to the right to a sound

3. follow a sound from left to right

4. locate a sound behind him

5. follow graduated sounds

6. imitate pounding a mallet

7. imitate ringing a bell

8. ring a bell and pound a mallet

9. imitate the sound of a bell

10. imitate the sound of a mallet

11. physically imitate the sound of a bell and the sound of a mallet when both are present

CRITERIA

The student will look to the left to sound as you make a noise to the left of him.

The student will look to the right to sound as you make a noise to the right of him.

The student will look from left to right to follow the sound stimulus you provide.

The student will look behind him as you provide a sound stimulus.

The student will follow the three grades of sound as you provide the stimulus.

The student will imitate pounding a mallet upon command after you have provided the model.

The student will imitate ringing a bell upon command after you have provided the model.

The student will ring a bell and pound a mallet upon command when both are present.

The student will imitate ringing a bell upon command when you ring it under a table.

The student will imitate pounding a mallet upon command when you pound it under a table.

The student will ring a bell upon command when the bell is being rung under a table and pound a mallet upon command when the mallet is being pounded under the table. The student should have both the mallet and the bell present on the table.

LANGUAGE DEVELOPMENT/Object Discrimination

Date_____ Name_____

OBJECTIVES

The student will:

1. give spoon

2. give spoon when spoon and fork are present

3. give fork

4. give fork and give spoon when both are present

5. give fork and give spoon when an extraneous object is present

6. give comb

7. give comb when both comb and toothbrush are present

8. give toothbrush

9. give toothbrush when both toothbrush and comb are present

10. give spoon and give toothbrush when both are present

11. give spoon and give toothbrush when an extraneous object is present

12. give cup

CRITERIA

The student will give the spoon upon command.

The student will give the spoon upon command when the fork is present.

The student will give the fork upon command.

The student will give the fork upon command and the spoon upon command when both are on the table.

The student will give the fork upon command and give the spoon upon command when both are on the table and an extraneous object is present.

The student will give the comb upon command.

The student will give the comb upon command and the toothbrush upon command when both are on the table.

The student will give the toothbrush upon command.

The student will give the toothbrush upon command when an extraneous object is present.

The student will give the spoon upon command and give the toothbrush upon command when both are present.

The student will give the toothbrush upon command and give the spoon upon command when an extraneous object is present.

The student will give the cup upon command.

(continued)

LANGUAGE DEVELOPMENT/Object Discrimination, continued

Date_____ Name_____

OBJECTIVES

The student will:

13. give cup when an extraneous object is present

14. give ball

15. give ball when both ball and cup are present

16. give ball and give cup when both are present

CRITERIA

The student will give the cup upon command when an extraneous object is present.

The student will give the ball upon command.

The student will give the ball upon command when both ball and cup are on the table.

The student will give the ball upon command and give the cup upon command when both are on the table.

LANGUAGE DEVELOPMENT/Concept Development

Date_____ Name_____

OBJECTIVES

The student will:
1. sit down

2. stand up

3. look

4. stop

5. come

6. open the door

7. close the door

8. *go to the _____

9. *give the _____

10. *put the _____ on the _____

11. *take the _____ off the _____

12. *pick up the _____

CRITERIA

The student will sit down upon command.

The student will stand up upon command.

The student will look at an object you are holding in front of him (same as Attending 1)

The student will stop upon command when you are walking with him. (If the student cannot walk have him engage in a similar activity.)

The student will come to you upon command from a distance of approximately five feet.

The student will open the door upon command.

The student will close the door upon command.

The student will go to the _____ upon command.

The student will give the _____ upon command.

The student will put the _____ on the _____ upon command.

The student will take the _____ off the _____ upon command.

The student will pick up the _____ upon command.

_____

*For Objectives 8 to 12, use nouns with which the student is familiar.

LANGUAGE DEVELOPMENT/Sound Imitation

Date_____ Name_____

OBJECTIVES

The student will imitate:

1. clapping hands

2. stamping feet

3. blowing on your hand

4. blowing a whistle

5. opening his mouth

6. closing his mouth

7. sticking out his tongue

8. the "ah" sound

9. the "oo" sound

CRITERIA

The student will clap hands upon command after you have provided a model (same as Physical Imitation 2).

The student will stamp his feet after you have provided a model.

The student will blow out a candle after you have provided a model (same as Physical Imitation 6a, b, or c).

The student will blow a whistle after you have provided a model (same as Physical Imitation 6a, b, or c).

The student will open his mouth after you have provided a model.

The student will close his mouth after you have provided a model.

The student will imitate sticking out his tongue after you have provided a model.

The student will imitate the "ah" sound after you have provided a model.

The student will imitate the "oo" sound after you have provided a model.

PHYSICAL EATING PROBLEMS

Date_____   Name_____

OBJECTIVES

The student will:

1. keep his tongue in his mouth

2. keep his lips closed

3. open his mouth

4. close his mouth

5. swallow

6. chew

7. bite with strength and chew

CRITERIA

The student will keep his tongue in his mouth while eating.

The student will keep his lips closed while eating.

The student will open his mouth upon command after a model has been provided (same as Sound Imitation 5).

The student will close his mouth upon command after a model has been provided (same as Sound Imitation 6a, b, or c).

The student will swallow while eating strained or solid foods.

The student will chew.

The student will bite a piece of candy and chew it before swallowing.

SECTION II

CHECKLISTS, OBJECTIVES, TASK ANALYSIS STEPS, AND IMPLEMENTATIONS

CHAPTER TEN

Motor
Development

If a student does not have adequate balance, you cannot expect him to successfully attend to his environment in a sitting or standing position. The student would be incapable of performing even a simple task if all his efforts were concentrated on maintaining or regaining his balance.

In the interim between beginning the balancing exercise and the time at which a student acquires these skills, there are several ways to facilitate proper balance so that you may begin teaching other tasks. The student can be placed in a relaxation chair if he has poor head control, or he can be propped up with pillows if his trunk control is inadequate. Be sure to look for signs of poor balance when working with all students. Does the student's head droop? Is he more attentive when he is supported in a chair?

The sequence of the Behavioral Checklist is developmental. Begin with the first Objective. If the student can master that Objective, place a check mark and the date on the line provided to the right of the first Objective. Proceed through the Checklist until the student encounters an Objective that is not in his repertoire. Stop at this point and determine the student's operant level on this particular task. You now have an observable record of which behaviors the student has in his repertoire and those on which you must train him.

NOTE: *Before training the student, you must consult a physical therapist for approval.*

BEHAVIORAL CHECKLIST FOR MOTOR DEVELOPMENT/Head and Trunk Control

OBJECTIVES

The student will:

1. hold his head erect without support when on his stomach or held over your shoulder _____
2. lift his head and upper chest when lying down _____
3. raise his head up and forward from a back-lying position _____
4. hold his head up when supported in a sitting position _____
5. hold his head in proper alignment when pulled to a sitting position _____

MOTOR DEVELOPMENT/Head and Trunk Control

OBJECTIVE 1

The student will hold his head erect without support when on his stomach or held over your shoulder after attaining five consecutive positive responses to a verbal command on each Step of the Task Analysis.

Task Analysis Steps

The student will:

1. let you hold his head up
2. let you hold his head up, and he will look at a dangling toy
3. let you hold his head up, and he will maintain the position for two seconds while looking at a dangling toy
4. let you hold his head up, and he will maintain the position for three seconds while looking at a dangling toy
5. let you hold his head up, and he will maintain the position for four seconds while looking at a dangling toy
6. let you hold his head up, and he will maintain the position for six seconds while looking at a dangling toy
7. let you hold his head up, and he will maintain the position for eight seconds while looking at a dangling toy
8. let you hold his head up, and he will maintain the position for ten seconds while looking at a dangling toy
9. lift his head to receive a reinforcer

MOTOR DEVELOPMENT/Head and Trunk Control

IMPLEMENTATION 1

MATERIALS:
Cage ball, carpeted barrel, dangling toy

PREREQUISITE SKILLS:
None

PROCEDURE:
A.   Determine student's reinforcement preferences
B.   Be certain the student is seated properly with support provided if needed
C.   Determine the student's operant level

The student is placed on a cage ball. The cage ball is then rolled so that the student's head is going closer to the floor. A normal reflex would be to lift the head. This can be stimulated through the use of physical prompts which will be faded later.

MOTOR DEVELOPMENT/Head and Trunk Control

OBJECTIVE 2 The student will lift his head and upper chest when lying down after attaining five consecutive positive responses to a verbal command on each Step of the Task Analysis.

Task Analysis Steps

The student will:

1. let you place his hands close to his sides in such a position that he can push himself up on them
2. place his hands close to his sides in such a position that he can push himself up on them
3. lift his head up in response to a dangling toy
4. lift his head and begin to lift his chest while following a dangling toy
5. move his forearms into a position to bear his weight
6. let you steady his arms while he lifts his chest while following a dangling toy
7. bear weight on his forearms while lifting his head and chest while following a dangling toy
8. lift his head and chest high when placed across a person's lap in a front-lying position
9. raise his head and chest up when in a front-lying position on a rounded inclined surface, such as a tire edge or a slant board
10. raise his hand and chest up high when rolled over a cylinder, barrel, or cage ball
11. lift his head and chest when his knees are tucked under him and pressure is applied to his buttocks in the direction of his heels

MOTOR DEVELOPMENT/Head and Trunk Control
IMPLEMENTATION 2

MATERIALS:

Cage ball, large covered barrel, slant board, mat, dangling noisy toy

PREREQUISITE SKILLS:

None

PROCEDURE:

A. Determine the student's reinforcement preference

B. Determine the student's operant level

1. Simply get the student used to the position. Lay him on his stomach with arms bent at elbows and hands at shoulder level.

2. The student will maintain the above position.

3. Dangle a toy in front of him; once you have his attention, raise the toy higher and higher. Try to get him to lift his head and chest. If there is a reinforcer the student particularly likes, that, too, can be dangled above him. The second time he must raise his head higher for the reinforcement.

4. Now reinforce him for lifting his chest. The next training session, reinforce for lifting head and chest.

5. Continue to reinforce as in 3 and 4. When the student raises high enough, his hands will gradually move into position.

6. Continue to reinforce and stimulate the student as in 3 and 5. Steady his arms (you can support at upper arm or elbows) while he lifts his chest. Unless the toy can be hung from the ceiling, a second person will be needed, one to dangle the toy and reinforce, the other to steady the student's arms. Once the student is up on his arms, support him and encourage him (praise—applaud) to stay in that position as long as possible.

7. Bearing weight on forearms will be easy for the student if you fade your support very gradually.

8. If the student is small enough, you can lay him across your knees in a front-lying position. Students who are too large to be held can be laid across a cage ball. Whether the student is on your lap or on a cage ball, the objective is the same. Have the student arch his back and hold his head and legs up. If you have a difficult time getting the student to respond, roll the cage ball so that the stu-

dent's head is close to the floor. As the student gets closer to the floor, he should automatically lift his head. Physical prompts are very useful also.

9. A cylinder, large barrel, or cage ball can be used to hold the student in a front-lying position. Roll the barrel slowly until the student's face is almost touching the floor. The student should automatically raise his head. Keep working with him until he can raise both head and chest.

10. A cylinder, large barrel, or cage ball can be used to hold the student in a front-lying position. Roll the barrel slowly until the student's face is almost touching the floor. The student should automatically raise his head. Keep working with him until he can raise both head and chest.

11. Tuck the student's knees under his chest and place his hands at shoulder level with elbows bent in. Apply pressure to the student's buttocks in the direction of his heels and he should lift his head and chest. Continue to perform this exercise until the student is in a position to be helped up on his elbows (not his hands).

MOTOR DEVELOPMENT/Head and Trunk Control

OBJECTIVE 3 The student will raise his head up and forward from a back-lying position after attaining five consecutive positive responses to a verbal command on each Step of the Task Analysis.

Task Analysis Steps

The student will:

1. let you turn his head from side-to-side while in a back-lying position
2. turn his head from side-to-side while in a back-lying position in response to a sound stimulus
3. turn his head from side-to-side while in a back-lying position in response to a verbal command
4. let you raise his head from a mid position while in a back-lying position
5. raise his head from a mid position while in a back-lying position in response to a sound stimulus
6. raise his head from a mid position while in a back-lying position in response to a verbal command
7. raise his head to look at a visual stimulus
8. maintain a head-erect position for at least thirty seconds while watching a visual stimulus, such as a mobile

MOTOR DEVELOPMENT/Head and Trunk Control

IMPLEMENTATION 3

MATERIALS:
Mat or table

PREREQUISITE SKILLS:
Student should be able to lift head from a front-lying position

PROCEDURE:
A. Determine the student's reinforcement preference
B. Determine the student's operant level

1. If the student is particularly rigid, start with relaxation exercises before trying to manipulate his head.
2. Reinforce the student for looking at a noise maker. Shake it to the right and reinforce the student for turning his head to the right. Shake the noise maker on the right until the student is turning in that direction. Do the same for the left, and then alternate from left to right until the student is turning his head from side to side.
3. This is similar to 2. Here, use the student's name or an expression he responds to.
4. The student will be lying on his back and you will lift his head from a mid position (head is centered, face is up).
5. Reinforce while using physical prompts to raise his head, then gradually fade out the prompts.
6. Reinforce while using physical prompts to raise his head, then gradually fade out the prompts.
7. Use the student's favorite toy or person. Once again, physical prompts and immediate reinforcement are the best helpers.

MOTOR DEVELOPMENT/Head and Trunk Control

OBJECTIVE 4 The student will hold his head up when supported in a sitting position after attaining five consecutive positive responses to a verbal command on each Step of the Task Analysis.

Task Analysis Steps

The student will:

1. let you hold him on your lap in a sitting position
2. assume a head-erect position momentarily in a sitting position
3. assume a head-erect position when pressure is applied to the base of the tailbone while in a sitting position
4. assume a head-erect position in response to a sound stimulus
5. assume a head-erect position in response to a verbal command while in a sitting position
6. assume a head-erect position in response to a visual stimulus while in a sitting position
7. let you put your hands on his shoulders while in a sitting position
8. regain a head-erect position when pulled forward from the shoulders far enough to lose head balance while in a sitting position
9. regain a head-erect position when pulled backward from the shoulders far enough to lose head balance while in a sitting position
10. regain a head-erect position when pulled to either side from the shoulders far enough to lose head balance while in a sitting position
11. hold his head up for at least one minute when supported in a sitting position while attending to a toy or mobile

MOTOR DEVELOPMENT/Head and Trunk Control

IMPLEMENTATION 4

MATERIALS:
Table

PREREQUISITE SKILLS:
None

PROCEDURE:
A.   Determine the student's reinforcement preference
B.   Determine the student's operant level

1–6.   The student can be sitting in your lap, on a table, or on a table with his legs dangling. During these Steps, the student can be held with maximum support. Once again, the use of prompts and proper fading techniques will be instrumental in attaining the desired behavior.

7.   Support the student in the sitting position by holding only his shoulders.

8.   Holding the student by the shoulders, pull him forward just far enough for him to lose his head balance. He should regain his head balance before proceeding to the next Step.

10.   Tilt the student to one side, manipulating only his shoulders, until he loses his head balance.

Any exercise to strengthen the neck muscles would be appropriate at this time. Ask your physical therapist for further suggestions.

MOTOR DEVELOPMENT/Head and Trunk Control

OBJECTIVE 5 The student will hold his head in proper alignment when pulled to a sitting position from a back-lying position after attaining five consecutive positive responses to a verbal command on each Step of the Task Analysis.

Task Analysis Steps

The student will:

1. raise his head up and forward from a back-lying position
2. let you grasp his hands
3. let you pull him up toward a sitting position
4. maintain proper head control and alignment when pulled toward a sitting position
5. maintain proper head alignment and control when returned to the mat from a sitting position

MOTOR DEVELOPMENT/Head and Trunk Control

IMPLEMENTATION 5

MATERIALS:
Mat

PREREQUISITE SKILLS:
None

PROCEDURE:

A. Determine the student's reinforcement preference
B. Determine the student's operant level

1. Any toys or vocalization can be utilized to prompt the student on this Step.

3. Begin with the student in a back-lying position. Holding both of his hands, slowly pull him to a sitting position. Lower him to the mat by holding his shoulders.

4–5. Encourage the student to lift his head by prompting and fading techniques.

   The student can be lying on his back with a favorite toy that he will want to see tucked into the waistband of his pants. He will try to lift his head to see it. A nuisance can be created by putting a bulky toy in the waistband. Encourage the student to remove it; he will have to lift his head to see it.

BEHAVIORAL CHECKLIST FOR MOTOR DEVELOPMENT/Sitting

OBJECTIVES

The student will:

1. go from a back-lying to a side-lying position   _____
2. go from a front-lying to a side-lying position   _____
3. sit with support   _____
4. sit without support   _____

MOTOR DEVELOPMENT/Sitting

OBJECTIVE 1

The student will go from a back-lying to a side-lying position after attaining five consecutive positive responses to a verbal command on each Step of the Task Analysis.

Task Analysis Steps

The student will:

1. turn his head to locate a sound stimulus when in a back-lying position
2. turn his head to follow a dangling toy when in a back-lying position
3. reach for a dangling toy while in a back-lying position
4. follow and reach for a dangling toy when it is taken to his side while in a back-lying position
5. let you put your hands on his hips while he attends to a dangling toy
6. let you roll his body toward the side as he follows the dangling toy from a back-lying position
7. go from a back-lying position to a side-lying position to reach for an object at his side
8. maintain a side-lying position while he attends to a toy

MOTOR DEVELOPMENT/Sitting

IMPLEMENTATION 1

MATERIALS:
   Dangling toy, rattle or noise maker, mat or table, blanket or pillow
PREREQUISITE SKILLS:
   None
PROCEDURE:
   A.   Determine the student's reinforcement preference
   B.   Determine the student's operant level

7.   When training the student to roll, a folded blanket or a pillow can be used to prop the student at an angle. If you want the student to turn to his left side, have the blanket or pillow under the right side of his back. Fade the prompt gradually as you consistently reward for the side-lying position.

MOTOR DEVELOPMENT/Sitting

OBJECTIVE 2
The student will go from a front-lying to a side-lying position after attaining five consecutive positive responses to a verbal command on each Step of the Task Analysis.

Task Analysis Steps

The student will:

1. lift and turn his head to the side to respond to a sound stimulus such as a rattle when in a front-lying position
2. lift and turn his head to the side to follow a dangling toy when in a front-lying position
3. reach for a dangling toy when it is taken to his side while in a front-lying position
4. reach for and follow a dangling toy when it is taken to his side while in a front-lying position
5. let you put your hands on his hips while he attends to the dangling toy
6. let you roll his body from the hips to a side-lying position while he attends to a dangling toy
7. roll from a front-lying to a side-lying position when reaching for a dangling toy
8. maintain a side-lying position while attending to a toy

MOTOR DEVELOPMENT/Sitting

IMPLEMENTATION 2

MATERIALS:
Folded blanket or pillow

PREREQUISITE SKILLS:
None

PROCEDURE:

A. Determine the student's reinforcement preference
B. Determine the student's operant level

7. When training the student to roll, a folded blanket can be used to prop the student at an angle. If you want the student to turn to his left side, have the blanket or pillow under the right side of the hips and chest. Fade this prompt gradually as you consistently reinforce for the side-lying position only.

MOTOR DEVELOPMENT/Sitting

OBJECTIVE 3
The student will sit with support after attaining five consecutive positive responses to a verbal command on each Step of the Task Analysis.

Task Analysis Steps

The student will:

1. be placed in a sitting position, legs apart, trunk weight forward
2. let you stabilize him in this position by placing your hands on his hips from behind
3. attempt to regain his position when tipped off balance in a forward direction
4. attempt to regain his position when tipped off balance to either side
5. attempt to regain his position when tipped off balance diagonally

MOTOR DEVELOPMENT/Sitting

IMPLEMENTATION 3

MATERIALS:

Mat, stuffed toy, hanging toys, ball, balloon, bubbles

PREREQUISITE SKILLS:

The student should be able to reach and grasp

PROCEDURE:

A. Determine the student's reinforcement preference

B. Determine the student's operant level

1. Give the student many different experiences in a high chair, relaxation chair, etc. Prop pillows around him and fold a towel or sheet to make a soft body strap. Show the student different objects to stimulate interest. Hang a brightly colored toy within his reach and encourage him to grasp it. As it becomes easy for him to grasp the toy, raise it higher or dangle it to the side of him. He will develop better head and trunk control as he reaches up or to the side.

   If the student will not reach for a toy or brightly colored object, dangle a feather that will tickle his nose. He will want to be rid of that nuisance. A balloon can also be hung in front of the student. Let it bounce off his face and encourage him to push it away.

   Students who are small enough should engage in games such as being bounced up and down and from side-to-side on your knee. Support the student by holding him around his lower ribs, and make a game of it by using nursery rhymes to bounce along with.

   Students who are too large to be bounced and held can be propped up in a corner with legs apart. Show him toys or roll a ball to him. Gradually have him sitting in the corner but not touching the walls. Give him a toy, then have him reach for it; place toys to the right and to the left so that he must reach for them. Dangle a balloon and encourage him to hit it, or blow a bubble and encourage him to catch it. A toy that requires two hands to hold should be presented; this will increase his ability to balance his trunk. Initiate games like pat-a-cake and peek-a-boo.

Any activity that will elicit reaching, grasping, and holding behaviors will aid in establishing appropriate trunk control.

3. Sit behind the student and gently push his shoulders forward. Do not let the student lose his balance completely. Gradually fade your physical prompts until he is regaining his balance unassisted.

4-5. Same as above.

MOTOR DEVELOPMENT/Sitting

OBJECTIVE 4
The student will sit without support after attaining five consecutive positive responses to a verbal command on each Step of the Task Analysis.

Task Analysis Steps

The student will:

1. assume or be placed in a sitting position
2. let you touch his arm while he is in a sitting position
3. regain his balance when slightly pushed forward from the shoulder
4. regain his balance when slightly pushed backward from the shoulder
5. regain his balance when slightly pushed to either side from the shoulder
6. regain his balance when slightly pushed in a diagonal slant from the shoulder
7. maintain a sitting position when playing with toys
8. maintain a sitting position when reaching for objects when playing

MOTOR DEVELOPMENT/Sitting

IMPLEMENTATION 4

MATERIALS:
Mat, stuffed toys, ball, balloon, hanging toy, bubbles

PREREQUISITE SKILLS:
The student should be able to reach, grasp, and release

PROCEDURE:
A. Determine the student's reinforcement preference
B. Determine the student's operant level

1. Give the student many different experiences in a high chair, relaxation chair, etc. Show the student different objects to stimulate interest. Hang a brightly colored toy within his reach and encourage him to grasp it. As it becomes easy for him to grasp the toy, raise it higher or dangle it to the side of him. He will develop better head and trunk control as he reaches up or to the side.

   If the student will not reach for a toy or brightly colored object, dangle a feather that will tickle his nose. He will want to be rid of that nuisance. A balloon can also be hung in front of the student. Let it bounce off his face and encourage him to push it away.

   Students who are small enough should engage in games such as being bounced up and down and from side-to-side on your knee. Support the student by holding his hands and make a game of it by using nursery rhymes to bounce along with.

   Students who are too large to be bounced and held can sit in a corner with legs apart. Show him toys or roll a ball to him. Gradually have him sitting in the corner but not touching the walls. Give him a toy, then have him reach for it; place toys to the right and to the left so that he must reach for them. Dangle a balloon and encourage him to hit it, or blow a bubble and encourage him to catch it. A toy that requires two hands to hold should be presented; this will increase his ability to balance his trunk. Initiate games like pat-a-cake and peek-a-boo. Any activity that will elicit reaching, grasping, and holding behaviors will aid in establishing appropriate trunk control.

BEHAVIORAL CHECKLIST FOR MOTOR DEVELOPMENT/Hand-Knee Position

OBJECTIVES

The student will:

1. go from a front-lying to a hand-knee position with assistance _____
2. go from a front-lying to a hand-knee position without assistance _____
3. maintain a hand-knee position with assistance _____
4. maintain a hand-knee position without assistance _____

MOTOR DEVELOPMENT/Hand-Knee Position

OBJECTIVE 1 The student will go from a front-lying to a hand-knee position with assistance after attaining five consecutive positive responses to a verbal command on each Step of the Task Analysis.

Task Analysis Steps

The student will:

1. let you place your hand under his hip bone in the pelvic area on one side of his body
2. let you raise up his hip by pulling up on that one side
3. flex his hip, knee, and arm on that side in a reflex response
4. let you flex his hip, knee, and arm on that side of his body if he does not have the needed reflex response
5. let you place your hand under the hip bone in the pelvic area on the other side of his body
6. let you raise up his hip by pulling up on that one side
7. flex his hip, knee, and arm on that side in a reflex response
8. let you flex his hip, knee, and arm on that side if he does not have the needed reflex response
9. let you place his hands near his shoulders flat on the floor in a position to bear weight
10. let you push his weight back on his heels by straightening his arms
11. push his weight back on his heels by straightening his arms
12. let you adjust his weight so that it is evenly distributed between hands and knees in a hand-knee kneeling position

MOTOR DEVELOPMENT/Hand-Knee Position

IMPLEMENTATION 1

MATERIALS:
  Mat
PREREQUISITE SKILLS:
  The student must have *good* head and trunk control
PROCEDURE:
  A. Determine the student's reinforcement preference
  B. Determine the student's operant level

  Once again, you will rely heavily on physical prompts. After you have the student in the hand-knee position and his weight is evenly distributed between hands and knees, try to fade physical prompts in maintaining that position.

MOTOR DEVELOPMENT/Hand-Knee Position

OBJECTIVE 2 The student will go from a front-lying to a hand-knee position without assistance after attaining five consecutive positive responses to a verbal command on each Step of the Task Analysis.

Task Analysis Steps

The student will:

1. Assume a hand-knee position with no assistance, even though he may not be able to maintain it without assistance

MOTOR DEVELOPMENT/Hand-Knee Position

IMPLEMENTATION 2

MATERIALS:
Mat

PREREQUISITE SKILLS:
The student must have *good* head and trunk control

PROCEDURE:
A. Determine the student's reinforcement preference
B. Determine the student's operant level

Proceed through the Task Analysis Steps of Objective 1, using physical prompts and fading to master Objective 2. Remember to reinforce immediately and to fade gradually.

MOTOR DEVELOPMENT/Hand-Knee Position

OBJECTIVE 3 The student will maintain a hand-knee position with assistance after attaining five consecutive positive responses to a verbal command on each Step of the Task Analysis.

Task Analysis Steps

The student will:

1. assume a hand-knee position as in Objective 1, or independently assume such a position
2. let you give support on his arm to maintain his extended position so that he can bear weight
3. let you give support at his hips and to bear part of his weight so that he can maintain his position
4. attend to an object or a toy dangling in front of him while maintaining his position, as an aid to maintaining his position

MOTOR DEVELOPMENT/Hand-Knee Position

IMPLEMENTATION 3

MATERIALS:
Mat, toys

PREREQUISITE SKILLS:
The student must be capable of going from a front-lying position to a hand-knee position with assistance

PROCEDURE:
A. Determine the student's reinforcement preference
B. Determine the student's operant level

1. The student will assume the hand-knee position, or you will position him.
2. You will support the student's arms.
3. You will hold the student at the hips to bear part of his weight.
4. The student will attend to a toy dangling in front of him as an aide is momentarily assisting him to maintain his position. Reinforce the student for independently maintaining this position five seconds, eight seconds, ten seconds, fifteen seconds, etc.

MOTOR DEVELOPMENT/Hand-Knee Position

OBJECTIVE 4 The student will maintain a hand-knee position without assistance after attaining five consecutive positive responses to a verbal command on each Step of the Task Analysis.

Task Analysis Steps

The student will:

1. assume or be placed in a hand-knee position
2. let you touch his shoulders and hips while in a hand-knee position
3. maintain his balance when pushed forward while in a hand-knee position
4. maintain his balance when pushed backward while in a hand-knee position
5. maintain his balance when pushed to either side while in a hand-knee position
6. maintain a hand-knee position without assistance

MOTOR DEVELOPMENT/Hand-Knee Position

IMPLEMENTATION 4

MATERIALS:
Mat

PREREQUISITE SKILLS:
The student must be capable of maintaining a hand-knee position with and without assistance for a limited period of time

PROCEDURE:
A. Determine the student's reinforcement preference
B. Determine the student's operant level

1–2. Before beginning Step 3, place the student in position and reinforce him for maintaining that hand-knee position for extended periods of time. Play music, dangle toys, or make sounds to interest him as he maintains that position.

3. Gently push the student forward; he should maintain his balance if he is assuming the proper position.

4. Gently push the student backward and observe his weight distribution.

5. Push the student from side to side and observe his shift in weight. Is he shifting the weight, or does he fall?

6. If he can adequately adjust to Steps 3–5, then he very definitely can maintain a hand-knee position without assistance. He will quite possibly need practice on one or more of the steps; remember, once again, to fade physical prompts gradually.

BEHAVIORAL CHECKLIST FOR MOTOR DEVELOPMENT/Standing

OBJECTIVES

The student will:

1. tolerate weight bearing on his feet while supported _____
2. support part of his body weight and actively bend and straighten his legs _____
3. balance his trunk _____
4. pull himself to a standing position from a squatting position _____
5. pull himself to a standing position from a hand-knee position _____
6. stand independently _____

MOTOR DEVELOPMENT/Standing

OBJECTIVE 1

The student will tolerate weight bearing on his feet while supported after attaining five consecutive positive responses to a verbal command on each Step of the Task Analysis.

Task Analysis Steps

The student will:

1. let you place your hands under his arms in a position of support for his body weight
2. let you lift him from under the arms so that he is suspended in space in a vertical position, head up, feet down
3. let you lower him vertically to the floor so that his feet come in contact with the floor
4. let you place his feet flat on the floor
5. let you allow his feet to bear some of the weight of his body while you support the rest
6. tolerate weight bearing without complaint, crying, or refusing to put weight on his feet

MOTOR DEVELOPMENT/Standing

IMPLEMENTATION 1

MATERIALS:
Mat

PREREQUISITE SKILLS:
The student must have good head and trunk control

PROCEDURE:
A. Determine the student's reinforcement preference
B. Determine the student's operant level

If the student proceeds through Task Analysis 1–6 without difficulty, play a game with him. Hold the student erect with his feet touching the floor. Lower and raise him with his feet always touching the floor and possibly supporting some of his body weight. You can do this to music, or simply with any words spoken in an up and down inflection. Be sure the inflection in your voice is going in the same direction as the student.

MOTOR DEVELOPMENT/Standing

OBJECTIVE 2

The student will support part of his body weight and actively bend and straighten his legs after attaining five consecutive positive responses to a verbal command on each Step of the Task Analysis.

Task Analysis Steps

The student will:

1. let you place your hands under his arms in a position to support his body weight
2. support part of his body weight on his feet, the other part supported by you from under his arms
3. let you bend his knees so that his body weight shifts downward
4. let you pull him up from under his arms so that his legs are straight again
5. bend his knees so that his body weight shifts downward
6. pull up against your support so that his legs are straight again
7. repeatedly bend and straighten his legs while supporting part of his body weight

MOTOR DEVELOPMENT/Standing

IMPLEMENTATION 2

MATERIALS:
Mat

PREREQUISITE SKILLS:
The student must have good head and trunk control
The student must tolerate weight bearing on his feet

PROCEDURE:
A. Determine the student's reinforcement preference
B. Determine the student's operant level

If the student proceeds through Task Analysis 1–6 without difficulty, play a game with him. Hold the student erect with his feet touching the floor. Lower and raise him with his feet always touching the floor and possibly supporting some of his body weight. You can do this to music, or simply with any words spoken in an up and down inflection. Be sure the inflection in your voice is going in the same direction as the student. If the student's legs appear to be weak, or if he has problems with flexor or extensor muscles, you might want to work on leg thrusts, knee flexions, and extensions.

MOTOR DEVELOPMENT/Standing

OBJECTIVE 3
The student will balance his trunk after attaining five consecutive positive responses to a verbal command on each Step of the Task Analysis.

Task Analysis Steps

The student will:

1. assume or be placed in a standing position
2. let you place your hands on his hips in a position of support
3. let you hold him firmly at the hips, as a base of support, letting his trunk move freely
4. let you tilt him forward far enough so that he loses trunk balance
5. regain his position and trunk balance when tilted forward, with your assistance
6. regain his position and trunk balance when tilted forward, independently
7. let you tilt him backward far enough so that he loses his trunk balance
8. regain his position and trunk balance when tilted backward, with your assistance
9. regain his position and trunk balance when tilted backward, independently
10. let you tilt him to either side far enough so that he loses his trunk balance
11. regain his position and trunk balance when tilted to either side, with your assistance
12. regain his position and trunk balance when tilted to either side, independently
13. let you change your support from the hips to the thighs
14. let you tilt him forward far enough so that he loses his trunk balance and position
15. regain his position and trunk balance when tilted forward, with your assistance
16. regain his position and trunk balance when tilted forward, independently
17. let you tilt him backward far enough so that he loses his trunk balance and position
18. regain his position and trunk balance when tilted backward, with your assistance
19. regain his position and trunk balance when tilted backward, independently
20. let you tilt him to either side far enough so that he loses his trunk balance and position
21. regain his position and trunk balance when tilted to either side, with your assistance
22. regain his position and trunk balance when tilted to either side independently

MOTOR DEVELOPMENT/Standing

IMPLEMENTATION 3

MATERIALS:
Mat

PREREQUISITE SKILLS:
None

PROCEDURE:
A. Determine the student's reinforcement preference
B. Determine the student's operant level

As you proceed through the Task Analysis Steps make sure you present them as a game. If you are too rough or push the student too hard, he will become frightened and want to sit down. Be certain you have the student's trust before beginning this particular task.

MOTOR DEVELOPMENT/Standing

OBJECTIVE 4 The student will pull himself to a standing position from a squatting position after attaining five consecutive positive responses to a verbal command on each Step of the Task Analysis.

Task Analysis Steps

The student will:

1. assume a squatting position with or without assistance
2. let you take him under the arms while he is in a squatting position
3. let you pull him up from a squatting position by pulling up from under the arms
4. let you return him to a squatting position
5. let you take his hands while he is in a squatting position
6. let you pull him to a standing position by pulling up on his hands
7. let you return him to a squatting position
8. take your hands while he is in a squatting position
9. pull himself to a standing position, using your hands for support
10. return to a squatting position
11. let you place his hands on another object, such as a table or rail
12. place his hands on another object, such as a table or rail
13. pull up on the stationary object until he is in a standing position

MOTOR DEVELOPMENT/Standing

IMPLEMENTATION 4

MATERIALS:
  Mat, table

PREREQUISITE SKILLS:
  The student must have adequate control of flexor and extensor muscles

PROCEDURE:
  A.   Determine the student's reinforcement preference
  B.   Determine the student's operant level

Play a bouncing game with the student. Hold the student in a standing position with his feet on the floor. Allow his knees to bend and then lift him up again. Do this to music or to any words spoken with an up and down inflection.

Also, you may play a game in which you tell the student to do what you do. Hold on to a table and squat, then lift yourself up again. Have the student stand next to you and also hold on to the table. An extra person may also be helpful in applying pressure to the student's shoulders when you go down and in gently lifting the student under the arms as you stand erect.

If the student's legs appear to be weak, work on leg thrusts and knee flexion and extensions.

MOTOR DEVELOPMENT/Standing

OBJECTIVE 5 The student will pull himself to a standing position from a hand-knee position after attaining five consecutive positive responses to a verbal command on each Step of the Task Analysis.

Task Analysis Steps

The student will:

1. assume a hand-knee position with or without assistance, as in Hand-Knee Position, Objective 3
2. let you take him by the shoulders while he is in a hand-knee position
3. let you shift his weight from a hand-knee position to a position in which his weight is on his heels, with little weight on his hands
4. shift his weight from a hand-knee position to a position in which his weight is on his heels, with little weight on his hands
5. let you take his hands so that he is in a kneel-sitting position
6. let you put his hands on a stationary object
7. hold on to the rail or stationary object for support
8. let you lift one of his legs and place his foot flat on the floor
9. lift one of his legs and place his foot flat on the floor
10. let you pull him up so that one leg straightens out, and the other straightens out as he reaches a standing position
11. pull himself to standing by straightening first one leg and then the other

MOTOR DEVELOPMENT/Standing

IMPLEMENTATION 5

MATERIALS:
Mat, table

PREREQUISITE SKILLS:
The student must have adequate control of flexor and extensor muscles

PROCEDURE:
A. Determine the student's reinforcement preference
B. Determine the student's operant level

3. If you pull the buttocks toward his heels, you will meet the criterion for this Step.

4. Now the buttocks should be resting on his heels with his hands hardly touching the floor.

Play a bouncing game with the student. Hold the student in a standing position with his feet on the floor. Allow his knees to bend and then left him up again. Do this to music or to any words spoken with an up and down inflection.

Also you may play a game in which you tell the student to do what you do. Hold on to a table and squat, then lift yourself up again. Have the student stand next to you and also hold on to a table. An extra person may also be helpful in applying pressure to the student's shoulders when you go down and in gently lifting the student under the arms as you stand erect.

If the student's legs appear to be weak, you will want to work on leg thrusts and knee flexion and extensions.

MOTOR DEVELOPMENT/Standing

OBJECTIVE 6 The student will stand independently after attaining five consecutive positive responses to a verbal command on each Step of the Task Analysis.

Task Analysis Steps

The student will:

1. pull himself to standing, or be placed in a standing position with assistance
2. stand while holding onto a stationary object, such as a rail or table, for support
3. stand while holding onto your hands for support
4. stand while holding onto one of your hands with one of his
5. stand independently

MOTOR DEVELOPMENT/Standing

IMPLEMENTATION 6

MATERIALS:
Mat, table, standing table
PREREQUISITE SKILLS:
None
PROCEDURE:
A. Determine the student's reinforcement preference
B. Determine the student's operant level

Place the student on a standing table and gradually increase the time that he stands and plays. The student can also be placed in the standing position in a corner of the room. Show him toys that he must reach for and encourage him to play pat-a-cake or try to catch bubbles, etc. As his balance begins to stabilize, have him stand a few inches in front of the wall and engage in the same activities.

Comments Made by the Physical Therapist

Suggested Readings

Altman, R., Talkington, L. W., and Cleland, C. C. 1972. Relative effectiveness of modeling and verbal instructions on severe retardates' gross motor performance. Psych. Repts. 31:695–698.

Auxter, D. 1971. Motor skill development in the profoundly retarded. Training School Bull. 68:5–9.

Bayley, N. 1969. Bayley Scales of Infant Development: Birth to Two Years. Psychological Corp., New York.

Chandler, S. S., and Adams, M. A. 1972. Multiply handicapped children motivated for ambulation through behavior modification. Phys. Ther. 52:3.

Cratby, B. J. 1974. Motor Activity and the Education of Retardates. 2nd Ed. Lea and Febeger, Philadelphia.

Frances, R. J., and Rarick, G. L. 1959. Motor characteristics of the mentally retarded. Am. J. Ment. Defic. 63:792–811.

Rice, H. K. 1968. Operant conditioning techniques for use in physical rehabilitation of multiply handicapped retarded patients. Phys. Ther. 48:342–346.

Wilson, V., and Parks, R. 1970. Promoting ambulation in the severely retarded child. Ment. Retard. 8:17–19.

CHAPTER ELEVEN

Eye-Hand Coordination

The goal of this program area is to establish and increase gross and fine motor coordination. A series of toys, designed for infants and toddlers, is used to facilitate reach, grasp, release, and higher levels of fine motor coordination.

Only the toys in the Materials List are to be used if rapid facilitation of the Task Analysis is expected. Any additional toys must have specific Task Analyses written for them.

BEHAVIORAL CHECKLIST FOR EYE-HAND COORDINATION

OBJECTIVES

The student will:

1.	make random patterns in shaving cream	_____
2.	make random patterns in finger paint	_____
3.	grasp a sound tube	_____
4.	release a sound tube	_____
5.	release a sound tube in a box	_____
6.	pick up a clutch ball	_____
7.	punch a balloon	_____
8.	reach for a soap bubble	_____
9.	spin the bubble on the mobile	_____
10.	spin the handle on the mobile	_____
11.	squeak the ball on the mobile	_____
12.	pull the handle on the merry-go-round	_____
13.	turn the knob on the busy box	_____
14.	turn the crank on the busy box	_____
15.	press the button on the busy box	_____
16.	push the car on the busy box	_____
17.	slide the door on the busy box	_____
18.	turn the telephone dial on the busy box	_____
19.	spin the wheel on the busy box	_____
20.	open the door on the busy box	_____
21.	open the drawer on the busy box	_____
22.	press the button on the surprise busy box	_____
23.	slide the knob on the surprise busy box	_____
24.	turn the knob on the surprise busy box	_____
25.	turn the dial on the surprise busy box	_____
26.	flip the switch on the surprise busy box	_____

27.	place three pegs in a peg board	_____
28.	remove stacking rings	_____
29.	randomly stack stacking rings	_____
30.	stack two stacking rings in order	_____
31.	nest nesting blocks	_____
32.	stack nesting blocks	_____
33.	nest nesting cups	_____
34.	stack nesting cups	_____
35.	place a circle in the form board	_____
36.	place a square in the form board	_____
37.	place a triangle in the form board	_____
38.	place a circle in the shape sorting box	_____
39.	place a square in the shape sorting box	_____
40.	place a triangle in the shape sorting box	_____
41.	assemble a three-piece puzzle	_____
42.	assemble a four-piece puzzle	_____
43.	assemble a five-piece puzzle	_____
44.	assemble a six-piece puzzle	_____
45.	trace a horizontal line with his finger	_____
46.	trace a vertical line with his finger	_____
47.	trace a horizontal curved line with his finger	_____
48.	trace an up and down curve with his finger	_____
49.	trace a circle, using a template	_____
50.	trace a square, using a template	_____
51.	trace a triangle, using a template	_____

EYE-HAND COORDINATION

OBJECTIVE 1

The student will make random patterns in shaving cream after attaining five consecutive positive responses to a verbal command on each Step of the Task Analysis.

Task Analysis Steps

The student will:

1. let you put his hand in the shaving cream
2. let you move his hand around in the shaving cream
3. move his hand around in a random pattern in the shaving cream

EYE-HAND COORDINATION

IMPLEMENTATION 1

MATERIALS:
Shaving cream (or whipped cream)
PREREQUISITE SKILLS:
None
PROCEDURE:
A. Determine the student's reinforcement preference
B. Be certain the student is seated properly with support provided if needed
C. Determine the student's operant level

The student can be standing if he is physically capable. If he is seated, he should be in the chair with a tray. If there is no tray, he should be at a table that is appropriate for his chair. The student should not have to reach above waist level to manipulate the cream.

EYE-HAND COORDINATION

OBJECTIVE 2

The student will make random patterns in finger paint after attaining five consecutive positive responses to a verbal command on each Step of the Task Analysis.

Task Analysis Steps

The student will:

1. let you put his hands in the finger paint
2. let you move his hands around in the finger paint
3. move his hands randomly in the finger paint

EYE-HAND COORDINATION

IMPLEMENTATION 2

MATERIALS:
Finger paints, paper to cover the entire table, table appropriate to the student's size

PREREQUISITE SKILLS:
None

PROCEDURE:
A. Determine the student's reinforcement preference
B. Be certain the student is seated properly with support provided if needed
C. Determine the student's operant level

   The student should be comfortably seated, feet touching the floor, hands at table, and the table at an appropriate level for the student. A standing table can also be used if the student is already using one.

EYE-HAND COORDINATION

OBJECTIVE 3
The student will grasp a sound tube after attaining five consecutive positive responses to a verbal command on each Step of the Task Analysis.

Task Analysis Steps

The student will:

1. let you hold his hand on the sound tube
2. let you place his hand around the sound tube
3. place his hand around the sound tube
4. grasp the sound tube

EYE-HAND COORDINATION

IMPLEMENTATION 3

MATERIALS:

Cylinder rattle—This is a small wooden rattle that can be purchased from Creative Playthings. It works well with smaller students, but the 1-inch diameter may be too small for students with large hands. A comparable rattle can be made from a cardboard paper roll. Roll the cardboard to a size that will accommodate the student's hand; place beans in it and cover with contact paper.

PREREQUISITE SKILLS:

The student should be able to reach

PROCEDURE:

A. Determine the student's reinforcement preference
B. Be certain the student is seated properly with support provided if needed
C. Determine the student's operant level

1. Sit across from the student to ensure proper attention. Get the student's attention (say his name, or use whatever method works for that particular student) and hold the tube in his direct line of vision, saying, "Do this." Place the sound tube in his hand and hold it there while you reinforce him.
2. Gain the student's attention; model the activity you wish him to engage in as you say, "Do this." Place the cylinder in the student's hand and reinforce him for holding it independently.
3. Gain the student's attention; model the activity as you say, "Do this." Place the cylinder in a position for the student to grasp it and reward him for doing so.
4. Gain the student's attention; model the activity as you say, "Do this." Place the cylinder within the student's reach and reward him for grasping and holding it.

EYE-HAND COORDINATION

OBJECTIVE 4

The student will release a sound tube after attaining five consecutive positive responses to a verbal command on each Step of the Task Analysis.

Task Analysis Steps

The student will:

1. let you take his hand off the sound tube
2. let you take his fingers off the sound tube
3. release the sound tube

EYE-HAND COORDINATION
IMPLEMENTATION 4

MATERIALS:

Cylinder rattle—This is a small wooden rattle that can be purchased from Creative Playthings. It works well with smaller students, but the 1-inch diameter may be too small for students with large hands. A comparable rattle can be made from a cardboard paper roll. Roll the cardboard to a size that will accommodate the student's hand; place beans in it, and cover with contact paper.

PREREQUISITE SKILLS:

The student should be able to reach

PROCEDURE:

A. Determine the student's reinforcement preference
B. Be certain the student is seated properly with support provided if needed
C. Determine the student's operant level

1. Gain the student's attention; model the activity as you say, "Do this." (As you model, exaggerate the removal of your fingers.) Remove the student's hand and drop the sound tube to the table. Reward the student immediately.
2. Gain the student's attention; model the activity as you say, "Do this." (As you model, exaggerate the removal of your fingers and hand.) Apply pressure to the base of the student's wrist to encourage him to release the sound tube.
3. Gain the student's attention; model the activity as you say, "Do this." Reward the student immediately.

EYE-HAND COORDINATION

OBJECTIVE 5
The student will release a sound tube in a box after attaining five consecutive positive responses to a verbal command on each Step of the Task Analysis.

Task Analysis Steps

The sound tube will be handed to the student and he will:

1. release the sound tube in a box upon the command, "Do this" after you have placed his hand in the box
2. release the sound tube in a box upon the command, "Do this" after you have placed his hand over the rim of the box
3. release the sound tube in a box upon the command, "Do this" after you have placed his hand even with the rim of the box
4. release the sound tube in a box upon the command, "Do this" after you have lifted his arm toward the box
5. independently release the sound tube in a box upon the command, "Do this"

EYE-HAND COORDINATION

IMPLEMENTATION 5

MATERIALS:

Cylinder rattle—This is a small wooden rattle that can be purchased from Creative Playthings. It works well with smaller students, but the 1-inch diameter may be too small for students with large hands. A comparable rattle can be made from a cardboard paper roll. Roll the cardboard to a size that will accommodate the student's hand; place beans in it and cover with contact paper. Large boxes—The boxes should be varied in height. The student should not have to lift his arm above shoulder level.

PREREQUISITE SKILLS:

The student should be able to reach

The student should be able to release the sound tube upon command

PROCEDURE:

A. Determine the student's reinforcement preference
B. Be certain the student is seated properly with support provided if needed
C. Determine the student's operant level

1. If the student is blind, the box should be covered with sandpaper or some other tactile material; train the student to:
    1. locate the box
    2. place his left hand on top of the box
    3. accept the sound tube with his right hand
    4. take the sound tube in his left hand and release it in the box

EYE-HAND COORDINATION

OBJECTIVE 6 The student will pick up a clutch ball after attaining five consecutive positive responses to a verbal command on each Step of the Task Analysis.

Task Analysis Steps

The student will:

1. let you put his hand on the clutch ball upon the command, "Do this"
2. let you hold the clutch ball with his hands upon the command, "Do this"
3. hold the clutch ball upon the command, "Do this"
4. let you use his arms to reach for the clutch ball; he will hold it upon command
5. let you position his arms next to the clutch ball; he will pick it up and hold it upon command
6. pick up the clutch ball upon the command, "Do this"

EYE-HAND COORDINATION

IMPLEMENTATION 6

MATERIALS:

Clutch ball (Creative Playthings)

PREREQUISITE SKILLS:

The student should be able to reach and grasp

PROCEDURE:

A. Determine the student's reinforcement preference
B. Be certain the student is seated properly with support provided if needed
C. Determine the student's operant level

1. The student can be positioned in a chair or lying on his back with the clutch ball hanging above him on a large string. After the shaping procedure, lay the student on his back with the ball hanging from a string that reaches to the floor. Be sure to place the ball where it will irritate the student, and he will push it away or play with it.
2. The above exercises can also be used with blind students along with the Creative Playthings texture ball. When using either ball, sew a few bells on it so that the blind student will easily find it hanging on the string.

EYE-HAND COORDINATION

OBJECTIVE 7 The student will punch a balloon after attaining five consecutive positive responses to a verbal command on each Step of the Task Analysis.

Task Analysis Steps

The student will:

1. look at the balloon upon the command, "Look"
2. let you use his hand to touch the balloon
3. let you use his hand to punch the balloon upon the command, "Do this"
4. let you direct his hand to the balloon, and he will punch it upon the command, "Do this"
5. punch the balloon independently upon the command, "Do this"

EYE-HAND COORDINATION

IMPLEMENTATION 7

MATERIALS:
Proper chair—The student should be seated with the necessary props provided. Make certain that the student's head is well balanced or that a relaxation chair is provided for this purpose. Balloon or punch ball, feather, cotton, and vinegar

PREREQUISITE SKILLS:
The student should be able to reach

PROCEDURE:
A. Determine the student's reinforcement preference
B. Be certain the student is seated properly with support provided if needed
C. Determine the student's operant level

If the student will not respond to this Objective tape a feather to the bottom of the balloon. Hang the balloon above the student, positioned to tickle his face. A piece of cotton or cloth can be soaked in vinegar and taped to the punch ball and positioned in front of the student's face. In either example, the balloon or ball should become a nuisance, and the student will be motivated to push it away.

This task can be adapted to the blind student by placing beans in the punch ball.

EYE-HAND COORDINATION

OBJECTIVE 8
The student will reach for a soap bubble after attaining five consecutive positive responses to a verbal command on each Step of the Task Analysis.

Task Analysis Steps

The student will:

1. look at the bubbles upon the command, "Look"
2. let you touch the bubble with his hand upon command when the bubble is held in front of him
3. let you position his hand by the bubble so that he will touch it upon command
4. touch the bubble upon command when it is held in front of him
5. let you use his hand to reach for the bubble upon command as it passes by
6. let you position his hand to reach for the bubble upon command as it passes by
7. reach for the bubble upon command as it passes by

EYE-HAND COORDINATION

IMPLEMENTATION 8

MATERIALS:
Proper chair, soap bubbles

PREREQUISITE SKILLS:
The student should be able to reach

PROCEDURE:
A. Determine the student's reinforcement preference
B. Be certain the student is seated properly with support provided if needed
C. Determine the student's operant level

2. Blow bubbles and catch one on the stick; model the act of touching the bubble as you say, "Do this."
3. Blow bubbles; model the act of reaching for them as you say, "Do this."
4. Blow bubbles and catch one on the stick; model breaking the bubble as you say, "Do this." Catch another bubble for the student to break as you slowly move it from right to left in front of him.
   Be sure to use bridging techniques when reinforcing the student.

EYE-HAND COORDINATION

OBJECTIVE 9
The student will spin the bubble on the mobile after attaining five consecutive positive responses to a verbal command on each Step of the Task Analysis.

Task Analysis Steps

The student will:

1. look toward the sound of the mobile
2. attend while the mobile is rotated for five seconds
3. let you touch the bubble with his hand
4. let you spin the bubble with his hand upon the command, "Do this"
5. spin the bubble with his hand upon the command, "Do this" after you have raised his arm to position
6. reach up and spin the bubble with his hand upon the command, "Do this"

EYE-HAND COORDINATION

IMPLEMENTATION 9

MATERIALS:
Fisher-Price Mobile, crib, playpen, or activity table
PREREQUISITE SKILLS:
The student should be able to reach, grasp, and release
PROCEDURE:
A. Determine the student's reinforcement preference
B. Be certain the student is seated properly with support provided if needed
C. Determine the student's operant level

The mobile must be within easy reach for each student. The student can be lying on his back or seated in his chair. An opportunity to play unassisted with this toy should also be provided.

The blind student can also enjoy this activity because each part provides a different auditory and tactile stimulation.

Sitting behind the student:

4. spin the bubble with your hand as you give the student the command, "Do this." The student will let you spin the bubble using his hand upon the command, "Do this." Reinforce immediately for the correct response.
5. spin the bubble with your hand as you give the command, "Do this." Raise the student's arm so that his hand is level with the bubble. Reinforce immediately when he spins the bubble.
6. spin the bubble with your hand as you give the command, "Do this." The student should do the same. Reinforce immediately for the correct response.

EYE-HAND COORDINATION

OBJECTIVE 10
The student will spin the handle on the mobile after attaining five consecutive positive responses to a verbal command on each Step of the Task Analysis.

Task Analysis Steps

The student will:

1. let you touch the handles with his hand upon the command, "Do this"
2. let you position his hand around the indented handles upon the command, "Do this"
3. let you position his hand around the indented handles upon the command, "Do this," maintaining the grasp for five seconds
4. grasp the indented handle upon the command, "Do this" after you have positioned his arm
5. grasp the indented handle independently upon the command, "Do this"

EYE-HAND COORDINATION

IMPLEMENTATION 10

MATERIALS:
Fisher-Price Mobile, crib, playpen, or activity table
PREREQUISITE SKILLS:
The student should be able to reach, grasp, and release
PROCEDURE:
A. Determine the student's reinforcement preference
B. Be certain the student is seated properly with support provided if needed
C. Determine the student's operant level

The mobile must be within easy reach for each student. The student can be lying on his back or seated in his chair. An opportunity to play unassisted with this toy should also be provided.

The blind student can also enjoy this activity because each part provides a different auditory and tactile stimulation.

Sitting behind the student:

2. hold the indented handle while you give the command, "Do this." Position the student's hand around the handle and reinforce.
3. hold the indented handle while you give the command, "Do this." Position the student's hand around the handle as you say, "Do this." He must maintain the grasp for five seconds. Reinforce immediately.
4. grasp the indented handle upon the command, "Do this." Position the student's arm so that his hand is level with the handle and he should grasp the handle. Reinforce immediately.
5. grasp the indented handle upon the command, "Do this." The student should imitate the movement independently. Reinforce immediately.

EYE-HAND COORDINATION

OBJECTIVE 11
The student will squeak the ball on the mobile after attaining five consecutive positive responses to a verbal command on each Step of the Task Analysis.

Task Analysis Steps

The student will:

1. let you touch the squeaky ball with his hand upon the command, "Do this"
2. let you position his hand upon the squeaky ball upon the command, "Do this"
3. let you squeeze the ball with his hand upon the command, "Do this"
4. squeeze the ball after his arm is positioned upon the command, "Do this"
5. squeeze the ball independently upon the command, "Do this"
6. squeak the ball upon the command, "Do this"

EYE-HAND COORDINATION
IMPLEMENTATION 11

MATERIALS:
Fisher-Price Mobile, crib, playpen, or activity table
PREREQUISITE SKILLS:
The student should be able to reach, grasp, and release
PROCEDURE:
A. Determine the student's reinforcement preference
B. Be certain the student is seated properly with support provided if needed
C. Determine the student's operant level

The mobile must be within easy reach for each student. The student can be lying on his back or seated in his chair. An opportunity to play unassisted with this toy should also be provided.

The blind student can also enjoy this activity because each part provides a different auditory and tactile stimulation.

Sitting behind the student:

2. grasp the squeaky ball upon the command, "Do this." Grasp the ball using the student's hand and reinforce immediately.
3. squeeze the ball upon the command, "Do this." Squeeze the ball using the student's hand and reinforce immediately.
4. squeeze the ball upon the command, "Do this." The student will then squeeze the ball after his arm has been lifted and his hand is level with the ball. Reinforce immediately.
5. squeeze the ball upon the command, "Do this." The student will then squeeze the ball independently. Reinforce immediately.
6. If the student did not make the ball squeak on previous trials, encourage him to apply more pressure. He may not be capable of this Step because he lacks the physical strength. If he cannot squeak the ball in three sessions, consider the task completed and go on to Objective 12.

EYE-HAND COORDINATION

OBJECTIVE 12 The student will pull the handle on the merry-go-round after attaining five consecutive positive responses to a verbal command on each Step of the Task Analysis.

Task Analysis Steps

The student will:

1. attend while the mobile is manipulated for five seconds
2. look toward the sound of the mobile
3. let you touch the handle with his hand
4. let you pull the handle and activate the merry-go-round with his hand upon the command, "Do this"
5. pull the handle upon the command, "Do this" after you have raised his arm to position
6. pull the handle independently upon the command, "Do this"

EYE-HAND COORDINATION

IMPLEMENTATION 12

MATERIALS:
Fisher-Price Merry-Go-Round Mobile, Fisher-Price Bluebird Mobile, Fisher-Price Jumping Jack

PREREQUISITE SKILLS:
The student should be able to reach, grasp, and release

PROCEDURE:
A. Determine the student's reinforcement preference
B. Be certain the student is seated properly with support provided if needed
C. Determine the student's operant level

1. Have the student seated in front of or lying under the mobile. The mobile should be within comfortable reach of the student. Work only on the middle handle to activate the merry-go-round. Each time the student successfully activates the merry-go-round, reinforce heartily with praise or a treat.

2. When stimulating a blind student to reach and grasp in this manner, choose a toy such as the Fisher-Price Bluebird. When the handle is pulled, it activates a music box, which has proven to be a greater reinforcement for the blind student. It is also an easier handle to pull; therefore, you may want to use it with students who are incapable of pulling the handle hard enough to activate the merry-go-round. Both of these toys provide their own built-in reinforcement, but you must still train with social praise or with edible reinforcers.

3. Touch the handle with the student's hand; praise him for it.

4. Pull the handle and activate the merry-go-round while giving the command, "Do this." Use the student's hand to pull the handle and activate the merry-go-round. Reinforce.

5. Pull the handle and activate the merry-go-round while giving the command, "Do this." Raise the student's arm so that the hand is positioned near the handle. The student will then pull the handle. Reinforce.

6. Pull the handle and activate the merry-go-round while giving the command, "Do this." The student should do the same. Reinforce.

EYE-HAND COORDINATION

OBJECTIVE 13 The student will turn the knob on the busy box after attaining five consecutive positive responses to a verbal command on each Step of the Task Analysis.

Task Analysis Steps

The student will:

1. let you put his hand on the turning knob
2. let you turn the knob with his hand upon the command, "Do this"
3. turn the knob with his hand upon the command, "Do this"

EYE-HAND COORDINATION

IMPLEMENTATION 13

MATERIALS:
Kohner Busy Box, Fisher-Price Musical Clock, Fisher-Price Musical Radio

PREREQUISITE SKILLS:
The student should be able to reach, grasp, and release. A student who is unable to grasp can still turn the knob if he can apply pressure with the palm of his hand and move his wrist.

PROCEDURE:
A. Determine the student's reinforcement preference
B. Be certain the student is seated properly with support provided if needed
C. Determine the student's operant level

The student should be correctly positioned in a chair with all outside stimuli absent. Remember to model the activity for each Step as you give the command, "Do this." If all the objects on the busy box are too confusing, you can use the Fisher-Price Musical Clock or Radio. The music presents reinforcement for both blind and retarded students.

After the student learns to manipulate the larger object, train him on the comparable but smaller object.

EYE-HAND COORDINATION

OBJECTIVE 14 The student will turn the crank on the busy box after attaining five consecutive positive responses to a verbal command on each Step of the Task Analysis.

Task Analysis Steps

The student will:

1. let you put his hand on the turn crank
2. let you turn the crank with his hand
3. turn the crank upon command

EYE-HAND COORDINATION

IMPLEMENTATION 14

MATERIALS:
Kohner Busy Box

PREREQUISITE SKILLS:
The student should be able to reach, grasp, and release. A student who is unable to grasp can still turn the crank if he can apply pressure with the palm of his hand and move his wrist.

PROCEDURE:
A. Determine the student's reinforcement preference
B. Be certain the student is seated properly with support provided if needed
C. Determine the student's operant level

The student should be correctly positioned in a chair with all outside stimuli absent. Remember to model the activity for each Step as you give the command, "Do this." If all the objects on the busy box are too confusing, any toy with a crank on it can be used as a replacement.

After the student learns to manipulate the larger object, train him on the comparable but smaller object.

EYE-HAND COORDINATION

OBJECTIVE 15 The student will press the button on the busy box after attaining five consecutive positive responses to a verbal command on each Step of the Task Analysis.

Task Analysis Steps

The student will:

1. let you put his hand on the button upon the command, "Do this"
2. let you push the button with his hand upon the command, "Do this"
3. press the button with his hand upon the command, "Do this"
4. let you touch the button with his finger upon command
5. let you press the button with his finger upon the command, "Do this"
6. push the button with his finger upon command

EYE-HAND COORDINATION

IMPLEMENTATION 15

MATERIALS:
Kohner Busy Box, Fisher-Price Pop-up Phone

PREREQUISITE SKILLS:
None

PROCEDURE:
A. Determine the student's reinforcement preference
B. Be certain the student is seated properly with support provided if needed
C. Determine the student's operant level

The student should be correctly positioned in a chair with all outside stimuli absent. Remember to model the activity for each Step as you give the command, "Do this." If the objects on the busy box are too confusing, the Fisher-Price Pop-up Phone offers more stimulation to those who cannot attend to one activity at a time on the busy box. The closeness of many buttons increases the chances of the student's initial success.

After the student learns to manipulate the larger object, train him on the comparable but smaller object.

EYE-HAND COORDINATION

OBJECTIVE 16
The student will push the car on the busy box after attaining five consecutive positive responses to a verbal command on each Step of the Task Analysis.

Task Analysis Steps

The student will:

1. let you touch the car with his hand
2. let you push the car to the right with his hand upon the command, "Do this"
3. let you push the car to the left with his hand upon the command, "Do this"
4. push the car to the left upon the command, "Do this"
5. push the car to the right upon the command, "Do this"

EYE-HAND COORDINATION

IMPLEMENTATION 16

MATERIALS:
Kohner Busy Box

PREREQUISITE SKILLS:
The student should be able to reach

PROCEDURE:
A. Determine the student's reinforcement preference
B. Be certain the student is seated properly with support provided if needed
C. Determine the student's operant level

The student should be correctly positioned in a chair with all outside stimuli absent. Remember to model the activity for each Step as you give the command, "Do this." If the objects on the busy box are too confusing, a small toy car that moves easily can be placed on a tray for the student to manipulate. A blind student can push a sound tube back and forth in a shallow box.

After the student learns to manipulate the car on the tray, he can be trained to push the busy box car.

EYE-HAND COORDINATION

OBJECTIVE 17
The student will slide the door on the busy box after attaining five consecutive positive responses to a verbal command on each Step of the Task Analysis.

Task Analysis Steps

The student will:

1. let you touch the slide door with his hand
2. let you slide the door open with his hand upon the command, "Do this"
3. slide the door open upon the command, "Do this"
4. let you slide the door closed with his hand upon the command, "Do this"
5. slide the door closed upon the command, "Do this"

EYE-HAND COORDINATION
IMPLEMENTATION 17

MATERIALS:
Kohner Busy Box

PREREQUISITE SKILLS:
The student should be able to reach

PROCEDURE:
A. Determine the student's reinforcement preference
B. Be certain the student is seated properly with support provided if needed
C. Determine the student's operant level

The student should be correctly positioned in a chair with all outside stimuli absent. Remember to model the activity for each Step as you give the command, "Do this." If all the objects on the busy box are too confusing, any toy with a crank on it can be used as a replacement.

After the student learns to manipulate the larger object, train him on the comparable but smaller object.

EYE-HAND COORDINATION

OBJECTIVE 18
The student will turn the telephone dial on the busy box after attaining five consecutive positive responses to a verbal command on each Step of the Task Analysis.

Task Analysis Steps

The student will:

1. let you put his finger in the dial upon command
2. let you put his finger in the dial and turn the dial upon the command, "Do this"
3. turn the dial upon the command, "Do this"

EYE-HAND COORDINATION

IMPLEMENTATION 18

MATERIALS:
Kohner Busy Box, Fisher-Price Dial-a-Phone

PREREQUISITE SKILLS:
The student should be able to reach. A student can be taught to turn the dial using the palm of his hand and a turn of his wrist. This should only be done when grasp and release are done by contractives.

PROCEDURE:
A. Determine the student's reinforcement preference
B. Be certain the student is seated properly with support provided if needed
C. Determine the student's operant level

The student should be correctly positioned in a chair with all outside stimuli absent. Remember to model the activity for each Step as you give the command, "Do this." If the objects on the busy box are too confusing, the Fisher-Price Dial-a-Phone has a dial much larger than the one found on the busy box. It is easier for many students to manipulate, as well. The Dial-a-Phone has a dial that, when activated, supplies more reinforcement to the student than the one found on the busy box.

After the student has been trained to manipulate the large dial, train him on the small busy box dial.

EYE-HAND COORDINATION

OBJECTIVE 19
The student will spin the wheel on the busy box after attaining five consecutive positive responses to a verbal command on each Step of the Task Analysis.

Task Analysis Steps

The student will:

1. let you touch and spin the wheel upon command
2. let you spin the wheel with his hand upon the command, "Do this"
3. spin the wheel upon the command, "Do this"

EYE-HAND COORDINATION

IMPLEMENTATION 19

MATERIALS:
Kohner Busy Box, Romper Room Spinning Tones

PREREQUISITE SKILLS:
None

PROCEDURE:
A. Determine the student's reinforcement preference
B. Be certain the student is seated properly with support provided if needed
C. Determine the student's operant level

The student should be correctly positioned in a chair with all outside stimuli absent. Remember to model the activity for each Step as you give the command, "Do this." If the objects on the busy box are too confusing, the Romper Room Spinning Tones offers three large wheels placed side by side. It produces reinforcement because each wheel makes a different tone as it spins. It is very good for the blind student because sound is an excellent reinforcement for these students.

After the student learns to manipulate the large object, train him on the comparable but smaller object.

EYE-HAND COORDINATION

OBJECTIVE 20 The student will open the door on the busy box after attaining five consecutive positive responses to a verbal command on each Step of the Task Analysis.

Task Analysis Steps

The student will:

1. let you touch the mirrored door with his hand
2. let you touch the knob of the door with his hand upon the command, "Do this"
3. let you open the door with his hand upon the command, "Do this"
4. open the door upon command

EYE-HAND COORDINATION

IMPLEMENTATION 20

MATERIALS:
Kohner Busy Box, Creative Playthings Pop-up Box
PREREQUISITE SKILLS:
The student should be able to reach, grasp, and release
PROCEDURE:
A. Determine the student's reinforcement preference
B. Be certain the student is seated properly with support provided if needed
C. Determine the student's operant level

The student should be correctly positioned in a chair with all outside stimuli absent. Remember to model the activity for each Step as you give the command, "Do this." If the objects on the busy box are too confusing, the Creative Playthings Pop-up Box can be opened in the same manner as the mirrored door. For reinforcement, a small doll pops up. The doll can be removed to place an edible reinforcer in the box. For the blind student, a rattle or string of bells could be placed in the box.

After the student learns to manipulate the larger object, train him on the comparable but smaller object.

EYE-HAND COORDINATION

OBJECTIVE 21
The student will open the drawer on the busy box after attaining five consecutive positive responses to a verbal command on each Step of the Task Analysis.

Task Analysis Steps

The student will:

1. let you position his hand on the drawer
2. let you open the drawer with his hand
3. open the drawer upon command

EYE-HAND COORDINATION

IMPLEMENTATION 21

MATERIALS:
Kohner Busy Box
PREREQUISITE SKILLS:
The student should be able to reach, grasp, and release
PROCEDURE:
A. Determine the student's reinforcement preference
B. Be certain the student is seated properly with support provided if needed
C. Determine the student's operant level

    The student should be correctly positioned in a chair with all outside stimuli absent. Remember to model the activity for each Step as you give the command, "Do this." If all the objects on the busy box are too confusing, any toy with a crank on it can be used as a replacement.
    After the student learns to manipulate the larger object, train him on the comparable but smaller object.

EYE-HAND COORDINATION

OBJECTIVE 22
The student will press the button on the surprise busy box after attaining five consecutive positive responses to a verbal command on each Step of the Task Analysis.

Task Analysis Steps

The student will:

1. let you put his hand on the button upon the command, "Do this"
2. let you press the button with his hand upon the command, "Do this"
3. press the button with his hand upon the command, "Do this"
4. let you touch the button with his finger upon command
5. let you press the button with his finger upon the command, "Do this"
6. press the button with his finger upon command

EYE-HAND COORDINATION

IMPLEMENTATION 22

MATERIALS:
Kohner Surprise Busy Box
PREREQUISITE SKILLS:
The student should be able to reach
PROCEDURE:
  A.   Determine the student's reinforcement preference
  B.   Be certain the student is seated properly with support provided if needed
  C.   Determine the student's operant level

    Although the surprise busy box offers more reinforcement than the busy box and less confusion in objects, problems may still arise. The extraneous objects can be masked with tape, or similar toys can be used.

    For all Task Analysis Steps in Objective 22, you should be seated next to the student and:

1.   touch the button with your hand as you say, "Do this." Take the student's hand and touch the button with it. If he does not resist, reinforce.
2.   press the button with your hand as you say, "Do this." Take the student's hand and press the button with it. If he cooperates, reinforce.
3.   press the button as you say, "Do this." The student should do the same, independently. If he does, reinforce.

    The Objective can be terminated here and credit given if the student cannot use a finger to manipulate the button.

EYE-HAND COORDINATION

OBJECTIVE 23 The student will slide the knob on the surprise busy box after attaining five consecutive positive responses to a verbal command on each Step of the Task Analysis.

Task Analysis Steps

The student will:

1. let you touch the sliding knob with his hand upon the command, "Do this"
2. let you slide the knob with his hand upon the command, "Do this"
3. slide the knob upon the command, "Do this"

EYE-HAND COORDINATION
IMPLEMENTATION 23

MATERIALS:
Kohner Surprise Busy Box

PREREQUISITE SKILLS:
The student should be able to reach

PROCEDURE:
A. Determine the student's reinforcement preference
B. Be certain the student is seated properly with support provided if needed
C. Determine the student's operant level

Although the surprise busy box offers more reinforcement than the busy box and less confusion in objects, problems may still arise. The extraneous objects can be masked with tape, or similar toys can be used.

For all Task Analysis Steps in Objective 23, you should be seated next to the student and:

1. touch the knob with your hand as you say, "Do this." The student should let you use his hand to do the same. If he does not resist, reinforce immediately.
2. slide the knob with your hand as you say, "Do this." The student should let you use his hand to do the same. If he does not resist, reinforce immediately.
3. slide the knob with your hand as you say, "Do this." The student should slide the knob independently.

EYE-HAND COORDINATION

OBJECTIVE 24 The student will turn the knob on the surprise busy box after attaining five consecutive positive responses to a verbal command on each Step of the Task Analysis.

Task Analysis Steps

The student will:

1. let you put his hand on the turning knob
2. let you turn the knob with his hand upon the command, "Do this"
3. turn the knob with his hand upon the command, "Do this

EYE-HAND COORDINATION

IMPLEMENTATION 24

MATERIALS:

Kohner Surprise Busy Box

PREREQUISITE SKILLS:

The student should be able to reach, grasp, and release

PROCEDURE:

A. Determine the student's reinforcement preference
B. Be certain the student is seated properly with support provided if needed
C. Determine the student's operant level

Although the surprise busy box offers more reinforcement than the busy box and less confusion in objects, problems may still arise. The extraneous objects can be masked with tape, or similar toys can be used.

For all Task Analysis Steps in Objective 24, you should be seated next to the student and:

1. touch the turning knob with your hand as you say, "Do this." Touch the turning knob with the student's hand. If he does not resist, reinforce him.
2. turn the turning knob with your hand as you say, "Do this." Turn the knob using the student's hand. If he cooperates, reinforce him.
3. turn the turning knob upon the command, "Do this." The student will then turn the knob independently. Reinforce immediately for the correct response.

EYE-HAND COORDINATION

OBJECTIVE 25 The student will turn the dial on the surprise busy box after attaining five consecutive positive responses to a verbal command on each Step of the Task Analysis.

Task Analysis Steps

The student will:

1. let you put his finger in the dial upon command
2. let you put his finger in the dial and turn the dial upon the command, "Do this"
3. turn the dial upon the command, "Do this"

EYE-HAND COORDINATION

IMPLEMENTATION 25

MATERIALS:
Kohner Surprise Busy Box, Fisher-Price Dial-a-Phone
PREREQUISITE SKILLS:
The student should be able to reach, grasp, and release
PROCEDURE:
A. Determine the student's reinforcement preference
B. Be certain the student is seated properly with support provided if needed
C. Determine the student's operant level

The student should be correctly positioned in a chair with all outside stimuli absent. Remember to model the activity for each Step as you give the command, "Do this." If the objects on the surprise busy box are too confusing, the Fisher-Price Dial-a-Phone has a dial much larger than the one found on the surprise busy box. It is easier for many students to manipulate, as well.

After the student has been trained to manipulate the large dial, he can then be trained on the smaller surprise busy box dial.

EYE-HAND COORDINATION

OBJECTIVE 26
The student will flip the switch on the surprise busy box after attaining five consecutive positive responses to a verbal command on each Step of the Task Analysis.

Task Analysis Steps

The student will:

1. let you place his hand on the switch upon the command, "Do this"
2. put his hand on the switch upon the command, "Do this"
3. let you flip the switch upon the command, "Do this"
4. flip the switch upon the command, "Do this"

EYE-HAND COORDINATION

IMPLEMENTATION 26

MATERIALS:
Kohner Surprise Busy Box

PREREQUISITE SKILLS:
The student should be able to reach

PROCEDURE:

A. Determine the student's reinforcement preference
B. Be certain the student is seated properly with support provided if needed
C. Determine the student's operant level

The student should be correctly positioned in a chair with all outside stimuli absent. Remember to model the activity for each Step as you give the command, "Do this." If all the objects on the surprise busy box are too confusing, any toy with a crank on it can be used as a replacement.

After the student learns to manipulate the larger object, train him on the comparable but smaller object.

EYE-HAND COORDINATION

OBJECTIVE 27 The student will place three pegs in a peg board after attaining five consecutive positive responses to a verbal command on each Step of the Task Analysis.

Task Analysis Steps

The student will:

1. let you use his hand to put a peg into the peg board upon command
2. let you use his hand to pick up the peg and position it by a hole in the peg board; he will then put the peg in the hole upon command
3. let you pick up the peg with his hand; he will then put the peg into the peg board upon command
4. pick up the peg and insert it into the peg board upon command
5. insert two pegs in the peg board upon command
6. insert three pegs in the peg board upon command

EYE-HAND COORDINATION

IMPLEMENTATION 27

MATERIALS:
Large knobbed pegs and matching board (Ideal, Special Ed.), double suction soap holder

PREREQUISITE SKILLS:
The student should be able to reach, grasp, and release

PROCEDURE:
A. Determine the student's reinforcement preference
B. Be certain the student is seated properly with support provided if needed
C. Determine the student's operant level

Place the peg board on the table using the suction holder to keep it in place. If the student has problems positioning the peg, tape over all holes but one; gradually phase out tape.

Make sure the student is properly seated with his feet touching the floor and the table at an appropriate level. He should be facing a bare wall with no distractions.

EYE-HAND COORDINATION

OBJECTIVE 28
The student will remove stacking rings after attaining five consecutive positive responses to a verbal command on each Step of the Task Analysis.

Task Analysis Steps

The student will:

1. let you grasp a stacking ring with his hand upon the command, "Do this"
2. let you remove a big stacking ring with his hand upon the command, "Do this"
3. remove the big stacking ring upon the command, "Do this" after you have used his hand to lift it to the top of the spindle
4. remove the big stacking ring upon the command, "Do this" after you have used his hand to lift it three-fourths of the way off
5. remove the big stacking ring upon the command, "Do this" after you have used his hand to lift it half way off
6. remove the big stacking ring upon the command, "Do this" after you have used his hand to lift it one-fourth of the way off
7. remove the stacking ring upon the command, "Do this" after you have positioned his hand on it
8. independently remove the stacking ring upon the command, "Do this"

EYE-HAND COORDINATION

IMPLEMENTATION 28

MATERIALS:
Fisher-Price Graduated Stacking Rings
PREREQUISITE SKILLS:
The student should be able to reach, grasp, and release
PROCEDURE:
A.   Determine the student's reinforcement preference
B.   Be certain the student is seated properly with support provided
     if needed
C.   Determine the student's operant level

1.   The student must be seated properly with the tray placed low
     enough to enable him to place the ring on the spindle. The
     graduated rings should be used because they are self-correcting
     and also the plastic rings are round and easier to grasp than the flat
     wooden ones on the straight spindle.
2.   The blind student can also master the activity. He should hold the
     spindle with his left hand and hold the ring in his right (if he is
     right-handed). He will bring his two hands together, thus finding the
     spindle and placing the ring on it.

EYE-HAND COORDINATION

OBJECTIVE 29

The student will randomly stack stacking rings after attaining five consecutive positive responses to a verbal command on each Step of the Task Analysis.

Task Analysis Steps

The student will:

1. let you use his hand to put the big stacking ring on upon the command, "Do this"
2. place the big stacking ring on, after you have used his hand to put it three-fourths of the way on, upon the command, "Do this"
3. place the big stacking ring on, after you have used his hand to put it half way on, upon the command, "Do this"
4. place the big stacking ring on, after you have used his hand to put it one-fourth of the way on, upon the command, "Do this"
5. place the big stacking ring on, after you have positioned his hand above the spindle, upon the command, "Do this"
6. place the big stacking ring on, after you have positioned his arm above the spindle, upon the command, "Do this"
7. place the large stacking ring on upon the command, "Do this"

EYE-HAND COORDINATION

IMPLEMENTATION 29

MATERIALS:
Fisher-Price Graduated Stacking Rings

PREREQUISITE SKILLS:
The student should be able to reach, grasp, and release

PROCEDURE:
A. Determine the student's reinforcement preference
B. Be certain the student is seated properly with support provided if needed
C. Determine the student's operant level

1. The student must be seated properly with the tray placed low enough to enable him to remove the ring from the spindle. To secure the toys to the table, a piece of Velcro can be glued to the table and to the bottom of the tray.
2. Be certain to model each activity as you give the command, "Do this."
3. The blind student can also master the activity. He should hold the spindle with his left hand and remove the rings with his right (if he is right-handed). Velcro can be used to attach bells to the spindle and to each ring.

EYE-HAND COORDINATION

OBJECTIVE 30 The student will stack two stacking rings in order after attaining five consecutive positive responses to a verbal command on each Step of the Task Analysis.

Task Analysis Steps

The student will:

1. place a large stacking ring on the spindle upon command, after you have positioned his arm above the spindle
2. place the large stacking ring on the spindle upon the command, "Do this"
3. place the large stacking ring on the spindle upon command, when a smaller stacking ring is taped to the table 10 inches from the large ring
4. place the large stacking ring on the spindle upon command, when a smaller stacking ring is taped to the table 8 inches from the large ring
5. place the large stacking ring on the spindle upon command, when a smaller stacking ring is taped to the table 8 inches from the large ring
6. place the large stacking ring on the spindle upon command, when the small stacking ring is taped to the table 5 inches from the large ring
7. place the large stacking ring on the spindle upon command, when the small stacking ring is taped to the table 3 inches from the large ring
8. place the large stacking ring on the spindle upon command, when the small stacking ring is taped to the table next to the large ring
9. place the large stacking ring on the spindle upon command, when the small stacking ring is lying next to the large ring
10. place the large stacking ring on the spindle upon command and place the small stacking ring on the spindle upon command, with physical assistance
11. place the large stacking ring on the spindle upon command and place the small stacking ring on the spindle upon command, with a gestural prompt
12. place the large stacking ring on the spindle upon command and place the small stacking ring on the spindle upon command
13. stack two stacking rings in order upon command

EYE-HAND COORDINATION

IMPLEMENTATION 30

MATERIALS:
Fisher-Price Graduated Stacking Rings

PREREQUISITE SKILLS:
The student should be able to reach, grasp, and release

PROCEDURE:
A. Determine the student's reinforcement preference
B. Be certain the student is seated properly with support provided if needed
C. Determine the student's operant level

The stacking rings selected for this exercise should be a large one (second ring from the bottom) and a small one (second ring from the top). These sizes will stress the size difference and help facilitate discrimination.

EYE-HAND COORDINATION

OBJECTIVE 31 The student will nest nesting blocks after attaining five consecutive positive responses to a verbal command on each Step of the Task Analysis.

Task Analysis Steps

The student will:

1. let you use his hands to place the small block inside the large block
2. will place the small block inside the larger block upon the command, "Do this" after you have used his hands to lift and position the small block over the large block
3. position and place the small block inside the large block upon the command, "Do this" after you have used his hands to lift the small block
4. place the small block on the large block upon the command, "Do this"
5. let you use his hands to place the medium block inside the large block upon the command, "Do this"
6. will place the medium block inside the large block upon the command, "Do this" after you have used his hands to lift and position the medium block over the large block
7. position and place the medium block inside the large block upon the command, "Do this" after you have used his hands to lift the medium block over the large block
8. place the medium block in the large block upon the command, "Do this"
9. let you use his hands to place the small block inside the medium block upon the command, "Do this"
10. place the small block inside the medium block upon the command, "Do this" after you have used his hands to lift and position the small block over the medium one
11. position and place the small block inside the medium block upon the command, "Do this" after you have used his hands to lift the small block

12. place the small block inside the medium block upon the command, "Do this"

EYE-HAND COORDINATION

IMPLEMENTATION 31

MATERIALS:
Creative Playthings Wooden Nesting Blocks

PREREQUISITE SKILLS:
The student should be able to reach, grasp, and release

PROCEDURE:

A. Determine the student's reinforcement preference
B. Be certain the student is seated properly with support provided if needed
C. Determine the student's operant level

1. The student must be seated properly with the table or tray low enough to accommodate the blocks for nesting. If the wooden blocks prove to be too heavy or cumbersome, they can also be purchased in cardboard.
2. This can also be adapted to the blind student. Have the large block held securely to the surface by suction. Have the student use one hand to find the opening of the block and the other hand to lift and insert the smaller block. Covering the blocks in a textured material may also help.

EYE-HAND COORDINATION

OBJECTIVE 32 The student will stack nesting blocks after attaining five consecutive positive responses to a verbal command on each Step of the Task Analysis.

Task Analysis Steps

The student will:

1. let you use his hands to place the small block on the large block upon the command, "Do this"
2. place the small block on the large block upon the command, "Do this" after you have used his hands to lift and position the small block over the large one
3. position and place the small block on the large block upon the command, "Do this" after you have used his hand to lift the small block
4. place the small block on the large block upon the command, "Do this"
5. let you use his hands to place the medium block on the large block upon the command, "Do this"
6. place the medium block on the large block upon the command, "Do this" after you have used his hands to lift and position the medium block over the large block
7. position and place the medium block on the large block upon the command, "Do this" after you have used his hands to lift the medium block
8. place the medium block on the big block upon the command, "Do this"
9. let you use his hands to place the small block on the medium block upon the command, "Do this"
10. place the small block on the medium block upon the command, "Do this" after you have used his hands to lift and position the small block over the medium block
11. position and place the small block on the medium block upon the command, "Do this" after you have used his hands to lift the small block
12. place the small block on the medium block upon the command, "Do this"

EYE-HAND COORDINATION

IMPLEMENTATION 32

MATERIALS:
Creative Playthings Wooden Nesting Blocks
PREREQUISITE SKILLS:
The student should be able to reach, grasp, and release
PROCEDURE:
A. Determine the student's reinforcement preference
B. Be certain the student is seated properly with support provided if
   needed
C. Determine the student's operant level

The student must be seated properly with the table or tray low enough to accommodate the blocks for stacking. The blocks should be held securely in place because some students may need two hands to lift the blocks. This can be done by taping the large block to the table and the medium block to the large block. As the student masters the task, the tape can be removed.

Remember that the modeling must be visually clear to the student.

This activity can be adapted to the blind student, just as in Implementation 31.

EYE-HAND COORDINATION

OBJECTIVE 33
The student will nest nesting cups after attaining five consecutive positive responses to a verbal command on each Step of the Task Analysis.

Task Analysis Steps

The student will:

1. let you place the small cup inside the large cup upon the command, "Do this"
2. place the small cup inside the large cup upon the command, "Do this" after you have used his hand to lift and position the small cup over the large one
3. position and place the small cup inside the large cup upon the command, "Do this" after you have used his hand to lift the small cup
4. place the small cup inside the large cup upon the command, "Do this"
5. let you use his hands to place the medium cup inside the large cup upon the command, "Do this"
6. place the medium cup inside the large cup upon the command, "Do this" after you have used his hands to lift and position the medium cup over the large cup
7. position and place the medium cup inside the large cup upon the command, "Do this" after you have used his hands to lift the medium cup
8. place the medium cup inside the large cup upon the command, "Do this"
9. let you use his hands to place the small cup inside the medium cup upon the command, "Do this"
10. place the small cup inside the medium cup upon the command, "Do this" after you have used his hands to lift and position the small cup over the medium cup
11. position and place the small cup inside the medium cup upon the command, "Do this" after you have used his hands to lift the small cup

12. place the small cup inside the medium cup upon the command, "Do this"

EYE-HAND COORDINATION

IMPLEMENTATION 33

MATERIALS:
Playskool Nesting Cups

PREREQUISITE SKILLS:
The student should be able to reach, grasp, and release

PROCEDURE:
A. Determine the student's reinforcement preference
B. Be certain the student is seated properly with support provided if needed
C. Determine the student's operant level

1. The student must be seated properly with the table or tray high enough to accommodate the cups for nesting.
2. Sit across from the student and model the activity as you give the command, "Do this."
3. The blind student can also engage in this activity. Have the large cup held securely by a suction cup so the student can use one hand to locate the opening of the cup and the other to place the small cup inside. The rewards should be heavy because this is not a reinforcing activity.

EYE-HAND COORDINATION

OBJECTIVE 34
The student will stack nesting cups after attaining five consecutive positive responses to a verbal command on each Step of the Task Analysis.

Task Analysis Steps

The student will:

1. let you use his hands to place the medium cup on the large cup
2. place the medium cup on the large cup, after you have used his hands to lift and position the medium cup on the large cup
3. position and place the medium cup on the large cup, after you have used his hands to lift the medium cup
4. place the medium cup on the large cup
5. let you use his hands to place the small cup on the medium cup
6. place the small cup on the medium cup, after you have used his hands to lift and position the small cup over the medium cup
7. position and place the small cup on the medium cup, after you have used his hands to lift the small cup
8. place the small cup on the medium cup

EYE-HAND COORDINATION

IMPLEMENTATION 34

MATERIALS:
 Playskool Nesting Cups
PREREQUISITE SKILLS:
 The student should be able to reach, grasp, and release
PROCEDURE:
 A. Determine the student's reinforcement preference
 B. Be certain the student is seated properly with support provided if
 needed
 C. Determine the student's operant level

   The student must be seated properly with the table or tray low
enough to accommodate the cups for stacking. The large cups should
be held securely in place with Velcro because some students may
encounter more difficulty in stacking than in previous exercises.
   The activity can be adapted to the blind student just as in Implementation 33.

EYE-HAND COORDINATION

OBJECTIVE 35 The student will place a circle in the form board after attaining five consecutive positive responses to a verbal command on each Step of the Task Analysis.

Task Analysis Steps

The student will:

1. let you use his hands to pick up the circle and place it in the form board
2. let you use his hands to pick up the circle and position it by the inset; he will place it in the form board
3. let you use his hands to pick up the circle and take it to the form board; he will place it in the inset
4. let you use his hands to pick up the circle; he will place it in the form board
5. pick up the circle and place it in the form board

EYE-HAND COORDINATION

IMPLEMENTATION 35

MATERIALS:
Creative Playthings Form Board, Montessori Form Trays

PREREQUISITE SKILLS:
The student should be able to reach

PROCEDURE:
A. Determine the student's reinforcement preference
B. Be certain the student is seated properly with support provided if needed
C. Determine the student's operant level

The student should be seated properly with the form board securely attached to the tray or table. If the student has problems with the form board because of other shapes on the board, a single inset from the Montessori tray can be used to eliminate confusion. If using the form board from Creative Playthings, make a template that will cover all other forms not being used.

For the blind student, the single inset would be best. Secure the inset to the surface, covering it with a textured material so it will be less difficult to find. Have the student find the inset with one hand as he positions the circle with the other.

EYE-HAND COORDINATION

OBJECTIVE 36
The student will place a square in the form board after attaining five consecutive positive responses to a verbal command on each Step of the Task Analysis.

Task Analysis Steps

The student will:

1. let you use his hands to pick up the square and place it in the form board
2. let you use his hands to pick up the square and position it by the inset; he will place it in the form board
3. let you use his hands to pick up the square and take it to the form board; he will place it in the form board
4. let you use his hands to pick up the square; he will place it in the form board
5. pick up the square and place it in the form board

EYE-HAND COORDINATION

IMPLEMENTATION 36

MATERIALS:
Creative Playthings Form Board, Montessori Form Trays

PREREQUISITE SKILLS:
The student should be able to reach into the proper inset

PROCEDURE:
  A. Determine the student's reinforcement preference
  B. Be certain the student is seated properly with support provided if
      needed
  C. Determine the student's operant level

    The student should be seated properly with the form board se-
curely attached to the tray or table. If the student has problems with the
form board because of the other shapes on the board, a single inset
from the Montessori tray can be used to eliminate confusion. If using the
form board from Creative Playthings, make a template that will cover all
other forms not being used, or mask the extraneous forms with tape
that corresponds to the color of the forms.
    For the blind student, the single inset would be best. Secure the
inset to the surface, covering it with a textured material so it will be less
difficult to find. Have the student find the inset with one hand as he
positions the square with the other.

EYE-HAND COORDINATION

OBJECTIVE 37

The student will place a triangle in the form board after attaining five consecutive positive responses to a verbal command on each Step of the Task Analysis.

Task Analysis Steps

The student will:

1. let you use his hands to pick up the triangle and place it in the form board
2. let you use his hands to pick up the triangle and position it by the inset; he will place it in the form board
3. let you use his hands to pick up the triangle and take it to the form board; he will place it in the form board
4. let you use his hands to pick up the triangle; he will place it in the form board
5. pick up the triangle and place it in the form board

EYE-HAND COORDINATION

IMPLEMENTATION 37

MATERIALS:
Creative Playthings Form Board, Montessori Form Trays

PREREQUISITE SKILLS:
The student should be able to reach into the proper inset

PROCEDURE:
A. Determine the student's reinforcement preference
B. Be certain the student is seated properly with support provided if needed
C. Determine the student's operant level

The student should be seated properly with the form board securely attached to the tray or table. If the student has problems with the form board because of other shapes on the board, a single inset from the Montessori tray can be used to eliminate confusion. If using the form board from Creative Playthings, make a template that will cover all other forms not being used.

For the blind student, a single inset would be best. Secure the inset to the surface, covering it with a textured material so it will be less difficult to find. Have the student find the inset with one hand as he positions the triangle with the other.

EYE-HAND COORDINATION

OBJECTIVE 38 The student will place a circle in the shape sorting box after attaining five consecutive positive responses to a verbal command on each Step of the Task Analysis.

Task Analysis Steps

The student will:

1. let you use his hands to pick up the circle and put it in the box
2. let you use his hands to pick up the circle and position it by the inset; he will put it in the box
3. let you use his hands to pick up the circle and take it to the form board; he will put it into the box
4. let you use his hands to pick up the circle; he will put it in the box
5. pick up the circle and place it in the box

EYE-HAND COORDINATION
IMPLEMENTATION 38

MATERIALS:

Creative Playthings Shape Sorting Box

PREREQUISITE SKILLS:

The student should be able to reach, grasp, and release

PROCEDURE:

A. Determine the student's reinforcement preference
B. Be certain the student is seated properly with support provided if needed
C. Determine the student's operant level

The student should be seated properly. The insets of the shape sorting box should be at the student's breast level. If you do not have a tray to manipulate, turn the box on its side or tilt it on a slant so the insets will be facing the student. If the student continues to have problems, tape over all the insets except for the shape you are working on. Go from a solid color tape that corresponds to the color of the box to a clear tape so the student will see them even if they cannot be used. Gradually fade out the tape altogether.

EYE-HAND COORDINATION

OBJECTIVE 39
The student will place a square in the shape sorting box after attaining five consecutive positive responses to a verbal command on each Step of the Task Analysis.

Task Analysis Steps

The student will:

1. let you use his hands to pick up the square and put it in the box
2. let you use his hands to pick up the square and position it by the inset; he will put it in the box
3. let you use his hands to pick up the square and take it to the box; he will put it in the box
4. let you use his hands to pick up the square; he will put it in the box
5. pick up the square and place it in the box

EYE-HAND COORDINATION

IMPLEMENTATION 39

MATERIALS:
Creative Playthings Shape Sorting Box

PREREQUISITE SKILLS:
The student should be able to reach, grasp, and release

PROCEDURE:
A. Determine the student's reinforcement preference
B. Be certain the student is seated properly with support provided if needed
C. Determine the student's operant level

The student should be seated properly. The insets of the shape sorting box should be at the student's breast level. If you do not have a tray to manipulate, turn the box on its side or tilt it on a slant so the insets will be facing the student. If the student continues to have problems, tape over all the insets except for the shape you are working on. Go from a solid color tape that corresponds to the color of the box to a clear tape so the student will see them even if they cannot be used. Gradually fade out the tape altogether.

EYE-HAND COORDINATION

OBJECTIVE 40 The student will place a triangle in the shape sorting box after attaining five consecutive positive responses to a verbal command on each Step of the Task Analysis.

Task Analysis Steps

The student will:

1. let you use his hands to pick up the triangle and put it in the box upon command
2. let you use his hands to pick up the triangle and position it by the inset; he will put it in the box
3. let you use his hands to pick up the triangle and take it to the box; he will put it in the box
4. let you use his hands to pick up the triangle; he will put it in the box
5. pick up the triangle and place it in the box

EYE-HAND COORDINATION

IMPLEMENTATION 40

MATERIALS:
Creative Playthings Shape Sorting Box

PREREQUISITE SKILLS:
The student should be able to reach, grasp, and release

PROCEDURE:
A. Determine the student's reinforcement preference
B. Be certain the student is seated properly with support provided if needed
C. Determine the student's operant level

The student should be seated properly. The insets of the shape sorting box should be at the student's breast level. If you do not have a tray to manipulate, turn the box on its side or tilt it on a slant so the insets will be facing the student. If the student continues to have problems, tape over all the insets except for the shape you are working on. Go from a solid color tape that corresponds to the color of the box to a clear tape so the student will see them even if they cannot be used. Gradually fade out the tape altogether.

EYE-HAND COORDINATION

OBJECTIVE 41
The student will assemble a three-piece puzzle after attaining five consecutive positive responses to a verbal command on each Step of the Task Analysis.

Task Analysis Steps

The student will:

1. let you use his hands to place the first puzzle piece in the inset upon command
2. let you use his hands to pick up the first puzzle piece and position it next to the inset; he will place it in the inset upon command
3. let you use his hands to pick up the first puzzle piece; he will place it in the inset upon command
4. place the first puzzle piece in the inset upon command
5. let you touch the second puzzle piece with his hand
6. let you hold the second puzzle piece with his hand
7. let you use his hands to place the second puzzle piece in the inset upon command
8. let you use his hands to pick up the second puzzle piece and position it next to the inset; he will place it in the inset upon command
9. let you use his hands to pick up the second puzzle; he will place it in the inset upon command
10. place the second puzzle piece in the inset upon command
11. let you touch the third puzzle piece with his hand
12. let you hold the third puzzle piece with his hand
13. let you use his hands to place the third puzzle piece in the inset upon command
14. let you use his hands to pick up the third puzzle piece and position it next to the inset; he will place it in the inset upon command
15. let you use his hands to pick up the third puzzle piece; he will place it in the inset upon command
16. place the third puzzle piece in the inset upon command

EYE-HAND COORDINATION

IMPLEMENTATION 41

MATERIALS:
Playskool three-piece puzzle
PREREQUISITE SKILLS:
The student should be able to reach, grasp, and release
PROCEDURE:
A. Determine the student's reinforcement preference
B. Be certain the student is seated properly with support provided if needed
C. Determine the student's operant level

The student must be seated properly. If he has a difficult time placing the puzzle pieces, a three-piece puzzle with knobs can be used. A bead can be glued to the center of each puzzle piece if new puzzles are hard to obtain.

If the other two pieces are causing distraction, make a template out of cardboard where only the piece you are working on shows through. If this is successful, make another template where one piece and the inset you are working on are exposed. Then go back to the entire puzzle.

EYE-HAND COORDINATION

OBJECTIVE 42

The student will assemble a four-piece puzzle after attaining five consecutive positive responses to a verbal command on each Step of the Task Analysis.

Task Analysis Steps

The student will:

1. let you use his hand to place the first puzzle piece in the inset upon command
2. let you use his hand to pick up the first puzzle piece and position it next to the inset; he will place it in the inset upon command
3. let you use his hand to pick up the first puzzle piece; he will place it in the inset upon command
4. place the first puzzle piece in the inset upon command
5. let you use his hand to touch the second puzzle piece
6. let you use his hand to hold the second puzzle piece
7. let you use his hand to place the second puzzle piece in the inset upon command
8. let you use his hand to pick up the second puzzle piece and position it next to the inset; he will place it in the inset upon command
9. let you use his hand to pick up the second puzzle piece; he will place it in the inset upon command
10. place the second puzzle piece in the inset upon command
11. let you use his hand to touch the third puzzle piece
12. let you use his hand to hold the third puzzle piece
13. let you use his hand to place the third puzzle piece in the inset upon command
14. let you use his hand to pick up the third puzzle piece and position it next to the inset; he will place it in the inset upon command
15. let you use his hand to pick up the third puzzle piece; he will place it in the inset upon command
16. place the third puzzle piece in the inset upon command
17. let you use his hand to touch the fourth puzzle piece
18. let you use his hand to hold the fourth puzzle piece
19. let you use his hand to place the fourth puzzle piece in the inset upon command
20. let you use his hand to pick up the fourth puzzle piece and position it next to the inset; he will place it in the inset upon command
21. let you use his hand to pick up the fourth puzzle piece; he will place it in the inset upon command
22. place the fourth puzzle piece in the inset upon command

EYE-HAND COORDINATION

IMPLEMENTATION 42

MATERIALS:
Playskool four-piece puzzle

PREREQUISITE SKILLS:
The student should be able to reach, grasp, and release

PROCEDURE:
A. Determine the student's reinforcement preference
B. Be certain the student is seated properly with support provided if needed
C. Determine the student's operant level

    The student must be seated properly. If he has a difficult time placing the puzzle pieces together, a four-piece puzzle with knobs can be used. A bead can be glued to the center of each puzzle piece if new puzzles are too hard to obtain.

    As the student is learning to place the first puzzle piece in the puzzle, the remaining three pieces should be intact. If they are causing distraction, make a template out of cardboard which has only the piece you are working on showing through. If this is successful, you can fade in the other puzzle pieces.

EYE-HAND COORDINATION

OBJECTIVE 43 The student will assemble a five-piece puzzle after attaining five consecutive positive responses to a verbal command on each Step of the Task Analysis.

Task Analysis Steps

The student will:

1. let you use his hand to place the first puzzle piece in the inset upon command
2. let you use his hand to pick up the first puzzle piece and position it next to the inset; he will place it in the inset upon command
3. let you use his hand to pick up the first puzzle piece; he will place it in the inset upon command
4. place the first puzzle piece in the inset upon command
5. let you use his hand to touch the second puzzle piece
6. let you use his hand to hold the second puzzle piece
7. let you use his hand to place the second puzzle piece in the inset upon command
8. let you use his hand to pick up the second puzzle piece and position it next to the inset; he will place it in the inset upon command
9. let you use his hand to pick up the second puzzle piece; he will place it in the inset upon command
10. place the second puzzle piece in the inset upon command
11. let you use his hand to touch the third puzzle piece
12. let you use his hand to hold the third puzzle piece
13. let you use his hand to place the third puzzle piece in the inset upon command
14. let you use his hand to pick up the third puzzle piece and position it next to the inset; he will place it in the inset upon command
15. let you use his hand to pick up the third puzzle piece; he will place it in the inset upon command
16. place the third puzzle piece in the inset upon command
17. let you use his hand to touch the fourth puzzle piece
18. let you use his hand to hold the fourth puzzle piece
19. let you use his hand to place the fourth puzzle piece in the inset upon command
20. let you use his hand to pick up the fourth puzzle piece and position it next to the inset; he will place it in the inset upon command
21. let you use his hand to pick up the fourth puzzle piece; he will place it in the inset upon command
22. place the fourth puzzle piece in the inset upon command
23. let you use his hand to touch the fifth puzzle piece
24. let you use his hand to hold the fifth puzzle piece
25. let you use his hand to place the fifth puzzle piece in the inset upon command
26. let you use his hand to pick up the fifth puzzle piece and position it next to the inset; he will place it in the inset upon command
27. let you use his hand to pick up the fifth puzzle piece; he will place it in the inset upon command
28. place the fifth puzzle piece in the inset upon command

EYE-HAND COORDINATION

IMPLEMENTATION 43

MATERIALS:
  Playskool five-piece puzzle
PREREQUISITE SKILLS:
  The student should be able to reach, grasp, and release
PROCEDURE:
  A. Determine the student's reinforcement preference
  B. Be certain the student is seated properly with support provided if
      needed
  C. Determine the student's operant level

The student must be seated properly. If he has a difficult time placing the puzzle pieces together, a five-piece puzzle with knobs can be used. A bead can be glued to the center of each puzzle piece if new puzzles are too hard to obtain.

As the student is learning to place the first puzzle piece in the puzzle, the remaining four pieces should be intact. If they are causing distraction, make a template out of cardboard which has only the piece you are working on showing through. If this is successful, you can fade in the other puzzle pieces.

EYE-HAND COORDINATION

OBJECTIVE 44 The student will assemble a six-piece puzzle after attaining five consecutive positive responses to a verbal command on each Step of the Task Analysis.

Task Analysis Steps

The student will:

1. let you use his hand to place the first puzzle piece in the inset upon command
2. let you use his hand to pick up the first puzzle piece and position it next to the inset; he will place it in the inset upon command
3. let you use his hand to pick up the first puzzle piece; he will place it in the inset upon command
4. place the first puzzle piece in the inset upon command
5. let you use his hand to touch the second puzzle piece
6. let you use his hand to hold the second puzzle piece
7. let you use his hand to place the second puzzle piece in the inset upon command
8. let you use his hand to pick up the second puzzle piece and position it next to the inset; he will place it in the inset upon command
9. let you use his hand to pick up the second puzzle piece; he will place it in the inset upon command
10. place the second puzzle piece in the inset upon command
11. let you use his hand to touch the third puzzle piece
12. let you use his hand to hold the third puzzle piece
13. let you use his hand to place the third puzzle piece in the inset upon command
14. let you use his hand to pick up the third puzzle piece and position it next to the inset; he will place it in the inset upon command
15. let you use his hand to pick up the third piece; he will place it in the inset upon command
16. place the third puzzle piece in the inset upon command
17. let you use his hand to touch the fourth puzzle piece
18. let you use his hand to hold the fourth puzzle piece
19. let you use his hand to place the fourth puzzle piece in the inset upon command
20. let you use his hand to pick up the fourth puzzle piece and position it next to the inset; he will place it in the inset upon command
21. let you use his hand to pick up the fourth puzzle piece; he will place it in the inset upon command
22. place the fourth puzzle piece in the inset upon command
23. let you use his hand to touch the fifth puzzle piece
24. let you use his hand to hold the fifth puzzle piece
25. let you use his hand to place the fifth puzzle piece in the inset upon command
26. let you use his hand to pick up the fifth puzzle piece and position it next to the inset; he will place it in the inset upon command
27. let you use his hand to pick up the fifth puzzle piece; he will place it in the inset upon command
28. place the fifth puzzle piece in the inset upon command
29. let you use his hand to touch the sixth puzzle piece
30. let you use his hand to hold the sixth puzzle piece
31. let you use his hand to place the sixth puzzle piece in the inset upon command
32. let you use his hand to pick up the sixth puzzle piece and position it next to the inset; he will place it in the inset upon command
33. let you use his hand to pick up the sixth puzzle piece; he will place it in the inset upon command
34. place the sixth puzzle piece in the inset upon command

EYE-HAND COORDINATION

IMPLEMENTATION 44

MATERIALS:
Playskool six-piece puzzle

PREREQUISITE SKILLS:
The student should be able to reach, grasp, and release

PROCEDURE:
A. Determine the student's reinforcement preference
B. Be certain the student is seated properly with support provided if needed
C. Determine the student's operant level

The student must be seated properly. If he has a difficult time placing the puzzle pieces together, a six-piece puzzle with knobs can be used. A bead can be glued to the center of each puzzle piece if new puzzles are too hard to obtain.

As the student is learning to place the first puzzle piece in the puzzle, the remaining five pieces should be intact. If they are causing distraction, make a template out of cardboard which has only the piece you are working on showing through. If this is successful, you can fade in the other puzzle pieces.

EYE-HAND COORDINATION

OBJECTIVE 45
The student will trace a horizontal line with his finger after attaining five consecutive positive responses to a verbal command on each Step of the Task Analysis.

Task Analysis Steps

The student will:

1. let you use his finger to trace a horizontal line
2. let you use his finger to trace three-fourths of a horizontal line; he will continue to trace the line to the end
3. let you use his finger to trace half of a horizontal line; he will continue to trace the line to the end
4. let you use his finger to trace one-fourth of a horizontal line; he will continue to trace the line to the end
5. trace a horizontal line

EYE-HAND COORDINATION

IMPLEMENTATION 45

MATERIALS:
12″ × 18″ white paper or poster board, black magic marker (thick)

PREREQUISITE SKILLS:
The student should be able to follow shapes in finger paints, sand, etc., with his finger

PROCEDURE:
A. Determine the student's reinforcement preference
B. Be certain the student is seated properly with support provided if needed
C. Determine the student's operant level

On a 12″ × 18″ white piece of poster board, draw a thick horizontal line in the middle. Place a reward (Fruit Loop) at the right end of the line. Place the student's finger on the left at the beginning of the line and hold his finger as you follow the line from left to right upon the command, "Do this." Gradually fade out manipulation of the student's finger.

EYE-HAND COORDINATION

OBJECTIVE 46
The student will trace a vertical line with his finger after attaining five consecutive positive responses to a verbal command on each Step of the Task Analysis.

Task Analysis Steps

The student will:

1. let you use his finger to trace a vertical line
2. let you use his finger to trace three-fourths of a vertical line; he will continue to trace the line to the end
3. let you use his finger to trace half of a vertical line; he will continue to trace the line to the end
4. let you use his finger to trace one-fourth of a vertical line; he will continue to trace the line to the end
5. trace a vertical line

EYE-HAND COORDINATION
IMPLEMENTATION 46

MATERIALS:
  12″ × 18″ white paper or poster board, black magic marker (thick)
PREREQUISITE SKILLS:
  The student should be able to follow shapes in finger paints, sand, etc., with his finger
PROCEDURE:
  A. Determine the student's reinforcement preference
  B. Be certain the student is seated properly with support provided if needed
  C. Determine the student's operant level

  On a 12″ × 18″ piece of paper, draw a thick vertical line down the middle. Place a reward (Fruit Loop, etc.) at the right end of the line. Place the student's finger on the left end of the line and hold the student's finger as you follow the line from left to right upon the command, "Do this." Gradually fade out manipulation of the student's finger.

EYE-HAND COORDINATION

OBJECTIVE 47
The student will trace a horizontal curved line with his finger after attaining five consecutive positive responses to a verbal command on each Step of the Task Analysis.

Task Analysis Steps

The student will:

1. let you use his finger to trace a horizontal curve
2. let you use his finger to trace three-fourths of a horizontal curve; he will continue to trace the line to the end
3. let you use his finger to trace half of a horizontal curve; he will continue to trace the line to the end
4. let you use his finger to trace one-fourth of a horizontal curve; he will continue to trace the line to the end
5. trace a horizontal curve

EYE-HAND COORDINATION

IMPLEMENTATION 47

MATERIALS:
12″ × 18″ white paper or poster board, black magic marker (thick)

PREREQUISITE SKILLS:
The student should be able to follow shapes in finger paints, sand, etc., with his hand

PROCEDURE:
A. Determine the student's reinforcement preference
B. Be certain the student is seated properly with support provided if needed
C. Determine the student's operant level

On a 12″ × 18″ piece of paper draw a line curved down the middle: ⌒ Place a reward at the right end of the line. Place the student's finger on the left at the beginning of the line and hold the student's finger as you follow the line from left to right upon the command, "Do this." Gradually fade out manipulation of the student's finger.

EYE-HAND COORDINATION

OBJECTIVE 48 The student will trace an up and down curve with his finger after attaining five consecutive positive responses to a verbal command on each Step of the Task Analysis.

Task Analysis Steps

The student will:

1. let you use his finger to trace the ∿ curve
2. let you use his finger to trace two-thirds of the curve; he will continue to trace the line to the end
3. let you use his finger to trace one-third of the curve; he will continue to trace the line to the end
4. trace the ∿ curve

EYE-HAND COORDINATION

IMPLEMENTATION 48

MATERIALS:
12″ × 18″ white paper or poster board, black magic marker (thick)

PREREQUISITE SKILLS:
The student should be able to follow shapes in finger paints, sand, etc., with his hand

PROCEDURE:
A. Determine the student's reinforcement preference
B. Be certain the student is seated properly with support provided if needed
C. Determine the student's operant level

On a 12″ × 18″ piece of white paper, draw a ⌇⌇⌇ line through the middle of the paper (left to right). Place a reward at the right end of the line. Place the student's finger on the left at the beginning of the line and hold the student's finger as you follow the line from left to right upon the command, "Do this." Gradually fade out manipulation of the student's finger.

EYE-HAND COORDINATION

OBJECTIVE 49
The student will trace a circle, using a template, after attaining five consecutive positive responses to a verbal command on each Step of the Task Analysis.

Task Analysis Steps

The student will:

1. let you use his hand to trace a circle
2. let you use his hand to trace three-fourths of a circle; he will finish one-fourth
3. let you use his hand to trace half of a circle; he will finish half
4. let you use his hand to trace one-fourth of a circle; he will finish three-fourths
5. trace a circle

EYE-HAND COORDINATION

IMPLEMENTATION 49

MATERIALS:

Circle template (made from cardboard), primary pencil

PREREQUISITE SKILLS:

Before beginning this exercise, you should have a large board or table covered with paper on which the student can scribble. Provide thick crayons or pencils for this activity. Using the student's hand, draw large circles on the board.

PROCEDURE:

A. Determine the student's reinforcement preference
B. Be certain the student is seated properly with support provided if needed
C. Determine the student's operant level

Have the student seated comfortably with the pencil correctly positioned in his hand. The template should be taped to the paper to eliminate slipping.

EYE-HAND COORDINATION

OBJECTIVE 50 The student will trace a square, using a template, after attaining five consecutive positive responses to a verbal command on each Step of the Task Analysis.

Task Analysis Steps

The student will:

1. let you use his hand to trace a square
2. let you use his hand to trace three-fourths of a square; he will finish it
3. let you use his hand to trace half of a square; he will finish it
4. let you use his hand to trace one-fourth of a square; he will finish it
5. trace a square

EYE-HAND COORDINATION

IMPLEMENTATION 50

MATERIALS:
Square template (made from cardboard), primary pencil

PREREQUISITE SKILLS:
Before beginning this exercise, you can have a large board or table covered with paper on which the student can scribble. Provide thick crayons or pencils for this activity. Using the student's hand, draw large squares on the board.

PROCEDURE:
A. Determine the student's reinforcement preference
B. Be certain the student is seated properly with support provided if needed
C. Determine the student's operant level

Have the student seated comfortably with a pencil correctly positioned in his hand. The template should be taped to the paper to eliminate slipping.

EYE-HAND COORDINATION

OBJECTIVE 51 The student will trace a triangle, using a template, after attaining five consecutive positive responses to a verbal command on each Step of the Task Analysis.

Task Analysis Steps

The student will:

1. let you use his hand to trace a triangle
2. let you use his hand to trace three-fourths of a triangle; he will finish one-fourth
3. let you use his hand to trace half of a triangle; he will finish half
4. let you use his hand to trace one-fourth of a triangle; he will finish three-fourths
5. trace a triangle

EYE-HAND COORDINATION

IMPLEMENTATION 51

MATERIALS:
Triangle template (made from cardboard), primary pencil

PREREQUISITE SKILLS:
Before beginning this exercise, a large board or table can be covered with paper on which the student can scribble. Provide thick crayons or pencils for this activity. Using the student's hand, draw a large triangle on the board.

PROCEDURE:
A. Determine the student's reinforcement preference
B. Be certain the student is seated properly with support provided if needed
C. Determine the student's operant level

Have the student seated comfortably with the pencil correctly positioned in his hand. The template should be taped to the paper to eliminate slipping.

Suggested Readings

Baer, D. M., Peterson, R. F., and Sherman, J. A. 1967. The development of imitation by reinforcing behavioral similarity to a model. J. Behav. 10:405–416.

Haeussermann, E. 1958. Developmental Potential of Pre-School Children. Grune and Stratton, New York.

House, B. J., and Zeaman, D. 1963. Miniature experiments in the discrimination learning of retardates. In: L. P. Lipsett and C. C. Spiker, eds., Advances in Child Development and Behavior, Vol. I. Academic Press, New York.

Keogh, B. K., and Keogh, J. F. 1967. Pattern copying and pattern walking performance of normal and educationally subnormal boys. Am. J. Ment. Defic. 71:1009–1013.

Lillard, P. P. 1972. Montessori: A Modern Approach. Schochen Books, New York.

Moore, R., and Goldiamond, I. 1964. Errorless establishment of visual discrimination using fading procedure. J. Exper. Anal. Behav. 7:269–272.

Morrison, D., and Pothier, P. 1972. The different remedial motor training programs and the development of mentally retarded pre-schoolers. Am. J. Ment. Defic. 77:251–258.

Terrace, H. S. 1963. Discrimination learning with and without errors. J. Exper. Anal. Behav. 6:1–27.

Terrace, H. S. 1963. Errorless transfer of a discrimination across two continua. J. Exper. Anal Behav. 6:223–232.

Webb, R. 1969. Sensory motor training of the profoundly retarded. Am. J. Ment. Defic. 74:283–294.

CHAPTER TWELVE

Language Development

Language development contains six major phases: attending, physical imitation, auditory training, object discrimination, concept development, and sound imitation. These phases are not dealt with in a linear fashion. A person's language development can be in several phases at the same time.

ATTENDING

The first of these phases is attending. It was designed to develop eye contact and cooperation. These attending behaviors are necessary for learning and are crucial to the training situation. It would be advisable to include these behaviors in a maintenance program on a regular basis.

PHYSICAL IMITATION

The physical imitation phase helps to establish gross and fine motor imitation. It is suggested that additional imitative behaviors should be added to the program. In her book, *Language Acquisition Program for the Retarded or Multiply Impaired,* Louise Kent suggests that simple object manipulation seems to be the easiest type of imitation. It is also easier to imitate visible movements, for example, clapping hands, than it is to imitate those behaviors that are not visible, such as sounds.

AUDITORY TRAINING

Auditory training establishes and increases discrimination of non-speech sounds and can also provide the sensitive assessor with a general indication of the student's hearing capabilities.

OBJECT DISCRIMINATION

The object discrimination phase helps to establish and increase receptive vocabulary. The objects designated in this program are not necessarily the ones to be used with every child. For optimum success, select objects that are important to the individual student.

CONCEPT DEVELOPMENT

Concept development establishes and increases receptive comprehension of verb-preposition phrases. This area also helps to bring the student's behavior under control. The tasks, stand up, sit down, come here, are first taught as behaviors to imitate and then as actions to perform in response to verbal command (Kent, 1974).

SOUND IMITATION

Sound imitation is the first step toward expressive language. The goal of this phase is to establish sound imitation behaviors. As soon as the student is imitating sounds, he can be recommended for a speech program and will enter an echoic phase of expressive language.

These six receptive phases build a foundation for expressive speech. This is a tedious program area and should be implemented with patience. Consulting a local speech therapist for special problems will aid in facilitation of this program.

BEHAVIORAL CHECKLIST FOR LANGUAGE DEVELOPMENT/Attending

OBJECTIVES

The student will:

1. fixate on an object upon the command, "Look" _____
2. follow a moving object in a horizontal pattern _____
3. follow a moving object in a vertical pattern _____
4. follow a moving object in a diagonal pattern _____
5. follow a moving object in a circular pattern _____
6. converge _____

LANGUAGE DEVELOPMENT/Attending

OBJECTIVE 1 The student will fixate on an object upon the command, "Look" after attaining five consecutive positive responses to a verbal command on each Step of the Task Analysis.

Task Analysis Steps

The student will:

1. look at an object upon command when his head is held in position
2. look at an object upon command when his chin is held in position
3. look at an object upon command when the object is directly in front of him
4. look at an object upon command when the object is to the right of him
5. look at the object upon command when the object is to the left of him

LANGUAGE DEVELOPMENT/Attending

IMPLEMENTATION 1

MATERIALS:
Bubbles, balloon, small toy, flashlight, pencil with face on end, treats

PREREQUISITE SKILLS:
None

PROCEDURE:
A. Determine the student's reinforcement preference
B. Be certain the student is seated properly with support provided if needed
C. Determine the student's operant level

The student should be seated comfortably, ensuring proper head support. If the student will not attend to any of the objects above, find a treat that he likes exceptionally well. Hold the treat for him to attend to and reinforce with a small portion of that item. (It should not be the same treat that he is attending to because you want your reinforcement to be immediate. For example, if the student is looking at an M&M candy, make sure he is looking at it while you are placing another M&M candy in his mouth.)

A student who is still uncooperative can have his training sessions during meal time. If he likes potatoes, hold a spoon of potatoes as you command him to look. As soon as he does so, reinforce him with another spoon of potatoes. Make sure the student gets the reinforcers while he is looking at the item you are holding. Only reinforce the behavior you want at the time it occurs.

LANGUAGE DEVELOPMENT/Attending

OBJECTIVE 2   The student will follow a moving object in a horizontal pattern after attaining five consecutive positive responses to a verbal command on each Step of the Task Analysis.

Task Analysis Steps

The student will:

1. attend to bubbles being blown (or flashlight moving in random manner)
2. *follow a bubble in a horizontal pattern upon command when his head is being manipulated
3. *follow a bubble in a horizontal pattern upon command when his chin is being manipulated
4. follow a bubble in a horizontal pattern upon command
5. follow a bubble in a horizontal pattern upon command when his head is held in position
6. follow a bubble in a horizontal pattern upon command when his chin is held in position
7. follow the bubble in a horizontal pattern upon command independently holding his head in position

---

*The student's head is manipulated slightly so that he will develop the idea of following the bubble with his eyes. The student should hold his head stationary independently; if he is physically incapable of doing this, the teacher or aide should hold his head. This is *not* considered a physical prompt.

LANGUAGE DEVELOPMENT/Attending

IMPLEMENTATION 2

MATERIALS:
Bubbles, balloon, small toy, flashlight, pencil with face on end, treats

PREREQUISITE SKILLS:
None

PROCEDURE:
A. Determine the student's reinforcement preference
B. Be certain the student is seated properly with support provided if needed
C. Determine the student's operant level

The student should be seated comfortably, ensuring proper head support. If the student will not attend to any of the objects above, find a treat that he likes exceptionally well. Hold the treat for him to attend to and reinforce with a small portion of that item. (It should not be the same treat that he is attending to because you want your reinforcement to be immediate.)

A student who is still uncooperative can have his training sessions during meal time. If he likes potatoes, hold a spoon of potatoes as you command him to look. As soon as he does so, reinforce him with another spoon of potatoes. Make sure the student gets the reinforcers while he is looking at the item you are holding. Only reinforce the behavior you want at the time it occurs.

LANGUAGE DEVELOPMENT/Attending

OBJECTIVE 3 The student will follow a moving object in a vertical pattern after attaining five consecutive positive responses to a verbal command on each Step of the Task Analysis.

Task Analysis Steps

The student will:

1. attend to bubbles being blown
2. *follow a bubble in a vertical pattern upon command when his head is being manipulated
3. *follow a bubble in a vertical pattern upon command when his chin is being manipulated
4. follow a bubble in a vertical pattern upon command
5. follow a bubble in a vertical pattern upon command when his head is held stationary
6. follow a bubble in a vertical pattern upon command when his chin is held stationary
7. follow a bubble in a vertical pattern upon command independently holding his head stationary

---

*The student's head is manipulated slightly so that he will develop the idea of following the bubble with his eyes. The student should hold his head stationary independently; if he is physically incapable of doing this, the teacher or aide should hold his head. This is *not* considered a physical prompt.

LANGUAGE DEVELOPMENT/Attending

IMPLEMENTATION 3

MATERIALS:
Bubbles, balloon, small toy, flashlight, pencil with face on end, treats

PREREQUISITE SKILLS:
None

PROCEDURE:
A. Determine the student's reinforcement preference
B. Be certain the student is seated properly with support provided if needed
C. Determine the student's operant level

The student should be seated comfortably, ensuring proper head support. If the student will not attend to any of the objects above, find a treat that he likes exceptionally well. Hold the treat for him to attend to and reinforce with a small portion of that item. (It should not be the same treat that he is attending to because you want your reinforcement to be immediate.)

A student who is still uncooperative can have his training sessions during meal time. If he likes potatoes, hold a spoon of potatoes as you command him to look. As soon as he does so, reinforce him with another spoon of potatoes. Make sure the student gets the reinforcers while he is looking at the item you are holding. Only reinforce the behavior you want at the time it occurs.

LANGUAGE DEVELOPMENT/Attending

OBJECTIVE 4 The student will follow a moving object in a diagonal pattern after attaining five consecutive positive responses to a verbal command on each Step of the Task Analysis.

Task Analysis Steps

The student will:

1. attend to bubbles being blown
2. *follow a bubble in a diagonal pattern upon command when his head is being manipulated
3. *follow a bubble in a diagonal pattern upon command when his chin is being manipulated
4. follow a bubble in a diagonal pattern upon command
5. follow a bubble in a diagonal pattern upon command when his head is held stationary
6. follow a bubble in a diagonal pattern upon command when his chin is held stationary
7. follow a bubble in a diagonal pattern upon command independently holding his head in position

---

*The student's head is manipulated slightly so that he will develop the idea of following the bubble with his eyes. The student should hold his head stationary independently; if he is physically incapable of doing this, the teacher or aide should hold his head. This is *not* considered a physical prompt.

LANGUAGE DEVELOPMENT/Attending

IMPLEMENTATION 4

MATERIALS:
Bubbles, balloon, small toy, flashlight, pencil with face on end, treats
PREREQUISITE SKILLS:
None
PROCEDURE:
A. Determine the student's reinforcement preference
B. Be certain the student is seated properly with support provided if needed
C. Determine the student's operant level

    The student should be seated comfortably, ensuring proper head support. If the student will not attend to any of the objects above, find a treat that he likes exceptionally well. Hold the treat for him to attend to and reinforce with a small portion of that item. (It should not be the same treat that he is attending to because you want your reinforcement to be immediate.)

    A student who is still uncooperative can have his training sessions during meal time. If he likes potatoes, hold a spoon of potatoes as you command him to look. As soon as he does so, reinforce him with another spoon of potatoes. Make sure the student gets the reinforcers while he is looking at the item you are holding. Only reinforce the behavior you want at the time it occurs.

LANGUAGE DEVELOPMENT/Attending

OBJECTIVE 5 The student will follow a moving object in a circular pattern after attaining five consecutive positive responses to a verbal command on each Step of the Task Analysis.

Task Analysis Steps

The student will:

1. attend to bubbles being blown
2. *follow a bubble in a circular pattern upon command when his head is being manipulated
3. *follow a bubble in a circular pattern upon command when his chin is being manipulated
4. follow a bubble in a circular pattern upon command
5. follow a bubble in a circular pattern upon command when his head is held in position
6. follow a bubble in a circular pattern upon command when his chin is held in position
7. follow a bubble in a circular pattern upon command independently holding his head stationary

---

*The student's head is manipulated slightly so that he will develop the idea of following the bubble with his eyes. The student should hold his head stationary independently; if he is physically incapable of doing this, the teacher or aide should hold his head. This is *not* considered a physical prompt.

LANGUAGE DEVELOPMENT/Attending

IMPLEMENTATION 5

MATERIALS:
Bubbles, balloon, small toy, flashlight, pencil with face on end, treats
PREREQUISITE SKILLS:
None
PROCEDURE:
A. Determine the student's reinforcement preference
B. Be certain the student is seated properly with support provided if needed
C. Determine the student's operant level

The student should be seated comfortably ensuring proper head support. If the student will not attend to any of the objects above, find a treat that he likes exceptionally well. Hold the treat for him to attend to and reinforce with a small portion of that item. (It should not be the same treat that he is attending to because you want your reinforcement to be immediate.)

A student who is still uncooperative can have his training sessions during meal time. If he likes potatoes, hold a spoon of potatoes as you command him to look. As soon as he does so, reinforce him with another spoon of potatoes. Make sure the student gets the reinforcers while he is looking at the item you are holding. Only reinforce the behavior you want at the time it occurs.

LANGUAGE DEVELOPMENT/Attending

OBJECTIVE 6 The student will look at an object (converge) after attaining five consecutive positive responses to a verbal command on each Step of the Task Analysis.

Task Analysis Steps

The student will:

1. look at a doll from two feet and look at it as it is brought within five inches of his nose
2. look at a bubble from two feet and look at it as it is brought to within five inches of his nose
3. look at a light from two feet and look at it as it is brought to within five inches of his nose

LANGUAGE DEVELOPMENT/Attending

IMPLEMENTATION 6

MATERIALS:
Bubbles, balloon, small toy, flashlight, pencil with face on end, treats
PREREQUISITE SKILLS:
None
PROCEDURE:
A. Determine the student's reinforcement preference
B. Be certain the student is seated properly with support provided if needed
C. Determine the student's operant level

The student should be seated comfortably, ensuring proper head support. If the student will not attend to any of the objects above, find a treat that he likes exceptionally well. Hold the treat for him to attend to and reinforce with a small portion of that item. (It should not be the same treat he is attending to because you want your reinforcement to be immediate.)

A student who is still uncooperative can have his training sessions during meal time. If he likes potatoes, hold a spoon of potatoes as you command him to look. As soon as he does so, reinforce him with another spoon of potatoes. Make sure the student gets the reinforcers while he is looking at the item you are holding. Only reinforce the behavior you want at the time it occurs.

BEHAVIORAL CHECKLIST FOR LANGUAGE DEVELOPMENT/Physical Imitation

The student will:

1. slap the table   _____
2. clap hands   _____
3. imitate ringing a bell   _____
4. imitate pounding a mallet   _____
5. ring a bell and pound a mallet   _____
6a. *blow a feather *or*   _____
6b. *blow out a candle *or*   _____
6c. *blow a whistle   _____

___

* No. 6a, b, and c are interchangeable. If the student can do one, he can receive credit for all.

LANGUAGE DEVELOPMENT/Physical Imitation

OBJECTIVE 1 The student will slap the table after attaining five consecutive positive responses to a verbal command on each Step of the Task Analysis.

Task Analysis Steps

The student will:

1. let you slap the table with his hand upon the command, "Do this"
2. slap the table with his hand upon the command, "Do this" after you have provided a gestural prompt
3. slap the table with his hand upon the command, "Do this"

LANGUAGE DEVELOPMENT/Physical Imitation

IMPLEMENTATION 1

MATERIALS:
Table
PREREQUISITE SKILLS:
None
PROCEDURE:
A. Determine the student's reinforcement preference
B. Be certain the student is seated properly with support provided if needed
C. Determine the student's operant level

The table should be low enough so the student can comfortably set his hands upon it. It will stimulate excitement if you hit the table several times (using one hand), smile, and/or make an exciting sound. Be sure not to frighten the student while engaging in this activity.

LANGUAGE DEVELOPMENT/Physical Imitation

OBJECTIVE 2 The student will clap hands after attaining five consecutive positive responses to a verbal command on each Step of the Task Analysis.

Task Analysis Steps

The student will:

1. let you clap his hands together upon the command, "Do this"
2. clap his hands together upon the command, "Do this" as you guide his wrists
3. clap his hands together upon the command, "Do this" as you guide his elbow
4. clap his hands together upon the command, "Do this"
5. *clap his hands together and play patty-cake

---

*Step 5 is not essential to complete the Objective.

LANGUAGE DEVELOPMENT/Physical Imitation

IMPLEMENTATION 2

MATERIALS:
None
PREREQUISITE SKILLS:
None
PROCEDURE:
  A. Determine the student's reinforcement preference
  B. Be certain the student is seated properly with support provided if needed
  C. Determine the student's operant level

    Encourage the student to clap his hands to patty-cake or any similar game. Do not encourage the student to clap for any good deed that he accomplishes, because this can turn into an undesirable behavior. Remember to reinforce only the behavior you want.

LANGUAGE DEVELOPMENT/Physical Imitation

OBJECTIVE 3
The student will imitate ringing a bell after attaining five consecutive positive responses to a verbal command on each Step of the Task Analysis.

Task Analysis Steps

The student will:

1. let you use his hand to pick up the bells and shake them upon the command, "Do this"
2. let you use his hand to pick up the bells and hold them; he will shake them upon the command, "Do this"
3. let you use his hand to pick up the bells; he will hold them and shake them upon the command, "Do this"
4. pick up the bells and shake them upon command after you have provided gestural prompts
5. pick up the bells and shake them upon command

LANGUAGE DEVELOPMENT/Physical Imitation

IMPLEMENTATION 3

MATERIALS:
Bells
PREREQUISITE SKILLS:
None
PROCEDURE:
A. Determine the student's reinforcement preference
B. Be certain the student is seated properly with support provided if needed
C. Determine the student's operant level

Training on this task can be done with or without grasp. If a student has to wear a hand splint for several minutes a day, this would be an appropriate task to train on while he is in the splint. Bells with handles can be used if the student has adequate grasping abilities. A cloth ring with small bells sewed on can function very well as a bracelet for the student whose grasp is not fine enough to lift the handle of a small bell.

LANGUAGE DEVELOPMENT/Physical Imitation

OBJECTIVE 4 The student will imitate pounding a mallet after attaining five consecutive positive responses to a verbal command on each Step of the Task Analysis.

Task Analysis Steps

The student will:

1. let you use his hand to pick up the mallet and pound it
2. let you use his hand to pick up and hold the mallet; he will pound it upon the command, "Do this"
3. let you use his hand to pick up the mallet; he will hold it and pound it upon the command, "Do this"
4. pick up and pound the mallet upon command after you have provided gestural prompts
5. pick up and pound the mallet upon command

LANGUAGE DEVELOPMENT/Physical Imitation

IMPLEMENTATION 4

MATERIALS:
Small mallet, which can be purchased through any vendor who furnishes equipment for rhythm bands. For the larger student, a mallet can be made with a dowel rod and a wooden block.

PREREQUISITE SKILLS:
None

PROCEDURE:
  A. Determine the student's reinforcement preference
  B. Be certain the student is seated properly with support provided if needed
  C. Determine the student's operant level

After the student has successfully completed this exercise as outlined in the Task Analysis, have him imitate pounding the mallet as you provide only an auditory stimulus.

LANGUAGE DEVELOPMENT/Physical Imitation

OBJECTIVE 5
The student will ring a bell and pound a mallet after attaining five consecutive positive responses to a verbal command on each Step of the Task Analysis.

Task Analysis Steps

The student will:

1. ring a bell upon the command, "Do this"
2. ring a bell upon the command, "Do this" when you are ringing another bell out of his line of vision
3. pound a mallet upon the command, "Do this"
4. pound a mallet upon the command, "Do this" when you are pounding another mallet out of his line of vision
5. ring a bell upon command when both the bell and the mallet are on the table
6. pound a mallet upon command when both the bell and the mallet are on the table

LANGUAGE DEVELOPMENT/Physical Imitation

IMPLEMENTATION 5

MATERIALS:

Bells with handles can be used if the student has adequate grasping abilities. A cloth ring with small bells sewed on can function very well as a bracelet for the student whose grasp is not fine enough to lift the handle of a small bell. A small mallet, which can be purchased through any vendor who furnishes equipment for rhythm bands. For the larger student, a mallet can be made with a dowel rod and a wooden block.

PREREQUISITE SKILLS:

None

PROCEDURE:

A. Determine the student's reinforcement preference
B. Be certain the student is seated properly with support provided if needed
C. Determine the student's operant level

It is imperative that each Step of this Objective be carried out explicitly because it becomes progressively more difficult. Before beginning, be certain the student can recognize and manipulate the bell and mallet.

Going back to Objectives 3 and 4, and taking the student through all Steps with only the auditory cues and no visual stimulation will alleviate the difficult problems that may occur with some students.

LANGUAGE DEVELOPMENT/Physical Imitation

OBJECTIVE 6a The student will blow a feather after attaining five consecutive positive responses to a verbal command on each Step of the Task Analysis.

Task Analysis Steps

The student will:

1. let you shape his lips in an oval by squeezing his cheeks
2. imitate blowing a feather upon command while his cheeks are held in position
3. blow a feather upon command

LANGUAGE DEVELOPMENT/Physical Imitation

IMPLEMENTATION 6a

MATERIALS:
Feather

PREREQUISITE SKILLS:
None

PROCEDURE:
A. Determine the student's reinforcement preference
B. Be certain the student is seated properly with support provided if needed
C. Determine the student's operant level

Hang a feather above the student so that it will touch his nose. This will sometimes stimulate the student to make the proper response.

A highly stimulating but messy version of this task is to put confetti on a tray and let the student blow it off. Make sure you are holding the student's hands. This is highly stimulating, and the student will want to get to the confetti any way he can.

LANGUAGE DEVELOPMENT/Physical Imitation

OBJECTIVE 6b The student will blow out a candle after attaining five consecutive positive responses to a verbal command on each Step of the Task Analysis.

Task Analysis Steps

The student will:

1. permit you to shape his lips in an oval by squeezing his cheeks
2. imitate blowing out a candle upon the command, "Do this" while his cheeks are held in position
3. blow out a candle upon command

LANGUAGE DEVELOPMENT/Physical Imitation

IMPLEMENTATION 6b

MATERIALS:
Candle

PROCEDURE:

A. Determine the student's reinforcement preference
B. Be certain the student is seated properly with support provided if needed
C. Determine the student's operant level

A highly stimulating but messy version of this task is to put confetti on a tray and let the student blow it off. Make sure you are holding the student's hands. This is highly stimulating, and the student will want to get to the confetti any way he can.

LANGUAGE DEVELOPMENT/Physical Imitation

OBJECTIVE 6c The student will blow a whistle after attaining five consecutive positive responses to a verbal command on each Step of the Task Analysis.

Task Analysis Steps

The student will:

1. let you shape his lips in an oval by squeezing his cheeks
2. imitate blowing a whistle upon command while his cheeks are held in position
3. blow a whistle upon command

LANGUAGE DEVELOPMENT/Physical Imitation
IMPLEMENTATION 6c

MATERIALS:
Plastic whistle, paper blow-out whistle
PROCEDURE:
A. Determine the student's reinforcement preference
B. Be certain the student is seated properly with support provided if needed
C. Determine the student's operant level

A paper whistle (New Year's type) provides added stimulus, and seeing the colored paper fill up with air provides additional reinforcement as well.

Suggestions for additional Objectives:

The student will:
point to nose
extend arms horizontally
put an object on the floor
pat stomach
put arms in front of you

BEHAVIORAL CHECKLIST FOR LANGUAGE DEVELOPMENT/Auditory Training

OBJECTIVES

The student will:

1. look to the left to a sound _____
2. look to the right to a sound _____
3. follow a sound from left to right _____
4. locate a sound behind him _____
5. follow graduated sounds _____
6. imitate pounding a mallet _____
7. imitate ringing a bell _____
8. ring a bell and pound a mallet _____
9. imitate the sound of a bell _____
10. imitate the sound of a mallet _____
11. physically imitate the sound of a bell and the sound of a mallet when both are present _____

LANGUAGE DEVELOPMENT/Auditory Training

OBJECTIVE 1 The student will look to the left to a sound after attaining five consecutive positive responses to a verbal command on each Step of the Task Analysis.

Task Analysis Steps

The student will:

1. play with a noisy rattle
2. be aware of the sound the rattle makes by following it in front of him
3. look at the rattle in front of him and follow the sound to the left of him
4. look to the left to the sound of the rattle

LANGUAGE DEVELOPMENT/Auditory Training

IMPLEMENTATION 1

MATERIALS:
Baby rattles of various sounds, noise makers, bells

PREREQUISITE SKILLS:
None

PROCEDURE:
A. Determine the student's reinforcement preference
B. Be certain the student is seated properly with support provided if needed
C. Determine the student's operant level

Before beginning the exercise, determine how loud or how soft the noise should be. Start with the soft sound of a baby rattle and then go on to increasingly noisier toys if the student does not respond. Many of these sounds will be new to the student. Be certain not to over stimulate him. Rapid fluttering of the eyelids is one of the most obvious signs of over-stimulation; watch for it and discontinue using that particular noise. The student should feel that this is a game and not something to be frightened of.

Often, you will be more successful with some students if you stand behind them. If a student attends to you rather than the noise, be certain to stand behind him.

LANGUAGE DEVELOPMENT/Auditory Training

OBJECTIVE 2
The student will look to the right to a sound after attaining five consecutive positive responses to a verbal command on each Step of the Task Analysis.

Task Analysis Steps

The student will:

1. play with the noise maker
2. be aware of the sound of the noise maker by following it in front of him
3. look at the noise maker in front of him and follow the sound to the right
4. look to the right to the sound of the rattle

LANGUAGE DEVELOPMENT/Auditory Training

IMPLEMENTATION 2

MATERIALS:
Baby rattles of various sounds, noise makers, bells

PREREQUISITE SKILLS:
None

PROCEDURE:
A. Determine the student's reinforcement preference
B. Be certain the student is seated properly with support provided if needed
C. Determine the student's operant level

Before beginning the exercise, determine how loud or how soft the noise should be. Start with the soft sound of a baby rattle and then go on to increasingly noisier toys if the student does not respond. Many of these sounds will be new to the student. Be certain not to over stimulate him. Rapid fluttering of the eyelids is one of the most obvious signs of over-stimulation; watch for it and discontinue using that particular noise. The student should feel that this is a game and not something to be frightened of.

Often, you will be more successful with some students if you stand behind them. If a student attends to you rather than to the noise, be certain to stand behind him.

LANGUAGE DEVELOPMENT/Auditory Training

OBJECTIVE 3 The student will follow a sound from left to right after attaining five consecutive positive responses to a verbal command on each Step of the Task Analysis.

Task Analysis Steps

The student will:

1. play with a noisy rattle
2. be aware of the noise the rattle makes by following it in front of him
3. look to the right to the rattle
4. look to the left to the rattle
5. look to the left to the rattle and, when the sound stops, look to the right to the sound beginning

LANGUAGE DEVELOPMENT/Auditory Training

IMPLEMENTATION 3

MATERIALS:
Baby rattles of various sounds, noise makers, bells

PREREQUISITE SKILLS:
None

PROCEDURE:
A. Determine the student's reinforcement preference
B. Be certain the student is seated properly with support provided if needed
C. Determine the student's operant level

Before beginning the exercise, determine how loud or how soft the noise should be. Start with the soft sound of a baby rattle and then go on to increasingly noisier toys if the student does not respond. Many of these sounds will be new to the student. Be certain not to over stimulate him. Rapid fluttering of the eyelids is one of the most obvious signs of over-stimulation; watch for it and discontinue using that particular noise. The student should feel that this is a game and not something to be frightened of.

Often, you will be more successful with some students if you stand behind them. If a student attends to you rather than to the noise, be certain to stand behind him.

LANGUAGE DEVELOPMENT/Auditory Training

OBJECTIVE 4
The student will locate a sound behind him after attaining five consecutive positive responses to a verbal command on each Step of the Task Analysis.

Task Analysis Steps

The student will:

1. play with a noisy rattle
2. follow the sound of the rattle
3. look to the right to the sound of the rattle
4. look to the left to the sound of the rattle
5. follow the sound from left to right
6. look around to the sound behind him
7. locate the sound behind him

LANGUAGE DEVELOPMENT/Auditory Training

IMPLEMENTATION 4

MATERIALS:
Baby rattles of various sounds, noise makers, bells

PREREQUISITE SKILLS:
None

PROCEDURE:
A. Determine the student's reinforcement preference
B. Be certain the student is seated properly with support provided if needed
C. Determine the student's operant level

Before beginning the exercise, determine how loud or how soft the noise should be. Start with the soft sound of a baby rattle and then go on to increasingly noisier toys if the student does not respond. Many of these sounds will be new to the student. Be certain not to over stimulate him. Rapid fluttering of the eyelids is one of the most obvious signs of over-stimulation; watch for it and discontinue using that particular noise. The student should feel that this is a game and not something to be frightened of.

Often, you will be more successful with some students if you stand behind them. If a student attends to you rather than to the noise, be certain to stand behind him.

LANGUAGE DEVELOPMENT/Auditory Training

OBJECTIVE 5 The student will follow graduated sounds after attaining five consecutive positive responses to a verbal command on each Step of the Task Analysis.

Task Analysis Steps

The student will:

1. play with a loud-sounding cylinder
2. follow the sound of the loud cylinder
3. look to the right to the sound of the loud cylinder
4. look to the left to the sound of the loud cylinder
5. follow the sound from left to right
6. locate the loud sound behind him
7. play with a medium-sounding cylinder
8. follow the sound of the medium cylinder
9. look to the right to the sound of the medium cylinder
10. look to the left to the sound of the medium cylinder
11. follow the sound from left to right
12. locate the medium sound behind him
13. play with a soft-sounding cylinder
14. follow the sound of the soft cylinder
15. look to the right to the sound of the soft cylinder
16. follow the sound from left to right
17. locate the soft sound behind him

LANGUAGE DEVELOPMENT/Auditory Training

IMPLEMENTATION 5

MATERIALS:

Montessori Sound Cylinders. The cylinders can also be made from salt boxes. Salt can be put in one for a soft sound, popcorn or rice for a medium sound, and big beans for a loud sound. Cover with contact paper to avoid "spilling the beans."

PREREQUISITE SKILLS:

None

PROCEDURE:

A. Determine the student's reinforcement preference
B. Be certain the student is seated properly with support provided if needed
C. Determine the student's operant level

Matching exercises can be created. Give the student three (or four) graduated sound cylinders from a matched set. Select one cylinder and shake it. Have the student find the same sound in his set. Be certain the two sets are made identically.

LANGUAGE DEVELOPMENT/Auditory Training

OBJECTIVE 6 The student will imitate pounding a mallet after attaining five consecutive positive responses to a verbal command on each Step of the Task Analysis.

Task Analysis Steps

The student will:

1. let you use his hand to pick up the mallet and pound it
2. let you use his hand to pick up and hold the mallet; he will pound it upon command
3. let you use his hand to pick up the mallet; he will hold it and pound it upon command
4. pick up and pound the mallet upon command after you have provided gestural prompts
5. pick up and pound the mallet upon command

LANGUAGE DEVELOPMENT/Auditory Training

IMPLEMENTATION 6

MATERIALS:

Small mallet, which can be purchased through any vendor who furnishes equipment for rhythm bands. For the larger student, a mallet can be made with a dowel rod and a wooden block; a pounding bench (made by Fisher-Price or Creative Playthings) comes complete with its own mallet

PREREQUISITE SKILLS:

None

PROCEDURE:

A. Determine the student's reinforcement preference
B. Be certain the student is seated properly with support provided if needed
C. Determine the student's operant level

After the student has successfully completed this exercise as outlined in the Task Analysis, have him imitate pounding the mallet as you provide only an auditory stimulus (model).

If the student will not pound the mallet on the table, you may try pounding it on a pounding bench. The sight of the pegs can be more reinforcing if the student has the coordination to pound the pegs through.

LANGUAGE DEVELOPMENT/Auditory Training

OBJECTIVE 7 The student will imitate ringing a bell after attaining five consecutive positive responses to a verbal command on each Step of the Task Analysis.

Task Analysis Steps

The student will:

1. let you use his hand to pick up the bells and shake them upon the command, "Do this"
2. let you use his hand to pick up the bells and hold them; he will shake them upon the command, "Do this"
3. let you use his hand to pick up the bells; he will hold them and shake them upon the command, "Do this"
4. pick up the bells and shake them upon command after you have provided gestural prompts
5. pick up the bells and shake them upon command

LANGUAGE DEVELOPMENT/Auditory Training

IMPLEMENTATION 7

MATERIALS:
Bells

PREREQUISITE SKILLS:
None

PROCEDURE:
A. Determine the student's reinforcement preference
B. Be certain the student is seated properly with support provided if needed
C. Determine the student's operant level

Training on this Objective can be done with or without grasp. If a student has to wear a hand splint for several minutes a day, this would be an appropriate Objective to train on while he is in the splint. Bells with handles can be used if the student has adequate grasping abilities. A cloth ring with small bells sewed on can function very well as a bracelet for the student whose grasp is not fine enough to lift the handle of a small bell.

LANGUAGE DEVELOPMENT/Auditory Training

OBJECTIVE 8 The student will ring a bell and pound a mallet after attaining five consecutive positive responses to a verbal command on each Step of the Task Analysis.

Task Analysis Steps

The student will:

1. ring a bell upon the command, "Do this"
2. ring a bell upon the command, "Do this" when you are ringing another bell out of his line of vision
3. pound a mallet upon the command, "Do this"
4. pound a mallet upon the command, "Do this" when you are pounding another mallet out of his line of vision
5. ring a bell upon command when both the bell and the mallet are on the table
6. pound a mallet upon command when both the bell and the mallet are on the table

LANGUAGE DEVELOPMENT/Auditory Training

IMPLEMENTATION 8

MATERIALS:
Bells with handles can be used if the student has adequate grasping abilities. A cloth ring with small bells sewed on can function very well as a bracelet for the student whose grasp is not fine enough to lift the handle of a small bell. A small mallet, which can be purchased through any vendor who furnishes equipment for rhythm bands. For the larger student, a mallet can be made with a dowel rod and a wooden block.

PREREQUISITE SKILLS:
The student should be able to imitate pounding a mallet and ringing a bell

PROCEDURE:
A. Determine the student's reinforcement preference
B. Be certain the student is seated properly with support provided if needed
C. Determine the student's operant level

It is imperative that each Step in this Objective be carried out explicitly because it becomes progressively more difficult. Before beginning be certain the student can recognize and manipulate the bell and mallet.

Going back to Objectives 6 and 7 and taking the student through all Steps with only the auditory cues and no visual stimulation will alleviate the difficult problems that may occur with some students.

LANGUAGE DEVELOPMENT/Auditory Training

OBJECTIVE 9 The student will imitate the sound of a bell after attaining five consecutive positive responses to a verbal command on each Step of the Task Analysis.

Task Analysis Steps

The student will:

1. ring the bell upon the command, "Do this"
2. ring the bell upon the command, "Do this" when you are ringing the bell out of his line of vision
3. let you use his hand to ring the bell upon the command, "Do this" when both the bell and the mallet are on the table and you are ringing another bell out of his line of vision
4. ring the bell upon the command, "Do this" after a gestural prompt, when both the bell and the mallet are on the table and you are ringing another bell out of his line of vision
5. ring the bell upon the command, "Do this" when both the bell and the mallet are on the table and you are ringing another bell out of his line of vision

LANGUAGE DEVELOPMENT/Auditory Training

IMPLEMENTATION 9

MATERIALS:
Bells with handles can be used if the student has adequate grasping abilities. A cloth ring with small bells sewed on can function very well as a bracelet for the student whose grasp is not fine enough to lift the handle of a small bell. A small mallet, which can be purchased through any vendor who furnishes equipment for rhythm bands. For the larger student, a mallet can be made with a dowel rod and a wooden block.

PREREQUISITE SKILLS:
The student should be able to imitate pounding a mallet and ringing a bell

PROCEDURE:
A. Determine the student's reinforcement preference
B. Be certain the student is seated properly with support provided if needed
C. Determine the student's operant level

Position the bell and the mallet on the table so that the bell is closer to the student. After the student has successfully completed the Steps twice, put the bell and the mallet next to each other. If the student continues to be distracted or has a difficult time, tape the mallet to the table. Remember to record it as a physical prompt.

LANGUAGE DEVELOPMENT/Auditory Training

OBJECTIVE 10 The student will imitate the sound of a mallet after attaining five consecutive positive responses to a verbal command on each Step of the Task Analysis.

Task Analysis Steps

The student will:

1. pound the mallet upon the command, "Do this"
2. pound the mallet upon the command, "Do this" when you are pounding another mallet under the table
3. let you use his hand to pound the mallet upon the command, "Do this" when both the mallet and the bell are on the table and you are pounding another mallet under the table
4. pound the mallet upon the command, "Do this" after a gestural prompt, when both the bell and the mallet are on the table and you are pounding another mallet under the table
5. pound the mallet upon the command, "Do this" when both the mallet and the bell are on the table and you are pounding another mallet under the table

LANGUAGE DEVELOPMENT/Auditory Training

IMPLEMENTATION 10

MATERIALS:

A small mallet can be purchased through any vendor who furnishes equipment for rhythm bands. For the larger student, a mallet can be made with a dowel rod and a wooden block. A pounding bench (Fisher-Price or Creative Playthings) comes with its own mallet.

PREREQUISITE SKILLS:

None

PROCEDURE:

A.   Determine the student's reinforcement preference
B.   Be certain the student is seated properly with support provided if needed
C.   Determine the student's operant level

If the student will not pound the mallet on the table, you may try pounding it on a pounding bench or toy xylophone.

LANGUAGE DEVELOPMENT/Auditory Training

OBJECTIVE 11 The student will physically imitate the sound of a bell and the sound of a mallet when both are present after attaining five consecutive positive responses to a verbal command on each Step of the Task Analysis.

Task Analysis Steps

The student will:

1. ring the bell upon the command, "Do this" when both the bell and the mallet are on the table

2. let you use his hand to ring the bell upon the command, "Do this" when both the bell and the mallet are on the table and you are ringing another bell under the table

3. ring the bell upon the command, "Do this" after a gestural prompt, when both the bell and the mallet are on the table and you are ringing another bell under the table

4. ring the bell upon the command, "Do this" when both the bell and the mallet are on the table and you are ringing another bell under the table

5. pound the mallet upon the command, "Do this" when both the bell and the mallet are on the table

6. let you use his hand to pound the mallet upon the command, "Do this" when both the bell and the mallet are on the table and you are pounding another mallet under the table

7. pound the mallet upon the command, "Do this" after a gestural prompt, when both the bell and the mallet are on the table and you are pounding another mallet under the table

8. ring the bell upon the command, "Do this" when both the bell and the mallet are on the table and you are ringing another bell under the table

9. pound the mallet upon the command, "Do this" when both the bell and the mallet are on the table and you are pounding another mallet under the table

LANGUAGE DEVELOPMENT/Auditory Training

IMPLEMENTATION 11

MATERIALS:

Bells with handles can be used if the student has adequate grasping abilities. A cloth ring with small bells sewed on can function very well as a bracelet for the student whose grasp is not fine enough to lift the handle of a small bell. A small mallet, which can be purchased through any vendor who furnishes equipment for rhythm bands. For the larger student, a mallet can be made with a dowel rod and a wooden block.

PREREQUISITE SKILLS:

The student should be able to imitate the sound of a mallet and the sound of a bell

PROCEDURE:

A. Determine the student's reinforcement preference
B. Be certain the student is seated properly with support provided if needed
C. Determine the student's operant level

The correct use of prompts will be instrumental in making a seemingly difficult task easy. Remember to fade all prompts gradually.

BEHAVIORAL CHECKLIST FOR LANGUAGE DEVELOPMENT/Object Discrimination

OBJECTIVES

The student will:

1. give spoon   _____
2. give spoon when spoon and fork are present   _____
3. give fork   _____
4. give fork and give spoon when both are present   _____
5. give fork and give spoon when an extraneous object is present   _____
6. give comb   _____
7. give comb when both comb and toothbrush are present   _____
8. give toothbrush   _____
9. give toothbrush when both toothbrush and comb are present   _____
10. give spoon and give toothbrush when both are present   _____
11. give spoon and give toothbrush when an extraneous object is present   _____
12. give cup
13. give cup when an extraneous object is present   _____
14. give ball   _____
15. give ball when both ball and cup are present   _____
16. give ball and give cup when both are present   _____

LANGUAGE DEVELOPMENT/Object Discrimination

OBJECTIVE 1 The student will give spoon after attaining five consecutive positive responses to a verbal command on each Step of the Task Analysis.

Task Analysis Steps

The student will:

1. let you use his hand to pick up the spoon and take it from him upon the command, "Give spoon"
2. pick up the spoon after you have gestured for him to do so; you will take it from him upon the command, "Give spoon"
3. pick up the spoon and give it to you upon the command, "Give spoon" after you have gestured for him to do so
4. pick up the spoon and give it to you upon the command, "Give spoon"

LANGUAGE DEVELOPMENT/Object Discrimination

IMPLEMENTATION 1

MATERIALS:
Spoon
PREREQUISITE SKILLS:
None
PROCEDURE:
A. Determine the student's reinforcement preference
B. Be certain the student is seated properly with support provided if needed
C. Determine the student's operant level

Spoons used for this Objective should look like the one the student uses each day. He should be exposed to the word "spoon" when he is using it to eat, and he should be asked to "Give spoon" at the beginning of each feeding session.

If tables are not available, a piece of masonite can be cut like this: to fit on a wheelchair or relaxation chair. Velcro straps can be attached to hold it securely.

LANGUAGE DEVELOPMENT/Object Discrimination

OBJECTIVE 2 The student will give spoon when spoon and fork are present after attaining five consecutive positive responses to a verbal command on each Step of the Task Analysis.

Task Analysis Steps

The student will:

1. let you use his hand to pick up the spoon when both spoon and fork are on the table
2. pick up the spoon upon the command, "Give spoon" after a gestural prompt, when both spoon and fork are on the table
3. pick up the spoon upon the command, "Give spoon" when both spoon and fork are present and the fork is taped to the table
4. pick up the spoon upon the command, "Give spoon" when both spoon and fork are on the table

LANGUAGE DEVELOPMENT/Object Discrimination

IMPLEMENTATION 2

MATERIALS:
Spoon, fork, table

PREREQUISITE SKILLS:
None

PROCEDURE:
A. Determine the student's reinforcement preference
B. Be certain the student is seated properly with support provided if needed
C. Determine the student's operant level

The spoons used for this task should look like the ones the student uses each day. He should be exposed to the word "spoon" when he is using it to eat, and he should be asked to "Give spoon" at the beginning of each feeding session.

For all discriminating tasks, "errorless discrimination" procedures can be used. When asking the student to give spoon, have the fork taped to the table and positioned further away from him. Gradually move the fork next to the spoon but still tape it to the table; finally, have the spoon and fork next to each other.

If tables are not available, a piece of masonite can be cut like this: ⌐⌐ to fit on a wheelchair or relaxation chair. Straps can be attached to hold it securely.

LANGUAGE DEVELOPMENT/Object Discrimination

OBJECTIVE 3 The student will give fork after attaining five consecutive positive responses to a verbal command on each Step of the Task Analysis.

Task Analysis Steps

The student will:

1. let you use his hand to pick up the fork upon the command, "Give fork"
2. pick up the fork after you have gestured for him to do so; you will then take it from him upon the command, "Give fork"
3. pick up the fork and give it to you upon the command, "Give fork" after you have gestured for him to do so
4. pick up the fork and give it to you upon the command, "Give fork"

LANGUAGE DEVELOPMENT/Object Discrimination

IMPLEMENTATION 3

MATERIALS:
Fork, table

PREREQUISITE SKILLS:
None

PROCEDURE:

A. Determine the student's reinforcement preference
B. Be certain the student is seated properly with support provided if needed
C. Determine the student's operant level

Forks used for this Objective should look like the one the student uses each day. He should be exposed to the word "fork" when he is using it to eat, and he should be asked to "Give fork" at the beginning of each feeding session.

If tables are not available, a piece of masonite can be cut like this: to fit on a wheelchair or relaxation chair. Velcro straps can be attached to hold it securely.

LANGUAGE DEVELOPMENT/Object Discrimination

OBJECTIVE 4 The student will give fork and give spoon when both are present after attaining five consecutive positive responses to a verbal command on each Step of the Task Analysis.

Task Analysis Steps

The student will:

1. pick up the fork upon the command, "Give fork" when both spoon and fork are on the table
2. pick up the spoon upon the command, "Give spoon" when both spoon and fork are on the table

LANGUAGE DEVELOPMENT/Object Discrimination

IMPLEMENTATION 4

MATERIALS:

Spoon, fork, table

PREREQUISITE SKILLS:

The student should be able to give fork and give spoon

PROCEDURE:

A. Determine the student's reinforcement preference
B. Be certain the student is seated properly with support provided if needed
C. Determine the student's operant level

The forks and spoons used for this Objective should look like the ones the student uses each day. He should be exposed to the words "fork" and "spoon" when he is using the utensils to eat. He should be asked to "Give fork" or "Give spoon" at the beginning of each feeding session.

For all discriminating tasks, "errorless discrimination" procedures can be used. When asking the student to give fork, have the spoon taped to the table and positioned further away from the student. Gradually move the spoon next to the fork, but still tape it to the table. Finally, have the fork and the spoon next to each other.

When asking the student to give spoon, have the fork taped to the table and positioned further away from the student. Gradually move the fork next to the spoon, but still tape it to the table. Finally, have the spoon and the fork next to each other.

When introducing a third item, it should be of a completely different size and color so that it will serve only as an extraneous object.

LANGUAGE DEVELOPMENT/Object Discrimination

OBJECTIVE 5 The student will give fork and give spoon when an extraneous object is present after attaining five consecutive positive responses to a verbal command on each Step of the Task Analysis.

Task Analysis Steps

The student will:

1. pick up the spoon upon the command, "Give spoon" when both spoon and fork are on the table
2. pick up the fork upon the command, "Give fork" when both spoon and fork are on the table
3. pick up the spoon upon the command, "Give spoon" when spoon, fork, and comb are on the table
4. pick up the fork upon the command, "Give fork" when spoon, fork, and comb are on the table
5. pick up the fork upon the command, "Give fork" and pick up the spoon upon the command, "Give spoon" when spoon, fork, and comb are on the table

LANGUAGE DEVELOPMENT/Object Discrimination

IMPLEMENTATION 5

MATERIALS:
Table, spoon, fork, comb

PREREQUISITE SKILLS:
The student should be able to give fork and give spoon

PROCEDURE:
A. Determine the student's reinforcement preference
B. Be certain the student is seated properly with support provided if needed
C. Determine the student's operant level

The articles used for this Objective should be those that the student sees each day. He should be exposed to the words "fork" and "spoon" when he is using the utensils to eat. He should be asked to "Give fork" or "Give spoon" at the beginning of each feeding session.

For all discriminating tasks, "errorless discrimination" procedures can be used. When asking the student to give fork, have the spoon taped to the table and positioned further away from the student. Gradually move the spoon next to the fork, but still tape it to the table. Finally, have the fork and the spoon next to each other.

When asking the student to give the spoon, have the fork taped to the table and positioned further away from the student. Gradually move the fork next to the spoon, but still tape it to the table. Finally, have the spoon and the fork next to each other.

When introducing a third item, it should be of a completely different size and color so that it will serve only as an extraneous object.

LANGUAGE DEVELOPMENT/Object Discrimination

OBJECTIVE 6 The student will give comb after attaining five consecutive positive responses to a verbal command on each Step of the Task Analysis.

Task Analysis Steps

The student will:

1. let you use his hand to pick up the comb and take it from him upon the command, "Give comb"
2. pick up the comb after you have gestured for him to do so; you will take it from him upon the command, "Give comb"
3. pick up the comb and give it to you upon the command, "Give comb" after you have gestured for him to do so
4. pick up the comb and give it to you upon the command, "Give comb"

LANGUAGE DEVELOPMENT/Object Discrimination

IMPLEMENTATION 6

MATERIALS:
Table, comb

PREREQUISITE SKILLS:
None

PROCEDURE:
A. Determine the student's reinforcement preference
B. Be certain the student is seated properly with support provided if needed
C. Determine the student's operant level

The comb used for this Objective should be the one used on the student each day. The aides on the wards should say, "Comb" and show the comb to the student as they use it each day. The student can hold it after his hair has been combed. Ask the student to "Give comb" before putting it away. If the student enjoys having his hair combed, ask him to give comb before combing his hair each day.

LANGUAGE DEVELOPMENT/Object Discrimination

OBJECTIVE 7 The student will give comb when both comb and toothbrush are present after attaining five consecutive positive responses to a verbal command on each Step of the Task Analysis.

Task Analysis Steps

The student will:

1. let you use his hand to pick up the comb when both a comb and a toothbrush are on the table
2. pick up the comb upon the command, "Give comb" after a gestural prompt has been given, when both a comb and a toothbrush are on the table
3. pick up the comb upon the command, "Give comb" when both a comb and a toothbrush are present and the toothbrush is taped on the table
4. pick up the comb upon the command, "Give comb" when both a comb and a toothbrush are on the table

LANGUAGE DEVELOPMENT/Object Discrimination

IMPLEMENTATION 7

MATERIALS:
Comb, toothbrush, table

PREREQUISITE SKILLS:
The student should be able to give comb

PROCEDURE:
A. Determine the student's reinforcement preference
B. Be certain the student is seated properly with support provided if needed
C. Determine the student's operant level

The toothbrush and the comb used for this Objective should look like the toothbrush and the comb the student sees each day. If the student has access to an appropriate chair, this task should be done in his room next to the stand where these two articles are kept. Have a resident aide or parent accentuate the comb in the student's daily routine.

For all discriminating tasks, "errorless discrimination" procedures can be used. When asking the student to give comb, have the toothbrush taped to the table and position it further away from the student. Gradually move the toothbrush next to the comb, but still tape it to the table. Finally, have the toothbrush and the comb next to each other.

If tables are not available, a piece of masonite can be cut like this: ⌐⌐ to fit on a wheelchair or relaxation chair. Velcro straps can be attached to hold it securely.

LANGUAGE DEVELOPMENT/Object Discrimination

OBJECTIVE 8 The student will give toothbrush after attaining five consecutive positive responses to a verbal command on each Step of the Task Analysis.

Task Analysis Steps

The student will:

1. let you use his hand to pick up the toothbrush upon the command, "Give toothbrush"
2. pick up the toothbrush after you have gestured for him to do so; you will then take it from him upon the command, "Give toothbrush"
3. pick up the toothbrush and give it to you upon the command, "Give toothbrush" after you have gestured for him to do so
4. pick up the toothbrush and give it to you upon the command, "Give toothbrush"

LANGUAGE DEVELOPMENT/Object Discrimination

IMPLEMENTATION 8

MATERIALS:
  Toothbrush, table
PREREQUISITE SKILLS:
  None
PROCEDURE:
  A. Determine the student's reinforcement preference
  B. Be certain the student is seated properly with support provided if needed
  C. Determine the student's operant level

   The toothbrush used for this Objective should look like the one the student sees each day. The parent or aide should be encouraged to say "toothbrush" and to show the toothbrush whenever they brush the student's teeth.

LANGUAGE DEVELOPMENT/Object Discrimination

OBJECTIVE 9 The student will give toothbrush when both toothbrush and comb are present after attaining five consecutive positive responses to a verbal command on each Step of the Task Analysis.

Task Analysis Steps

The student will:

1. let you use his hand to pick up the toothbrush upon the command, "Give toothbrush" when both a comb and a toothbrush are on the table
2. pick up the toothbrush upon the command, "Give toothbrush" after a gestural prompt has been given, when both a comb and a toothbrush are on the table
3. pick up the toothbrush upon the command, "Give toothbrush" when both a comb and a toothbrush are present and the comb is taped to the table
4. pick up a toothbrush upon the command, "Give toothbrush" when both a comb and a toothbrush are on the table

LANGUAGE DEVELOPMENT/Object Discrimination

IMPLEMENTATION 9

MATERIALS:
 Toothbrush, comb, table

PREREQUISITE SKILLS:
 The student should be able to give comb and give toothbrush

PROCEDURE:
 A. Determine the student's reinforcement preference
 B. Be certain the student is seated properly with support provided if needed
 C. Determine the student's operant level

   The toothbrush and the comb used for this Objective should look like those the student sees each day. If the student has access to an appropriate chair, this exercise should be done in his room or wherever his toothbrush and comb are kept. Have a resident aide or parent accentuate these articles during the student's daily routine.

   For all discriminating tasks, "errorless discrimination" procedures can be used. When asking the student to "Give toothbrush," have the comb taped to the table and position it further away from the student. Gradually move the comb next to the toothbrush, but still tape it to the table. Finally, have the toothbrush and the comb next to each other.

   If tables are not available, a piece of masonite can be cut like this: ⌐⌐ to fit on a wheelchair or relaxation chair. Velcro straps can be attached to hold it securely.

LANGUAGE DEVELOPMENT/Object Discrimination

OBJECTIVE 10 The student will give spoon and give toothbrush when both are present after attaining five consecutive positive responses to a verbal command on each Step of the Task Analysis.

Task Analysis Steps

The student will:

1. pick up the spoon upon the command, "Give spoon" when both a spoon and a toothbrush are on the table
2. pick up the toothbrush upon the command, "Give toothbrush" when both a spoon and a toothbrush are on the table

LANGUAGE DEVELOPMENT/Object Discrimination

IMPLEMENTATION 10

MATERIALS:
  Toothbrush, comb, table
PREREQUISITE SKILLS:
  None
PROCEDURE:
  A. Determine the student's reinforcement preference
  B. Be certain the student is seated properly with support provided if
      needed
  C. Determine the student's operant level

The toothbrush and the comb used for this Objective should look like those the student sees each day. If the student has access to an appropriate chair, this exercise should be done in his room or wherever his toothbrush and comb are kept. Have the resident aide or parent accentuate these articles during the student's daily routine.

For all discriminating tasks, "errorless discrimination" procedures can be used. When asking the student to give toothbrush, have the comb taped to the table and position it further away from the student. Gradually move the comb next to the toothbrush but still tape it to the table. Finally, have the toothbrush and the comb next to each other.

If tables are not available, a piece of masonite can be cut like this: ⌐⌐ to fit on a wheelchair or relaxation chair. Velcro straps can be attached to hold it securely.

LANGUAGE DEVELOPMENT/Object Discrimination

OBJECTIVE 11 The student will give spoon and give toothbrush when an extraneous object is present after attaining five consecutive positive responses to a verbal command on each Step of the Task Analysis.

Task Analysis Steps

The student will:

1. pick up the spoon upon the command, "Give spoon" when both a spoon and a toothbrush are on the table
2. pick up the toothbrush upon the command, "Give toothbrush" when both a spoon and a toothbrush are on the table
3. pick up the spoon upon the command, "Give spoon" when a spoon, a toothbrush, and a cup are on the table
4. pick up the toothbrush upon the command, "Give toothbrush," and pick up the spoon upon the command, "Give spoon," when a spoon, a toothbrush, and a cup are on the table

LANGUAGE DEVELOPMENT/Object Discrimination

IMPLEMENTATION 11

MATERIALS:
 Spoon, toothbrush, cup, table
PREREQUISITE SKILLS:
 None
PROCEDURE:
 A. Determine the student's reinforcement preference
 B. Be certain the student is seated properly with support provided if needed
 C. Determine the student's operant level

    The spoon, toothbrush, and cup used for this Objective should look like those the student sees each day. If the student has access to an appropriate chair, this exercise should be done in his room or wherever his toothbrush, spoon, and cup are kept. Have the resident aide or parent accentuate these articles during the student's daily routine.

    For all discriminating tasks, "errorless discrimination" procedures can be used. When asking the student to "give spoon," have the toothbrush and the cup taped to the table and position them further away from the student. Gradually move the toothbrush and cup next to the spoon, but still tape them to the table. Finally, have the toothbrush and the comb next to each other. Use the same procedure when asking the student to give toothbrush.

    If tables are not available, a piece of masonite can be cut like this: ⌐⌐ to fit on a wheelchair or relaxation chair. Velcro straps can be attached to hold it securely.

LANGUAGE DEVELOPMENT/Object Discrimination

OBJECTIVE 12
The student will give cup after attaining five consecutive positive responses to a verbal command on each Step of the Task Analysis.

Task Analysis Steps

The student will:

1. let you use his hand to pick up the cup upon the command, "Give cup"
2. pick up the cup after you have gestured for him to do so; you will then take it from him upon the command, "Give cup"
3. pick up the cup and give it to you upon the command, "Give cup" after you have gestured for him to do so
4. pick up the cup and give it to you upon the command, "Give cup"

LANGUAGE DEVELOPMENT/Object Discrimination

IMPLEMENTATION 12

MATERIALS:
  Cup, table

PREREQUISITE SKILLS:
  None

PROCEDURE:

  A. Determine the student's reinforcement preference
  B. Be certain the student is seated properly with support provided if needed
  C. Determine the student's operant level

The cup used for this Objective should look like the one the student uses each day. He should be exposed to the word "cup" when he is using one, and he should be asked to "Give cup" at the beginning of each feeding session.

If tables are not available, a piece of masonite can be cut like this: ⌐‾⌐ to fit on a wheelchair or relaxation chair. Velcro straps can be attached to hold it securely.

LANGUAGE DEVELOPMENT/Object Discrimination

OBJECTIVE 13 The student will give cup when an extraneous object is present after attaining five consecutive positive responses to a verbal command on each Step of the Task Analysis.

Task Analysis Steps

The student will:

1. let you use his hand to pick up the cup upon the command, "Give cup" when both a cup and a ball are on the table
2. pick up the cup upon the command, "Give cup" after a gestural prompt has been given when both a cup and a ball are on the table
3. pick up the cup upon the command, "Give cup" when both a cup and a ball are present, and the ball is taped to the table
4. pick up the cup upon the command, "Give cup" when both a cup and a ball are on the table

LANGUAGE DEVELOPMENT/Object Discrimination

IMPLEMENTATION 13

MATERIALS:
Cup, ball, table

PREREQUISITE SKILLS:
The student should be able to give cup

PROCEDURE:
A. Determine the student's reinforcement preference
B. Be certain the student is seated properly with support provided if needed
C. Determine the student's operant level

Tape the ball to the table and position it further away than the cup from the student. Gradually move the ball next to the cup, but still tape it to the table. Finally, have the cup and the ball next to each other; still tape the ball, and then remove the tape.

If tables are not available, a piece of masonite can be cut like this: ⌐⌐ to fit on a wheelchair or relaxation chair. Velcro straps can be attached to hold it securely.

LANGUAGE DEVELOPMENT/Object Discrimination

OBJECTIVE 14
The student will give ball after attaining five consecutive positive responses to a verbal command on each Step of the Task Analysis.

Task Analysis Steps

The student will:

1. let you use his hand to pick up the ball upon the command, "Give ball"
2. pick up the ball after you have gestured for him to do so; you will then take it from him upon the command, "Give ball"
3. pick up the ball and give it to you upon the command, "Give ball" after you have gestured for him to do so
4. pick up the ball and give it to you upon the command, "Give ball"

LANGUAGE DEVELOPMENT/Object Discrimination

IMPLEMENTATION 14

MATERIALS:
Ball

PREREQUISITE SKILLS:
None

PROCEDURE:
A. Determine the student's reinforcement preference
B. Be certain the student is seated properly with support provided if needed
C. Determine the student's operant level

The ball used for this Objective should look like the one the student sees most frequently. He should be exposed to the word "ball" when playing with it. Do not have the student throw you the ball upon command, "Give ball"; he may generalize this behavior to the other objects.

LANGUAGE DEVELOPMENT/Object Discrimination

OBJECTIVE 15
The student will give ball when both ball and cup are present after attaining five consecutive positive responses to a verbal command on each Step of the Task Analysis.

Task Analysis Steps

The student will:

1. let you use his hand to pick up the ball upon the command, "Give ball" when both a cup and a ball are on the table
2. pick up the ball upon the command, "Give ball" after a gestural prompt has been given, when both a cup and a ball are on the table
3. pick up the ball upon the command, "Give ball" when both a cup and a ball are present and the cup is taped to the ball
4. pick up the ball upon the command, "Give ball" when both a cup and a ball are on the table

LANGUAGE DEVELOPMENT/Object Discrimination

IMPLEMENTATION 15

MATERIALS:
Ball, cup, table

PREREQUISITE SKILLS:
The student should be able to give ball and give cup

PROCEDURE:
A. Determine the student's reinforcement preference
B. Be certain the student is seated properly with support provided if needed
C. Determine the student's operant level

Tape the cup to the table and position it further away from the student than the ball. Gradually move the ball next to the cup, but still tape it to the table. Finally, have the ball and the cup next to each other, still taping the ball and then removing the tape.

If tables are not available, a piece of masonite can be cut like this: to fit on a wheelchair or relaxation chair. Velcro straps can be attached to hold it securely.

LANGUAGE DEVELOPMENT/Object Discrimination

OBJECTIVE 16 The student will give ball and give cup when both are present after attaining five consecutive positive responses to a verbal command on each Step of the Task Analysis.

Task Analysis Steps

The student will:

1. give ball upon the command, "Give ball" when both a cup and a ball are on the table
2. give cup upon the command, "Give cup" when both a cup and a ball are on the table

LANGUAGE DEVELOPMENT/Object Discrimination

IMPLEMENTATION 16

MATERIALS:
  Ball, cup, table
PREREQUISITE SKILLS:
  None
PROCEDURE:
  A.   Determine the student's reinforcement preference
  B.   Be certain the student is seated properly with support provided if
       needed
  C.   Determine the student's operant level

  For all discriminating tasks, "errorless discrimination" procedures
can be used. When asking the student to give ball, have the cup taped
to the table and positioned further away from him. Gradually move the
cup next to the ball, but still tape it to the table. Finally, have the ball and
the cup next to each other and do not use tape.

  When asking the student to give cup, have the ball taped to the
table and positioned further away from him. Gradually move the ball
next to the cup, but still tape it to the table. Finally, have the ball and
the cup next to each other using no tape.

  This should not be the end of the Object Discrimination Objectives.
These have only been an example of the techniques to use. All objects
in the student's environment can be taught in the same fashion.

  When training the student to recognize objects or picture cards,
you should use "errorless discrimination."

  Suggestions for other object discrimination objectives:

The student will:

  recognize body parts
  recognize room parts
  recognize food

BEHAVIORAL CHECKLIST FOR LANGUAGE DEVELOPMENT/Concept Development

OBJECTIVES

The student will:

1. sit down   _____
2. stand up   _____
3. look   _____
4. stop   _____
5. come   _____
6. open the door   _____
7. close the door   _____
8. *go to the _____   _____
9. *give the _____   _____
10. *put the _____ on the _____   _____
11. *take the _____ off the _____ _____
12. *pick up the _____   _____

---

*For Objectives 8 to 12, use nouns with which the student is familiar.

LANGUAGE DEVELOPMENT/Concept Development

OBJECTIVE 1

The student will sit down after attaining five consecutive positive responses to a verbal command on each Step of the Task Analysis.

Task Analysis Steps

The student will:

1. let you seat him upon the command, "Sit down" when he is standing in front of a chair
2. sit down upon command when he is standing in front of a chair
3. let you seat him upon command when he is in a group of other students
4. sit down upon command when he is in a group of students
5. let you seat him upon command when he is engaged in an extraneous activity
6. sit down upon command when he is engaged in an extraneous activity

LANGUAGE DEVELOPMENT/Concept Development

IMPLEMENTATION 1

MATERIALS:
Chair

PREREQUISITE SKILLS:
None

PROCEDURE:
A. Determine the student's reinforcement preference
B. Determine the student's operant level

Stand the student in front of a chair. Upon the command, "Sit down," physically place him in the chair and reinforce immediately. You should use as much inflection in your voice as possible when saying, "Sit down."

Bring the student to his feet and repeat the procedure until he can sit independently upon command. Remember to fade the prompts gradually.

LANGUAGE DEVELOPMENT/Concept Development

OBJECTIVE 2 The student will stand up after attaining five consecutive positive responses to a verbal command on each Step of the Task Analysis.

Task Analysis Steps

The student will:

1. let you lift him from his chair upon the command, "Stand up"
2. stand up upon command when he is seated
3. let you lift him from his chair when he is in a group of students
4. stand up upon command when he is seated in a group of students
5. let you lift him from his seat upon command when he is engaged in an extraneous activity
6. stand up upon command when he is engaged in an extraneous activity

LANGUAGE DEVELOPMENT/Concept Development

IMPLEMENTATION 2

MATERIALS:
  Chair
PREREQUISITE SKILLS:
  None
PROCEDURE:
  A. Determine the student's reinforcement preference
  B. Determine the student's operant level

The student should be seated in a chair. Upon the command, "Stand up," physically bring the student to his feet and reinforce immediately. You should use as much inflection in your voice as possible when saying, "Stand up."

Have the student sit down upon command and repeat the above procedure.

LANGUAGE DEVELOPMENT/Concept Development

OBJECTIVE 3 The student will look after attaining five consecutive positive responses to a verbal command on each Step of the Task Analysis.

Task Analysis Steps

The student will:

1. look at an object upon the command, "Look" when his head is held in position
2. look at an object upon command when his chin is held in position
3. look at an object upon command when the object is directly in front of him
4. look at an object upon command when the object is to the right of him
5. look at an object upon command when the object is to the left of him

LANGUAGE DEVELOPMENT/Concept Development

IMPLEMENTATION 3

MATERIALS:
  None
PREREQUISITE SKILLS:
  None
PROCEDURE:
  A. Determine the student's reinforcement preference
  B. Determine the student's operant level

Note: If the student has completed the Checklist for Attending, he will
  have acquired this behavior. Remediation may be needed. See
  Attending, Objectives 1 to 6.

LANGUAGE DEVELOPMENT/Concept Development

OBJECTIVE 4
The student will stop after attaining five consecutive responses to a verbal command on each Step of the Task Analysis.

Task Analysis Steps

The student will:

1. let you walk him down the hall, bringing his body to a halt upon the command, "Stop"
2. stop upon command when you walk down the hall with him (you stop each time you give the command)
3. stop upon command as he walks toward you down the hall

LANGUAGE DEVELOPMENT/Concept Development

IMPLEMENTATION 4

MATERIALS:
  None
PREREQUISITE SKILLS:
  None
PROCEDURE:
  A. Determine the student's reinforcement preference
  B. Determine the student's operant level

Walk down the hall with the student. Each time you give the command, "Stop," you and the student should stop, and he should be reinforced immediately. Have the student walk down the hall or across the room to you. Give the command, "Stop" and, if the student stops immediately, give special priase and go to him immediately and reward him.

While the student is playing, give the command, "Stop." As the student successfully carries out the command, reward him.

LANGUAGE DEVELOPMENT/Concept Development

OBJECTIVE 5 The student will come after attaining five consecutive positive responses to a verbal command on each Step of the Task Analysis.

Task Analysis Steps

The student will:

1. let you bring him to you upon the command, "Come" from three feet away
2. come to you upon command from three feet away
3. come to you upon command from six feet away
4. come to you upon command when engaged in play three feet away
5. come to you upon command when engaged in play six feet away

LANGUAGE DEVELOPMENT/Concept Development

IMPLEMENTATION 5

MATERIALS:
  None
PREREQUISITE SKILLS:
  None
PROCEDURE:
  A.   Determine the student's reinforcement preference
  B.   Determine the student's operant level

Begin by having the student come to you when he is within arms' reach, so that you may have adequate control over his situation. A corner is often a good place for the student to be standing; this way he cannot back off or be distracted by what is occurring behind him.

Always remember to reinforce immediately and have an extra-strong reinforcer when the student is more than three feet away.

LANGUAGE DEVELOPMENT/Concept Development

OBJECTIVE 6 The student will open the door after attaining five consecutive positive responses to a verbal command on each Step of the Task Analysis.

Task Analysis Steps

The student will:

1. let you touch the door knob with his hand
2. let you hold the door knob with his hand
3. let you turn the knob and open the door with his hand upon the command, "Open the door"
4. let you turn the knob with his hand; he will push the door open upon command
5. turn the knob and open the door upon command after you have placed his hand on the knob
6. open the door upon command

LANGUAGE DEVELOPMENT/Concept Development

IMPLEMENTATION 6

MATERIALS:
Door

PREREQUISITE SKILLS:
None

PROCEDURE:
A. Determine the student's reinforcement preference
B. Determine the student's operant level

Opening the door could be done each time the student leaves a room. The reinforcement would sometimes be leaving the room, as well as the edible reinforcement the student would receive.

Opening the door should not be done as an isolated task, or you will be training what may turn into an inappropriate behavior. The student will want to play with the door, opening and closing it.

LANGUAGE DEVELOPMENT/Concept Development

OBJECTIVE 7

The student will close the door after attaining five consecutive positive responses to a verbal command on each Step of the Task Analysis.

Task Analysis Steps

The student will:

1. let you touch the door knob with his hand
2. let you hold the door knob with his hand
3. let you hold the door knob and pull the door shut with his hand upon the command, "Shut the door"
4. pull the door shut upon command

LANGUAGE DEVELOPMENT/Concept Development
IMPLEMENTATION 7

MATERIALS:
Door
PREREQUISITE SKILLS:
None
PROCEDURE:
A. Determine the student's reinforcement preference
B. Determine the student's operant level

Closing the door could be done each time the student leaves a room. The reinforcement would sometimes be leaving the room, as well as the edible reinforcement the student would receive.

Closing the door should not be done as an isolated task, or you will be training what may turn into an inappropriate behavior. The student will want to play with the door, opening and closing it.

LANGUAGE DEVELOPMENT/Concept Development

OBJECTIVE 8 The student will go to the _____ after attaining five consecutive positive responses to a verbal command on each Step of the Task Analysis. (Window and door are used in this Task Analysis.)

Task Analysis Steps

The student will:

1. let you take him to the window upon the command, "Go to the window"
2. go to the window from a distance of three feet upon the command, "Go to the window"
3. go to the window from across the room upon the command, "Go to the window"
4. let you take him to the door upon the command, "Go to the door"
5. go to the door from a distance of three feet upon the command, "Go to the door"
6. go to the door from across the room upon the command, "Go to the door"

LANGUAGE DEVELOPMENT/Concept Development

IMPLEMENTATION 8

MATERIALS:
Window, door

PREREQUISITE SKILLS:
None

PROCEDURE:
A. Determine the student's reinforcement preference
B. Determine the student's operant level

The student should first know where the object is that he will be told to go to. He should be in surroundings in which he spends the major portion of his time. Before asking the student to go to a door, for example, be certain he knows what a door is and that there is not more than one door to confuse him.

Take the student to the door upon command and, finally, verbally command the student to go to the door. Remember to fade these prompts gradually and to reinforce immediately. Have the reinforcer near the door.

LANGUAGE DEVELOPMENT/Concept Development

OBJECTIVE 9 The student will give the _____ after attaining five consecutive positive responses to a verbal command on each Step of the Task Analysis. (Cup and spoon are used in this Task Analysis.)

Task Analysis Steps

The student will:

1. let you use his hand to pick up a spoon and give it to you upon the command, "Give spoon"
2. let you use his hand to pick up a spoon; he will give it to you upon the command, "Give spoon"
3. pick up a spoon and give it to you upon the command, "Give spoon"
4. let you use his hand to pick up a cup and give it to you upon the command, "Give cup"
5. let you use his hand to pick up a cup; he will give it to you upon the command, "Give cup"
6. pick up a cup and give it to you upon the command, "Give cup"
7. pick up a cup and give it to you upon the command, "Give cup," and pick up a spoon upon the command, "Give spoon"
8. pick up a cup and a spoon upon the command, "Give cup and spoon"

LANGUAGE DEVELOPMENT/Concept Development

IMPLEMENTATION 9

MATERIALS:
Cup, spoon
PREREQUISITE SKILLS:
None
PROCEDURE:
A. Determine the student's reinforcement preference
B. Be certain the student is seated properly with support provided if needed
C. Determine the student's operant level

Always start with an object you are certain the student already knows. You do not want to teach two behaviors at one time. Use prompts, but remember to fade them gradually.

LANGUAGE DEVELOPMENT/Concept Development

OBJECTIVE 10
The student will put the _____ on the _____ after attaining five consecutive positive responses to a verbal command on each Step of the Task Analysis. (Spoon and box are used in this Task Analysis.)

Task Analysis Steps

The student will:

1. let you use his hand to pick up and put a spoon on a box upon the command, "Spoon on"
2. let you use his hand to pick up the spoon and position it above the box; he will then place it on the box upon the command, "Spoon on"
3. let you use his hand to pick up the spoon and position it near the box; he will then place it on the box upon the command, "Spoon on"
4. let you use his hand to pick up the spoon; he will place in on the box upon the command, "Spoon on"
5. let you direct his hand to the spoon; he will pick up the spoon and place it on the box upon the command, "Spoon on"
6. pick up the spoon and place it on the box upon the command, "Spoon on"

LANGUAGE DEVELOPMENT/Concept Development

IMPLEMENTATION 10

MATERIALS:
Spoon, box, table

PREREQUISITE SKILLS:
None

PROCEDURE:
A. Determine the student's reinforcement preference
B. Be certain the student is seated properly with support provided if needed
C. Determine the student's operant level

The language used is extremely important in concept development tasks. The command should be, "Spoon on" unless the student already knows the word for box. He will not know if the action he is performing is called "on" or "box."

When engaging in concept development for the spastic student, a head pointer could be used to push the spoon *on* a sheet of paper.

The blind student can surely benefit from this Objective. Be sure the objects being used (spoon, box) are textured so that there is no problem in determining where the object should be placed.

LANGUAGE DEVELOPMENT/Concept Development

OBJECTIVE 11 The student will take the _____ off the _____ after attaining five consecutive positive responses to a verbal command on each Step of the Task Analysis. (Spoon and box are used in this Task Analysis.)

Task Analysis Steps

The student will:

1. let you use his hand to pick up a spoon and take it off a box upon the command, "Spoon off"
2. let you use his hand to pick up the spoon and raise it above the box; he will remove the spoon upon the command, "Spoon off"
3. let you use his hand to pick up the spoon; he will remove it from the box upon the command, "Spoon off"
4. let you direct his hand near the spoon; he will pick it up and remove it from the box upon the command, "Spoon off"
5. pick up and remove the spoon from the box upon the command, "Spoon off"

LANGUAGE DEVELOPMENT/Concept Development

IMPLEMENTATION 11

MATERIALS:
Spoon, box, table

PREREQUISITE SKILLS:
None

PROCEDURE:
A. Determine the student's reinforcement preference
B. Be certain the student is seated properly with support provided if needed
C. Determine the student's operant level

Once again, be extremely careful with the language being used. Any extra words will only confuse the student. Use of inflection will help in the understanding of the on-off concept.

The area on which the student is putting the spoon can be altered to different boxes, books, etc.

LANGUAGE DEVELOPMENT/Concept Development

OBJECTIVE 12 The student will pick up the _____ after attaining five consecutive positive responses to a verbal command on each Step of the Task Analysis. (Spoon is used in this Task Analysis.)

Task Analysis Steps

The student will:

1. let you use his hand to pick up a spoon upon the command, "Pick up spoon"
2. pick up a spoon upon command after you have positioned his hand by the spoon
3. pick up a spoon upon the command, "Pick up spoon"

LANGUAGE DEVELOPMENT/Concept Development

IMPLEMENTATION 12

MATERIALS:
Spoon

PREREQUISITE SKILLS:
None

PROCEDURE:
A. Determine the student's reinforcement preference
B. Be certain the student is seated properly with support provided if needed
C. Determine the student's operant level

As the student is being pattern-fed, give the command to pick up the spoon each time it is picked up. Once the student has learned to pick up the spoon, go on to other objects such as a ball, fork, cup, toy car, etc.

BEHAVIORAL CHECKLIST FOR LANGUAGE DEVELOPMENT/Sound Imitation

OBJECTIVES

The student will imitate:

1. clapping hands   _____
2. stamping feet   _____
3. blowing on your hand   _____
4. blowing a whistle   _____
5. opening his mouth   _____
6. closing his mouth   _____
7. sticking out his tongue _____
8. the "ah" sound   _____
9. the "oo" sound   _____

LANGUAGE DEVELOPMENT/Sound Imitation

OBJECTIVE 1
The student will imitate clapping hands after attaining five consecutive positive responses to a verbal command on each Step of the Task Analysis.

Task Analysis Steps

The student will:

1. let you clap his hands
2. let you clap his hands upon the command, "Do this" after you have clapped your hands to demonstrate
3. let you clap his hands, controlling wrists only, upon command after you have clapped your hands to demonstrate
4. clap his hands upon the command, "Do this" after you clap your hands to demonstrate

LANGUAGE DEVELOPMENT/Sound Imitation

IMPLEMENTATION 1

MATERIALS:
  None
PREREQUISITE SKILLS:
  None
PROCEDURE:
  A. Determine the student's reinforcement preference
  B. Be certain the student is seated properly with support provided if needed
  C. Determine the student's operant level

Try to make a game out of this Objective. You can recite pat-a-cake to it so that it will be fun for the student.

LANGUAGE DEVELOPMENT/Sound Imitation

OBJECTIVE 2 The student will imitate stamping feet after attaining five consecutive positive responses to a verbal command on each Step of the Task Analysis.

Task Analysis Steps

The student will:

1. let you stamp the floor with his foot
2. let you stamp the floor with his foot upon the command, "Do this"
3. let you stamp the floor with his foot upon the command, "Do this" after you have stamped your foot to demonstrate
4. let you stamp his foot, controlling the leg only, upon the command, "Do this" after you have stamped your foot to demonstrate
5. stamp his foot upon the command, "Do this" after you have stamped your foot to demonstrate

LANGUAGE DEVELOPMENT/Sound Imitation

IMPLEMENTATION 2

MATERIALS:
   None
PREREQUISITE SKILLS:
   None
PROCEDURE:
   A.   Determine the student's reinforcement preference
   B.   Be certain the student is seated properly with support provided if
        needed
   C.   Determine the student's operant level

   This Objective should be done to music if at all possible. If it is not
done to music, the student may display these behaviors at an inappropriate time.

LANGUAGE DEVELOPMENT/Sound Imitation

OBJECTIVE 3 The student will imitate blowing on your hand after attaining five consecutive positive responses to a verbal command on each Step of the Task Analysis.

Task Analysis Steps

The student will:

1. let you form his lips in a small "O"
2. assume an "O" lip position upon the command, "Do this" accompanied by a demonstration
3. let you blow on his hand
4. let you blow on his hand and put it in front of his lips upon the command, "Do this"
5. let you blow on his hand, and he will attempt to do the same upon the command, "Do this"
6. let you blow on his hand, and he will do the same upon the command, "Do this"

LANGUAGE DEVELOPMENT/Sound Imitation

IMPLEMENTATION 3

MATERIALS:
Cotton, strip of paper, confetti

PREREQUISITE SKILLS:
None

PROCEDURE:
A. Determine the student's reinforcement preference
B. Be certain the student is seated properly with support provided if needed
C. Determine the student's operant level

Some alternatives to this Objective would be to place a cotton ball on the table and demonstrate blowing the cotton ball. Accentuate your lip movement and encourage the student to blow the cotton ball. The same can be done with a strip of paper placed close to the mouth.

For an extremely stimulating exercise, place confetti on the table and encourage him to blow it off. Be certain the student's hands are not into the confetti; it will be a great temptation.

LANGUAGE DEVELOPMENT/Sound Imitation

OBJECTIVE 4 The student will imitate blowing a whistle after attaining five consecutive positive responses to a verbal command on each Step of the Task Analysis.

Task Analysis Steps

The student will:

1. attend as you blow the whistle
2. let you hold the whistle to his lips upon command after you have given a demonstration of blowing a whistle
3. let you use his hand to hold the whistle to his lips upon command after you have given a demonstration of blowing the whistle
4. hold the whistle to his lips upon command after you have given a demonstration of blowing the whistle
5. hold the whistle and let you place his lips around it upon command after you have given a demonstration of blowing the whistle
6. hold the whistle in his mouth upon command after you have given a demonstration of blowing a whistle
7. blow the whistle upon the command, "Do this" after a demonstration

LANGUAGE DEVELOPMENT/Sound Imitation

IMPLEMENTATION 4

MATERIALS:
Whistle

PREREQUISITE SKILLS:
None

PROCEDURE:
A. Determine the student's reinforcement preference
B. Be certain the student is seated properly with support provided if needed
C. Determine the student's operant level

    A whistle may not be stimulating enough for some students. In those instances, try a party horn that makes a sound and has a tissue paper extender.

LANGUAGE DEVELOPMENT/Sound Imitation

OBJECTIVE 5 The student will imitate opening his mouth after attaining five consecutive positive responses to a verbal command on each Step of the Task Analysis.

Task Analysis Steps

The student will:

1. let you open his mouth
2. open his mouth after you have manipulated it open as a model
3. open his mouth upon command after you have given a demonstration
4. open his mouth upon command

LANGUAGE DEVELOPMENT/Sound Imitation

IMPLEMENTATION 5

MATERIALS:
None

PREQUISITE SKILLS:
None

PROCEDURE:

A. Determine the student's reinforcement preference
B. Be certain the student is seated properly with support provided if needed
C. Determine the student's operant level

LANGUAGE DEVELOPMENT/Sound Imitation

OBJECTIVE 6
The student will imitate closing his mouth after attaining five consecutive positive responses to a verbal command on each Step of the Task Analysis.

Task Analysis Steps

The student will:

1. permit you to close his mouth
2. close his mouth upon command after you have manipulated it closed as a model
3. close his mouth upon command after you have given a demonstration

LANGUAGE DEVELOPMENT/Sound Imitation

IMPLEMENTATION 6

MATERIALS:
  None

PREREQUISITE SKILLS:
  None

PROCEDURE:
  A. Determine the student's reinforcement preference
  B. Be certain the student is seated properly with support provided if needed
  C. Determine the student's operant level

    When reinforcing the student for this Objective, be certain you are reinforcing only the behavior you want. Do not use candy, cereal, or any other edibles that would require the student to open his mouth. A bottle with a long thin tip (a hair tint bottle) can be used to squirt Kool-Aid or another sweet liquid into the student's mouth while his mouth is still closed.

LANGUAGE DEVELOPMENT/Sound Imitation

OBJECTIVE 7
The student will imitate sticking out his tongue after attaining five consecutive positive responses to a verbal command on each Step of the Task Analysis.

Task Analysis Steps

The student will:

1. let you open his mouth and, through the use of a tongue depressor, the tongue will extend out of his mouth
2. let you open his mouth; he will stick out his tongue upon command after you have given a demonstration
3. open his mouth and stick out his tongue upon command after you have given a demonstration
4. open his mouth slightly and stick out his tongue upon command after you have given a demonstration
5. stick out his tongue upon command after you have given a demonstration

LANGUAGE DEVELOPMENT/Sound Imitation

IMPLEMENTATION 7

MATERIALS:
Tongue depressor

PREREQUISITE SKILLS:
None

PROCEDURE:
A. Determine the student's reinforcement preference
B. Be certain the student is seated properly with support provided if needed
C. Determine the student's operant level

After the student has opened his mouth, use the tongue depressor to touch down on the back of the tongue. Immediately reinforce. If you are using a liquid reinforcer, make sure you squirt only a small amount into his mouth, under the tongue or on the tip. A large squirt straight into the mouth will go straight down the throat and cause coughing and discomfort. Pudding would be a good reinforcer. You could put a small amount on the tip of the student's tongue; the student should have no fear of discomfort.

LANGUAGE DEVELOPMENT/Sound Imitation

OBJECTIVE 8 The student will imitate the "ah" sound after attaining five consecutive positive responses to a verbal command on each Step of the Task Analysis.

Task Analysis Steps

The student will:

1. let you open his mouth and hold his tongue down with a depressor while you say, "ah"
2. say "ah" upon command after you hold his mouth open and his tongue down with a depressor
3. say "ah" upon command while you hold his mouth slightly open
4. say "ah" upon command

LANGUAGE DEVELOPMENT/Sound Imitation

IMPLEMENTATION 8

MATERIALS:
Tongue depressor

PREREQUISITE SKILLS:
None

PROCEDURE:
A. Determine the student's reinforcement preference
B. Be certain the student is seated properly with support provided if needed
C. Determine the student's operant level

The student will be reinforced first for any sound that he makes. Once you have the student responding, do not reinforce until he makes a sound similar to "ah." Finally, reinforce only the "ah" sound. The student can stand and hold hands with you as you both go in a circle when "ah" is being sung or said. As soon as the student stops saying the sound, the activity should also stop.

LANGUAGE DEVELOPMENT/Sound Imitation

OBJECTIVE 9
The student will imitate the "oo" sound upon command after attaining five consecutive positive responses to a verbal command on each Step of the Task Analysis.

Task Analysis Steps

The student will:

1. permit you to apply pressure to his cheeks so that his lips will form an "O" upon the command, "Say oo"
2. permit you to shape his mouth in an "O" upon the command, "Say oo"
3. say "oo" while you hold his mouth in position upon the command, "Say oo"
4. say "oo" upon command after a demonstration

LANGUAGE DEVELOPMENT/Sound Imitation

IMPLEMENTATION 9

MATERIALS:
None

PREREQUISITE SKILLS:
None

PROCEDURE:
A. Determine the student's reinforcement preference
B. Be certain the student is seated properly with support provided if needed
C. Determine the student's operant level

The student will first be rewarded for any sound he makes. Once you have the student responding, do not reinforce until he makes a sound similar to "oo." Finally, reinforce only the "oo" sound. The student can stand and hold hands with you as you both go in a circle (or dance) while "oo" is being sung or said. As soon as the student stops saying the sound, the activity should also stop. If a speech therapist is not available, a checklist can be made of the following vowels and consonants.

Vowel sounds:

ah	as	in	author
ee	as	in	beep
oh	as	in	spoke
oo	as	in	loop
i	as	in	line
eh	as	in	effort
i	as	in	little

Consonant imitation:

p, n, m, b, h, w, v, k, t, g, f, y, d, th, l, s, z, r, wh, sh, pah, bah, mah, hah, wah, nah, pee, bee, mee, hee, wee, nee

Suggested Readings

Baer, D. M., Peterson, R. F., and Sherman, J. A. 1967. The development of imitation by reinforcing behavioral similarity to a model. J. Exper. Anal. Behav. 10:405–416.

Baer, D. M., and Sherman, J. A. 1964. Reinforcement control of generalized imitation in young children. J. Exper. Child Psych. 1:37–49.

Baker, E. E. 1967. Aligning speech evaluation and behavioral objectives. Speech Teacher 16:158–160.

Brison, D. W. 1966. A non-talking child in kindergarten: An application of behavior therapy. J. School Psych. 4:65–69.

Gray, B., and Fygetakis, L. 1968. The development of language as a function of programmed conditioning. Behav. Res. Ther. 6:455–460.

Gray, B., and Ryan, B. 1974. A Language Program for the Nonlanguage Child. Research Press, Champaign, Ill.

Guess, D. 1969. A functional analysis of receptive language and productive speech: Acquisition of the plural morphems. J. Appl. Behav. Anal. 2:55–64.

Kent, L. R. 1974. Pre-verbal section. In: Language Acquisition Program for the Retarded or Multiply Impaired. Research Press, Champaign, Ill.

Peterson, R. F. 1968. Imitation: A basic behavioral mechanism. In: H. H. Sloane, Jr., and B. D. MacAulay (eds.), Operant Procedures in Remedial Speech and Language Training. Houghton-Mifflin, Boston.

Salzinger, K., Feldman, R. S., Cowan, J. E., and Salzinger, S. 1965. Operant conditioning of verbal behavior of two young speech-deficient boys. In: L. Krasner and L. P. Ullman, eds., Research in Behavior Modification. Holt, Rinehart & Winston, New York.

Walker, H. M., and Buckley, N. K. 1968. The use of positive reinforcement in conditioning attending behavior. J. Appl. Behav. Anal. 1:245–250.

CHAPTER THIRTEEN

Physical Eating Problems

Problems with chewing, swallowing, tongue thrust, etc., are prevalent among the profoundly retarded population. These problems limit the types of food the student can eat, as well as his speech potentials. When viewing the whole person these seem to be the obvious problems needing immediate remediation. However, the techniques of brushing and icing can be harmful if not performed under the direction of a physical therapist.

Note: *Be certain to seek out the approval of your physical therapist before beginning these activities.*

BEHAVIORAL CHECKLIST FOR PHYSICAL EATING PROBLEMS

OBJECTIVES

The student will:

1. keep his tongue in his mouth _____
2. keep his lips closed _____
3. open his mouth _____
4. close his mouth _____
5. swallow _____
6. chew _____
7. bite with strength and chew _____

PHYSICAL EATING PROBLEMS

OBJECTIVE 1
The student will keep his tongue in his mouth after attaining five consecutive positive responses to a verbal command on each Step of the Task Analysis.

Task Analysis Steps

The student will:

1. retract his tongue when you apply pressure to the back of the tongue for five to ten seconds; do this three times a day
2. retract his tongue when you apply pressure under the chin before swallowing; do this three times a day
3. retract his tongue, touching the hard palate with the tip of the tongue when the hard palate is brushed; do this three times a day
4. retract his tongue, touching the hard palate with the tip of the tongue when the hard palate is iced; do this three times a day

PHYSICAL EATING PROBLEMS

IMPLEMENTATION 1

MATERIALS:
Rotating brush (rotary brushes used for mixing drinks can also be used), tongue depressor, ice, 1-inch paint brush

PREREQUISITE SKILLS:
None

PROCEDURE:
- A. Determine the student's reinforcement preference
- B. Be certain the student is seated properly with support provided if needed
- C. Determine the student's operant level

1. This exercise is to be done three times a day. Take a tongue depressor and apply pressure to the back of the student's tongue. The tongue will retract; reward immediately with a liquid reinforcer. (Make sure the dispenser is such that the student will not have to open his mouth.) Remember to reinforce only the behavior you want.
2. If the student's tongue is protruding, squirt a liquid into his mouth and apply pressure under the chin. The tongue will retract and you can further reward the student with pudding. Be certain to use pudding; the edible reinforcer here will not be immediate. Do this three times a day.
3. Brush the student's hard palate with a soft 1-inch brush. This will tickle and cause the student to retract the tongue and touch his hard palate with the tip of the tongue. Do this three times a day.
4. Rub the student's hard palate with a piece of ice. (An ice cube can be run under water until it has a rounded edge.) A tray used for popsicles is exceptionally good for making ice cubes for this exercise.

This exercise also causes a tickling feeling, which will cause the student to touch his hard palate with the tip of his tongue. This exercise should be done three times a day.

Not all of the above exercises will work with all students. At least two of them should be followed through three times a day. If the tongue is flabby, it can be firmed up by stimulating the sides with a rotary brush.

PHYSICAL EATING PROBLEMS

OBJECTIVE 2
The student will keep his lips closed after attaining five consecutive positive responses to a verbal command on each Step of the Task Analysis.

Task Analysis Steps

The student will:

1. close his lips after brushing around the mouth for one and a half minutes; do this three times a day
2. close his lips after icing* around the mouth three times; do this three time a day
3. pinch his lips together as you pull the spoon out of his mouth

---

*Note: Ice, wipe, ice, wipe, ice, wipe

PHYSICAL EATING PROBLEMS

IMPLEMENTATION 2

MATERIALS:
 Rotary brush, ice, spoon
PREREQUISITE SKILLS:
 None
PROCEDURE:
 A. Determine the student's reinforcement preference
 B. Be certain the student is seated properly with support provided if needed
 C. Determine the student's operant level

1. Brush lightly around the mouth and encourage the student to close his lips.
2. Ice around the mouth three times a day. Use the following procedure: ice, wipe, ice, wipe, ice, wipe. While you are icing, close your lips in the same fashion you want the student to imitate. You should not need imitation procedures in this task, but it would not interfere with the exercise if you used them.

PHYSICAL EATING PROBLEMS

OBJECTIVE 3

The student will open his mouth after attaining five consecutive positive responses to a verbal command on each Step of the Task Analysis.

Task Analysis Steps

The student will:

1. let you open his mouth
2. open his mouth after you have manipulated it open as a model
3. open his mouth upon command after you have given a demonstration
4. open his mouth upon command

PHYSICAL EATING PROBLEMS

IMPLEMENTATION 3

MATERIALS:
  None
PREREQUISITE SKILLS:
  None
PROCEDURE:
  A. Determine the student's reinforcement preference
  B. Be certain the student is seated properly with support provided if needed
  C. Determine the student's operant level

PHYSICAL EATING PROBLEMS

OBJECTIVE 4
The student will close his mouth after attaining five consecutive positive responses to a verbal command on each Step of the Task Analysis.

Task Analysis Steps

The student will:

1. let you close his mouth
2. close his mouth upon command after you have manipulated it closed as a model
3. close his mouth upon command after you have given a demonstration
4. close his mouth upon command

PHYSICAL EATING PROBLEMS

IMPLEMENTATION 4

MATERIALS:
None

PREREQUISITE SKILLS:
None

PROCEDURE:
- A. Determine the student's reinforcement preference
- B. Be certain the student is seated properly with support provided if needed
- C. Determine the student's operant level

When reinforcing the student for this Objective, be certain you are reinforcing only the behavior you want. Do not use candy, cereal, or any other edibles that would require the student to open his mouth. A bottle with a long thin tip (a hair tint bottle) can be used to squirt Kool-Aid or another sweet liquid into the student's mouth while his mouth is still closed.

PHYSICAL EATING PROBLEMS

OBJECTIVE 5
The student will swallow after attaining five consecutive positive responses to a verbal command on each Step of the Task Analysis.

Task Analysis Steps

The student will:

1. swallow when pressure is applied to the back of his tongue for five to ten seconds; do this three times a day.
2. swallow when you walk a swizzle stick from the front of his tongue to the back for five to ten seconds; do this three times a day
3. swallow when the mid-line of his throat is stroked for five to ten seconds; do this three times a day.

PHYSICAL EATING PROBLEMS

IMPLEMENTATION 5

MATERIALS:
Swizzle stick, tongue depressor

PREREQUISITE SKILLS:
None

PROCEDURE:

A. Determine the student's reinforcement preference
B. Be certain the student is seated properly with support provided if needed
C. Determine the student's operant level

The student's neck should not be extended because it makes swallowing more difficult. His head should be slightly flexed, as during feeding.

1. Using a tongue depressor, gently apply pressure to the back of his tongue.
2. Walk the swizzle stick down the student's tongue—from front to back.
3. Stroke as rhythmically as possible. The strokes should be firm but not so firm that the student feels pressure on his throat.

PHYSICAL EATING PROBLEMS

OBJECTIVE 6
The student will chew after attaining five consecutive positive responses to a verbal command on each Step of the Task Analysis.

Task Analysis Steps

The student will:

1. let you manipulate his jaw in a chewing motion
2. let you manipulate his jaw to bite the bubble gum
3. manipulate his jaw to bite the bubble gum
4. let you manipulate his jaw in a chewing motion while bubble gum is in his mouth
5. move his jaw in a chewing motion while bubble gum is in his mouth
6. chew bubble gum

PHYSICAL EATING PROBLEMS

IMPLEMENTATION 6

MATERIALS:
  String, gauze, bubble gum
PREREQUISITE SKILLS:
  None
PROCEDURE:
  A. Determine the student's reinforcement preference
  B. Be certain the student is seated properly with support provided if needed
  C. Determine the student's operant level

  Be certain the student does not have cavities. If he does, do not use bubble gum.

1. Put a piece of bubble gum in a warm glass of water to soften it.
2. Wrap the softened gum in a piece of gauze.
3. Attach a long piece of string (tightly) to the bubble gum wrapped in gauze.
    The student will have to bite down on the gauze to taste the sweetness of the gum. As you use the long string to pull the bubble gum from side to side in the student's mouth, you will be encouraging the student to chew in a rotary motion.

PHYSICAL EATING PROBLEMS

OBJECTIVE 7
The student will bite with strength and chew after attaining five consecutive positive responses to a verbal command on each Step of the Task Analysis.

Task Analysis Steps

The student will:

1. bite off a soft piece of candy with his front teeth rather than with his molars
2. bite off a potato chip with his front teeth rather than with his molars
3. bite off a piece of celery with his front teeth rather than with his molars

PHYSICAL EATING PROBLEMS

IMPLEMENTATION 7

MATERIALS:
  Foods of various textures
PREREQUISITE SKILLS:
  None
PROCEDURE:
  A. Determine the student's reinforcement preference
  B. Be certain the student is seated properly with support provided if needed
  C. Determine the student's operant level

   If the student has a severe biting reflex (bites hard every time the front of his mouth and teeth are touched) he should be fed into the side of his mouth. Spoons or other utensils should be covered with vinyl to reduce gum and tooth damage.

SECTION III

APPENDICES

APPENDIX ONE

Materials List

MOTOR DEVELOPMENT MATERIALS LIST

Head and Trunk Control

Objective 1: Cage ball, carpeted barrel, dangling toy
Objective 2: Cage ball, large covered barrel, slant board, mat, dangling noisy toy
Objective 3: Mat or table
Objective 4: Table
Objective 5: Mat

Sitting

Objective 1: Dangling toy, rattle or noise maker, mat or table, blanket or pillow
Objective 2: Folded blanket or pillow
Objective 3: Mat, stuffed toy, hanging toys, ball, balloon, bubbles
Objective 4: Mat, stuffed toys, ball, balloon, hanging toy, bubbles

Hand-Knee Position

Objective 1: Mat
Objective 2: Mat
Objective 3: Mat, toys
Objective 4: Mat

Standing

Objective 1: Mat
Objective 2: Mat
Objective 3: Mat
Objective 4: Mat, table
Objective 5: Mat, table
Objective 6: Mat, table, standing table

EYE-HAND COORDINATION MATERIALS LIST

Objective 1: Shaving and whipped creams
Objective 2: Finger paints, paper to cover entire table, table appropriate to the student's size
Objective 3: Cylinder rattle or sound tube
Objective 4: Cylinder rattle or sound tube
Objective 5: Cylinder rattle or sound tube, large boxes
Objective 6: Clutch ball (Creative Playthings)
Objective 7: Proper chair, balloon or punch ball, feather, cotton, and vinegar
Objective 8: Proper chair, soap bubbles
Objective 9: Fisher-Price Mobile, crib, playpen, or activity table
Objective 10: Fisher-Price Mobile, crib, playpen, or activity table
Objective 11: Fisher-Price Mobile, crib, playpen, or activity table
Objective 12: Fisher-Price Merry-Go-Round Mobile, Fisher-Price Bluebird Mobile, Fisher-Price Jumping Jack
Objective 13: Kohner Busy Box or Fisher-Price Musical Clock, Fisher-Price Musical Radio
Objective 14: Kohner Busy Box
Objective 15: Kohner Busy Box or Fisher-Price Pop-Up Phone
Objective 16: Kohner Busy Box
Objective 17: Kohner Busy Box
Objective 18: Kohner Busy Box or Fisher-Price Dial-a-Phone
Objective 19: Kohner Busy Box or Romper Room Spinning Tone
Objective 20: Kohner Busy Box or Creative Playthings Pop-Up Box

Objective 21: Kohner Busy Box
Objective 22: Kohner Surprise Busy Box
Objective 23: Kohner Surprise Busy Box
Objective 24: Kohner Surprise Busy Box
Objective 25: Kohner Surprise Busy Box or Fisher-Price Dial-a-Phone
Objective 26: Kohner Surprise Busy Box
Objective 27: Large-knobbed pegs and matching board (Ideal—Special Ed.), double suction soap holder
Objective 28: Fisher-Price Graduated Stacking Rings
Objective 29: Fisher-Price Graduated Stacking Rings
Objective 30: Fisher-Price Graduated Stacking Rings
Objective 31: Creative Playthings Wooden Nesting Blocks
Objective 32: Creative Playthings Wooden Nesting Blocks
Objective 33: Playskool Nesting Cups
Objective 34: Playskool Nesting Cups
Objective 35: Creative Playthings Form Board, Montessori Form Trays (Preston $100.00)
Objective 36: Creative Playthings Form Board, Montessori Form Trays (Preston $100.00)
Objective 37: Creative Playthings Form Board, Montessori Form Trays (Preston $100.00)
Objective 38: Creative Playthings Shape Sorting Box
Objective 39: Creative Playthings Shape Sorting Box
Objective 40: Creative Playthings Shape Sorting Box
Objective 41: Playskool three-piece puzzle

Objective 42: Playskool four-piece puzzle
Objective 43: Playskool five-piece puzzle
Objective 44: Playskool six-piece puzzle
Objective 45: 12″ × 18″ white paper or poster board, black magic marker (thick)
Objective 46: 12″ × 18″ white paper or poster board, black magic marker (thick)
Objective 47: 12″ × 18″ white paper or poster board, black magic marker (thick)
Objective 48: 12″ × 18″ white paper or poster board, black magic marker (thick)
Objective 49: Circle template (made from cardboard), primary pencil
Objective 50: Square template (made from cardboard), primary pencil
Objective 51: Triangle template (made from cardboard), primary pencil

LANGUAGE DEVELOPMENT MATERIALS LIST

Attending

Objective 1: Bubbles, balloon, small toy, flashlight, pencil with face on end, treats
Objective 2: Bubbles, balloon, small toy, flashlight, pencil with face on end, treats
Objective 3: Bubbles, balloon, small toy, flashlight, pencil with face on end, treats
Objective 4: Bubbles, balloon, small toy, flashlight, pencil with face on end, treats
Objective 5: Bubbles, balloon, small toy, flashlight, pencil with face on end, treats
Objective 6: Bubbles, balloon, small toy, flashlight, pencil with face on end, treats

Physical Imitation

Objective 1: Table
Objective 2: None

Objective 3: Bells
Objective 4: Small mallet
Objective 5: Bells with handles, small mallet
Objective 6a: Feather
Objective 6b: Candle
Objective 6c: Plastic whistle, paper blow-out whistle

Auditory Training

Objective 1: Baby rattles of various sounds, noise makers, bells
Objective 2: Baby rattles of various sounds, noise makers, bells
Objective 3: Baby rattles of various sounds, noise makers, bells
Objective 4: Baby rattles of various sounds, noise makers, bells
Objective 5: Montessori Sound Cylinders (approximately $50.00)
Objective 6: Small mallet
Objective 7: Bells
Objective 8: Bells with handles, small mallet
Objective 9: Bells with handles, small mallet
Objective 10: Small mallet
Objective 11: Bells with handles, small mallet

Object Discrimination

Objective 1: Spoon
Objective 2: Spoon, fork, table
Objective 3: Fork, table
Objective 4: Spoon, fork, table
Objective 5: Table, spoon, fork, comb
Objective 6: Table, comb
Objective 7: Comb, toothbrush, table
Objective 8: Toothbrush, table
Objective 9: Toothbrush, comb, table
Objective 10: Toothbrush, comb, table
Objective 11: Spoon, toothbrush, cup, table

Objective 12: Cup, table
Objective 13: Cup, ball, table
Objective 14: Ball
Objective 15: Ball, cup, table
Objective 16: Ball, cup, table

Concept Development

Objective 1: Chair
Objective 2: Chair
Objective 3: None
Objective 4: None
Objective 5: None
Objective 6: Door
Objective 7: Door
Objective 8: Window, door
Objective 9: Cup, spoon
Objective 10: Spoon, box, table
Objective 11: Spoon, box, table
Objective 12: Spoon

Sound Imitation

Objective 1: None
Objective 2: None
Objective 3: Cotton, strip of paper, confetti
Objective 4: Whistle
Objective 5: None
Objective 6: None
Objective 7: Tongue depressor
Objective 8: Tongue depressor
Objective 9: None

PHYSICAL EATING PROBLEMS MATERIALS LIST

Objective 1: Rotating brush, tongue depressor, ice, 1-inch paint brush
Objective 2: Rotary brush, ice, spoon

Objective 3: None
Objective 4: None
Objective 5: Swizzle stick, tongue depressor
Objective 6: String, gauze, bubble gum
Objective 7: Foods of various textures

APPENDIX TWO

Answers TO Chapter Questions

CHAPTER ONE ANSWERS

1. Operant psychology is a behavioral science that develops practical techniques for producing changes in socially significant behaviors.

2.

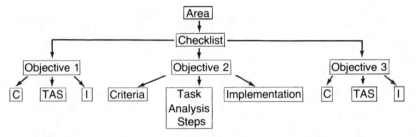

3. Behavioral Objective

4. a. Make communication clear to everyone involved in the behavior change process.
   b. Provides a consistent description for everyone observing the individual.

5.

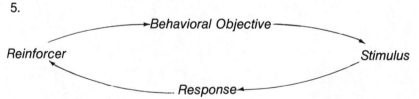

6. A Behavioral Objective states specifically what behavior is to be observed.
   The stimulus is the event which precedes and sets the occasion for the response.
   The response is the activity the person performs.
   Reinforcers are the things or events following a behavior that will increase the possibility of the behavior occurring again.

7. On the choice of Objectives.
8. It provides information on the effectiveness of the reinforcer.
9. Through feedback, the student lets you know if there are instructional problems.
10. Stimulus—instructional material questions
Response—answers to chapter questions
Reinforcer—learning to use the program progressing through the book

CHAPTER TWO ANSWERS

1. a. The teacher should possess a tool to assess the whole person.
   b. A prescription to direct teaching needs is imperative for remediation.
2. Equipment and environment
3. Only one area should be assessed each day.
4. Table, chair, cerebral palsy chair, mat, cabinet
5. It will minimize outside stimulation.
6. False
7. After the room is ready and the correct toy has been selected, the student can be brought to the assessment room.
8. Assessment area
   Name
   Date
9. Direct observation
10. A check mark for a correct response and a blank space for an incorrect response.
11. Any Objective and criterion taken from pages 76 to 92 will be acceptable.
12. Assure reliability among raters if the criterion is consistent.
13.

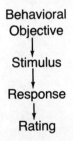

Behavioral
Objective
↓
Stimulus
↓
Response
↓
Rating

14. Behavioral Objectives state specifically what behavior is to be observed.
   The stimulus is the event which precedes and sets the occasion for the response.
   The response is the activity the person performs.
   The rating is a check mark (√) if the response is positive and a blank if the response is negative.
15. Verbal command
   Demonstration
   Toy
16. Rating—because the instructional cycle trains the behavior, the assessment chain merely assesses the behavior.
17. The instructional cycle has a reinforcing component and the assessment chain has a rating component.
18. The illustrations must contain a verbal command, a demonstration of the desired response, and a toy.
19. When the student has been assessed.

CHAPTER THREE ANSWERS

1. False—all Checklists are reviewed before remediation begins.
2. Viewing the entire Checklist
3. B
4. It would be the first blank space encountered in one area of a Checklist (i.e., Attending).
5. The student would be training on one Objective from several areas.
6. The student cannot follow a moving object circularly.
7. Training time
8. Three
9. a. Target the first deficit behavior within a Checklist area
   b. List the Objectives and select three that are most similar or that present the least amount of conflict in training.
10. No—each student should have an individual assessment which outlines his specific problems.

CHAPTER FOUR ANSWERS

1. Task Analysis

2. It is a set of skills the student is to accomplish to perform the target response.
3. The operant level is the last Step within the Task Analysis that the student has already assimilated in his behavioral repertoire.
4. An Objective is prescribed.
5. A reinforcer is the thing or event following a behavior that will increase the possibility of the behavior occurring again.
6. No—everyone has different likes and dislikes.
7. A survey can be taken in which one would record the food, toys, and activities that interest the student.
8. Immediate
9. Less effective it will be.
10. Any example is acceptable if verbal praise and/or a pat on the back occur before the edible reinforcer.
11. Continuous
12. After the student has learned the desired response, continuous reinforcement is no longer necessary.
13. Intermittent
14. True
15. A prompt is assistance given by the trainer to the student to help him perform the response.
16. Physical, gestural, and verbal
17. The example must describe a physical manipulation by the trainer.
18. The example must describe a gesture made by the trainer.
19. The example must describe a verbal command given by the trainer.
20. Fading

CHAPTER FIVE

Reinforcement Questions I

1. a. No
   b. Yes—a reinforcer was given for the inappropriate behaviors of crying, kicking, and screaming.
   c. Cookie
   d. When Harry is quiet.
2. The only items we can be positive about are that a reinforcement is given; it occurs immediately after the desirable behavior and there is an appropriate state of deprivation. If Hazel continues this procedure, there should be an increase in the behavior.
3. a. No
   b. He could have told her that he appreciated the ckicken dinner but that he would like to try different types of meals in the future.
   c. No
4. a. She is reinforcing politeness in asking permission to go out and play.
   b. The reinforcement is a kiss and permission to play outside.
5. a. Irma received praise for her new clothes and was able to buy beautiful gifts for her grandchildren.
6. As you read your story, check off each item on the reinforcement review. Include any item you missed.
7. Clyde was receiving juice all day. An appropriate state of deprivation did not exist.
8. a. Debbie was doing this for attention.
   b. Her mother would strengthen the behavior.
   c. Debbie should get attention when remaining dry and not when screaming.
   d. The reinforcer is the mother's attention.
9. a. Praise and treats
   b. The people working with Louie must refrain from giving him praise or treats.
   c. Louie will not respond to the training because an appropriate level of deprivation will not be established.

Reinforcement Questions II

1. Yes
2. Yes
3. Yes
4. Yes
5. No

CHAPTER FIVE ANSWERS

1. Model
2. Five

3. Third
4. Increase
5. Decrease
6. False
7. Physical
   Gestural
   Verbal
8. False
9. False
10. Most of the prompts are included in the instructions. When the prompts are not included, it should be the responsibility of the teacher, nurse, or psychologist.

Questions for Parents on Prompting and Fading

1. Prompting
2. Verbal, gestural, command, gesture, physical
3. No
4. True
5. Five
6. Verbal command alone
7. Fading
8. Begin again with the last successful prompt.
9. Yes
10. Gradually

CHAPTER SIX ANSWERS

1. Ivan
2. Auditory training
3. 3
4. 2
5. Cheese bits
6. Terry
7. Gestural
8. A (√) indicates a successful response.
9. A (0) indicates an unsuccessul response.
10. A training session is ended:
    a. after a student makes five consecutive positive responses to one prompt.
    b. after five consecutive incorrect responses.
    c. after ten incorrect responses.
    d. after twenty trials.
11. The total in a session.
12. The total plus (0) in a session.
13. The total consecutive (√) in a session.

CHAPTER SEVEN ANSWERS

1. What the learner will be doing.
2. c., d.
3. Observable acts
4. Any phrase that states an observable act is acceptable
5. The student will _____ after attaining five consecutive positive responses to a verbal command on each Step of the Task Analysis.
6. It breaks the behavior down into easy-to-teach steps.
7. 1. What is your goal?
   2. What are your entering behaviors?
   3. What steps lie between the goal and the entering behavior?
8. 3a. List the skills for that Objective.
   3b. Sequence the skills.
9. See page 226.
10. See page 194.

CHAPTER EIGHT ANSWERS

1. A maintenance program is instituted.
2. One
3. During a fifteen-minute maintenance session, a stimulus is provided in the appropriate environment.
4. Objective 4 should be placed on a maintenance schedule.
5. Motor Development, Eye-Hand Coordination, Language, Eating
6. One can say that a behavior has generalized from the training area to the appropriate environment if a student can operate a busy box in the training area as well as on the ward floor. Behavior has also generalized if the student has been trained on the first

three Objectives of a Checklist and suddenly can master Objective 4 without training.

7. It will tell you if generalization has occurred and if there is a need for maintenance.

8. a

9. Feedback
   Observable record

10. c

APPENDIX THREE

Answers TO Chapter Stories

STORY 1-A

1. Objective—3, Eye-Hand Coordination
   Stimulus—command
   toy
   demonstration
   Response—Sammy drops the sound tube into the box.
   Reinforcer—The teacher squirted Kool-Aid into Sammy's mouth, but it was not a reinforcer because he didn't like it.
2. The correct response indicated that the appropriate Objective had been selected. If the response doesn't occur again, it will tell you that the reinforcer was not effective.
3. Sammy did not find the Kool-Aid to be reinforcing.

STORY 1-B

1. Objective—4, Motor Development/Sitting
   Stimulus—command
   Response—no response
   Reinforcer—Miss Terry was not able to reinforce because the behavior did not occur.
2. Because there was no response and all alternative stimulus situations were tried, we know that the Objective is inappropriate. The training sessions have never been reinforced in two months and they may become aversive.
3. There was no feedback on the reinforcer because an opportunity to use it never arose. A further indication of an inappropriate Objective.

STORY 1-C

1. Objective—14, Eye-Hand Coordination
   Stimulus—verbal command
   toy

demonstration
Response—inappropriately pushes button
Reinforcer—aggravating teacher
A solution to this problem would consist of masking out the other objects on the busy surprise box.

STORY 2-A

1. Objective—1, Sound Imitation
Stimulus—an inappropriate command
no demonstration
Response—none
Rating—Sonya cannot clap her hands upon command
2. He is arbitrarily assigning the same Objective to all the students.

STORY 2-B

Objective—1, Object Discrimination
Stimulus—no demonstration
command
Response—laughing
Rating—blank

STORY 2-C

1. Attending, look
2. The teacher gives a command and uses a physical prompt. Prompting is not allowed during assessment.
3. The student looks at the doll. No—the teacher is physically manipulating the student's head.
4. Yes, the use of a reinforcer when the teacher hugs the student.

STORY 3-A

Objective:

1. 11, Eye-Hand Coordination
2. 6, Auditory Training, or 4, Physical Imitation
3. 3, Sound Imitation

STORY 3-B

Objective:

1. 3, Motor Development/Head and Trunk Control
2. 1, Physical Eating Problems
3. 1, Attending

STORY 3-C

Mother to Train at Home:

Object Discrimination Objective 1

Hospital Training:

1. Auditory Training, Objective 11, or Physical Imitation, Objective 5
2. Eye-Hand Coordination, Objective 34
3. Concept Development, Objective 1

STORY 4-A

1. Use physical, gestural, and verbal prompts appropriately.
2. Fade prompts from physical to gestural to verbal.
3. Use a bridging technique during reinforcement.
4. Reinforce immediately after the appropriate behavior occurs.
5. Go on to the next Step after the student responds with five consecutive responses to a verbal command.

STORY 4-B

1. She did not prescribe an Objective for each student based on his individual needs. She should go back and administer individual assessment.
2. She did not determine an operant level. The teacher should do this after each individual assessment.
3. The student's reinforcement preference was not determined. The teacher should do this before training begins.

4. The reinforcement schedule is not appropriate because we are not sure which students are learning a new behavior.
5. The aide is doing an excellent job using Steps 1,3, and 4.

STORY 4-C

1. The teacher did not determine an operant level.
2. The aide was using a verbal prompt for all students when some probably needed a physical or gestural prompt.

STORY 6-A

See data sheet

STORY 6-B

Trial—2
Step—2
Trainer Signature—Jerry
Day and Date—12/2/76
Prompt—gestural

STORY 6-C

1. In Trial 1, Myrtle did not end the training session after five consecutive correct responses.
2. In Trial 2, Myrtle did not end the training session after five consecutive correct responses.
3. In Trial 3, Myrtle did not stop after five consecutive responses.
4. In Trial 4, Myrtle went on to a new Step before Step 2 was complete. Also, she continued training after five consecutive incorrect responses
5. She returned to the appropriate Step but not to the appropriate prompt. Also, she continued training after five consecutive incorrect responses.

DATA SHEET

Name **Sally** Objective **7**

Area **Eye-Hand Coordination** Reinforcers **peppermint patties**

TRIAL **1**

1	2	3	4	5	6	7	8	9	10
11	12	13	14	15	16	17	18	19	20

Step **2**

Trainer signature **your name**

Day and Date **today's date**

Prompt **gestural**

1. Correct responses _____
2. Total responses _____
3. Highest number consecutive responses _____

TRIAL ___

1	2	3	4	5	6	7	8	9	10
11	12	13	14	15	16	17	18	19	20

Step ___

Trainer signature _____

Day and Date _____

Prompt _____

1. Correct responses _____
2. Total responses _____
3. Highest number consecutive responses _____

TRIAL ___

1	2	3	4	5	6	7	8	9	10
11	12	13	14	15	16	17	18	19	20

Step ___

Trainer signature _____

Day and Date _____

Prompt _____

1. Correct responses _____
2. Total responses _____
3. Highest number consecutive responses _____

TRIAL ___

1	2	3	4	5	6	7	8	9	10
11	12	13	14	15	16	17	18	19	20

Step ___

Trainer signature _____

Day and Date _____

Prompt _____

1. Correct responses _____
2. Total responses _____
3. Highest number consecutive responses _____

TRIAL ___

1	2	3	4	5	6	7	8	9	10
11	12	13	14	15	16	17	18	19	20

Step ___

Trainer signature _____

Day and Date _____

Prompt _____

1. Correct responses _____
2. Total responses _____
3. Highest number consecutive responses _____

STORY 8-A

Elaine should be assessed on the therapy evaluation form. Immediate feedback should be given after assessment so that Elaine's problems can be eliminated.

STORY 8-B

1. Provide a maintenance program for the newly acquired Objectives.
2. No—She can institute a maintenance program.
3. It should be spent on maintenance since all the Objectives have been mastered in the training area.

APPENDIX FOUR

Selected Bibliography

Ayllon, T., and Roberts, M. 1974. Eliminating discipline problems by strengthening academic performance. J. Appl. Behav. Anal. 1:71–76.

Baer, D. M., Wolf, M. M., and Risley, T. R. 1968. Some current dimensions of applied behavior analysis. J. Appl. Behav. Anal. 1:91–97.

Baer, D. M., and Wolf, M. M. 1968. The reinforcement contingency in preschool and remedial education. R. D. Hess and Baer, R. M. eds., Early Education: Current Theory, Research and Practice. Aldine, Chicago.

Bandura, A., (ed.). 1974. Psychological Modeling: Conflicting Theories. Lieber-Atherton, New York.

Bandura, A., Ross, E., and Ross, S. A. 1963. Vicarious reinforcement and imitative learning. J. Abnorm. Soc. Psych. 67:601–607.

Barton, E. S. 1970. Inappropriate speech in a severely retarded child: A case study in language conditioning and generalization. J. Appl. Behav. Anal. 4:299–307.

Becker, W. C. 1971. Parents Are Teachers. Research Press, Champaign, Ill.

Becker, W. C. 1969. Teaching Children: A Child Management Program for Parents. Engleman-Becker Corporation, Champaign, Ill.

Bradfield, R. H. 1970. Behavior Modification: The Human Effort. Fearon Publishers, Belmont, Calif.

Doke, L. A., and Risley, T. R. 1972. The organization of day-care environments: Required versus optional Activities. J. Appl. Behav. Anal. 5:405–420.

Doll, E. A. 1965. The Vineland Social Maturity Scale. American Guidance Service, Circle Pines, Minnesota.

Foster, R. 1974. Camelot Behavioral Checklist. Camelot Behavioral Systems, Parsons, Kanses.

Gagné, R. M. 1965. The Conditions of Learning. Holt, Rinehart, & Winston, New York.

Gray, B. B., and Ryan, B. P. 1974. A Language Program for the Non-language Child. Research Press, Champaign, Ill.

Gunzburg, R. 1900. Primary Progress Assessment Chart of Social Development. Bristol, Indiana.

Hihira, K. Foster, R. Shellhaas, M. and Leland, H. 1975. AAMD Adaptive Behavior Scale. American Association on Mental Deficiency, Washington, D.C.

Jakobovits, L., and Miron, M. (eds.). 1967. Readings in the Psychology of Language. Prentice-Hall, Englewood Cliffs, N.J.

Keller, F. S. 1969. A programmed system of instruction. Ed. Tech. Monogr. 2:1–26.

Kent, L. 1974. Language Acquisition Program for the Retarded or Multiply Impaired. Research Press, Champaign, Ill.

Mykelbust, H. 1957. Auditory Disorders in Children. Grune and Stratton, New York.

Nelson, G. L., Cone, J. D., and Christopher, R. 1975. Training correct utensil use in retarded children. Am. J. Ment. Defic. 80:114–22.

O'Leary, D. K., and O'Leary, S. (eds.). 1972. Classroom Management: The Successful Use of Behavior Modification. Pergamon Press, New York.

Rood, M. An Introduction to Treatment Techniques. Printed and Distributed by Intermediate School District, County of Macomb, Mich.

Smith. D. E. P., and Smith, J. M. 1968. Teacher's Manual for the Michigan Language Program. Ann Arbor Publishers, Ann Arbor Mich.

Smith, W. L. 1971. Ending the isolation of the handicapped. Am. Ed. November:29–33.

Tate, B. G. 1972. Case Study: Control of Chronic Self-Injurious Behavior by Conditioning Procedures. Reprint from Behavior Therapy, 3(1), by Academic Press, New York.

U.S. Congressional and Administrative News. 1974. 93d Congress Educational Amendments of 1974. P.L. 93–380, p. 4257.

U.S. Congressional and Administrative News. 1974. 93d Congress, Vol. 3, p. 4138.

Vulpe, S. G. 1900. Vulpe Assessment Battery. National Institute on Mental Retardation of the Canadian Association for the Mentally Retarded, Canada.

Walls, R. T. 1975. Behavior Checklists. A paper presented at the Behavior Assessment in Clinical Psychology Conference, West Virginia University.

Williams, R. L 1975. Teaching a Multiply-Handicapped Child Receptive Language and Self-Feeding Skills. From a paper first presented at the First Annual Mid-western Association of Behavior Analysis, Chicago, May, 1975.

Student Assessment Chart

Following are five Student Assessment Charts. They are filled out according to each student's baseline level, and they show the students' completed Objectives.

STUDENT ASSESSMENT CHART
CA- student 2K

Objective Number

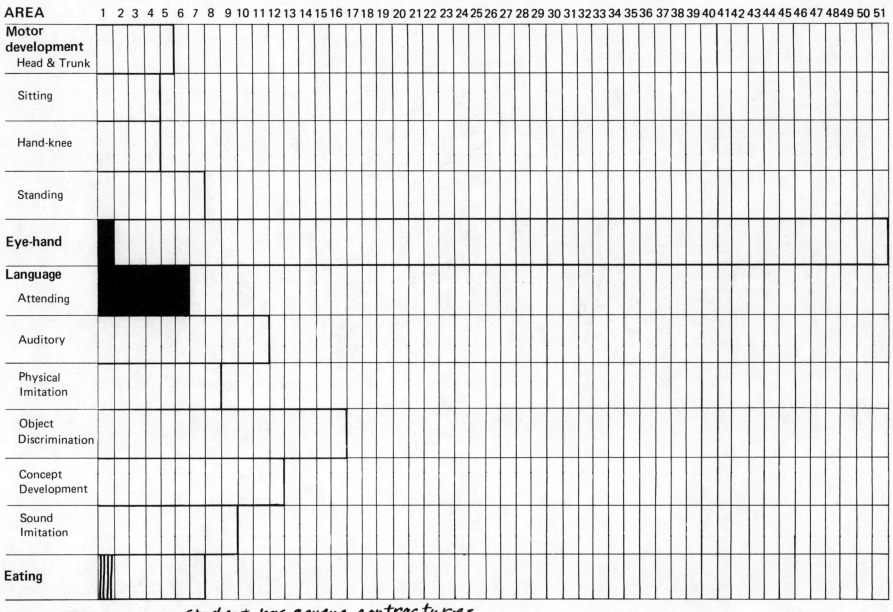

| AREA | 1 | 2 | 3 | 4 | 5 | 6 | 7 | 8 | 9 | 10 | 11 | 12 | 13 | 14 | 15 | 16 | 17 | 18 | 19 | 20 | 21 | 22 | 23 | 24 | 25 | 26 | 27 | 28 | 29 | 30 | 31 | 32 | 33 | 34 | 35 | 36 | 37 | 38 | 39 | 40 | 41 | 42 | 43 | 44 | 45 | 46 | 47 | 48 | 49 | 50 | 51 |

Motor development
Head & Trunk

Sitting

Hand-knee

Standing

Eye-hand

Language
Attending

Auditory

Physical Imitation

Object Discrimination

Concept Development

Sound Imitation

Eating

Baseline ■   Comments: *Student has severe contractures*

Completed Objectives ▥

423

STUDENT ASSESSMENT CHART
CA - Student 2D
Objective Number

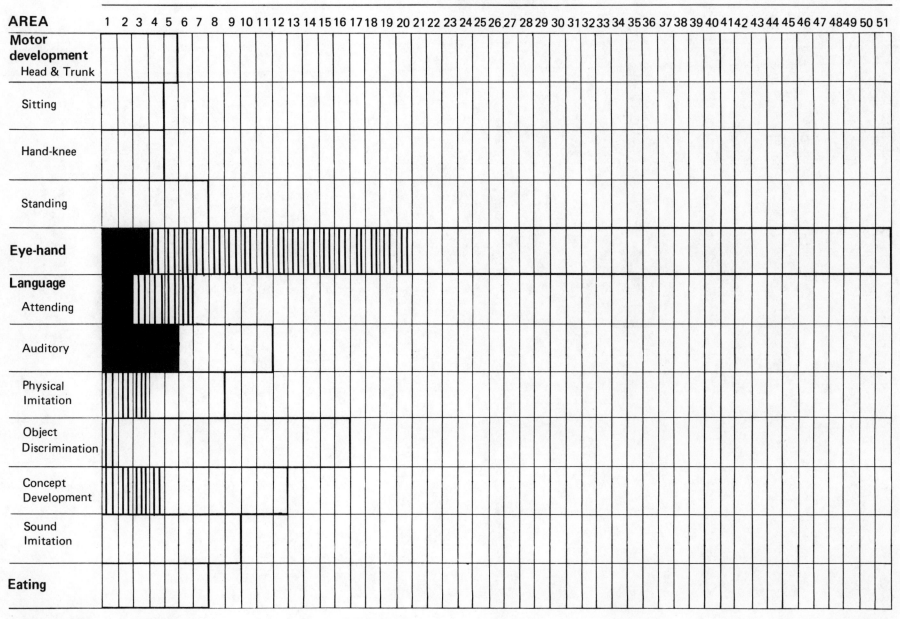

AREA	1 2 3 4 5 6 7 8 9 10 11 12 13 14 15 16 17 18 19 20 21 22 23 24 25 26 27 28 29 30 31 32 33 34 35 36 37 38 39 40 41 42 43 44 45 46 47 48 49 50 51

Motor development
Head & Trunk

Sitting

Hand-knee

Standing

Eye-hand

Language
Attending

Auditory

Physical Imitation

Object Discrimination

Concept Development

Sound Imitation

Eating

Baseline ■

Completed Objectives ▥

Comments:

STUDENT ASSESSMENT CHART

CA Student 1 J

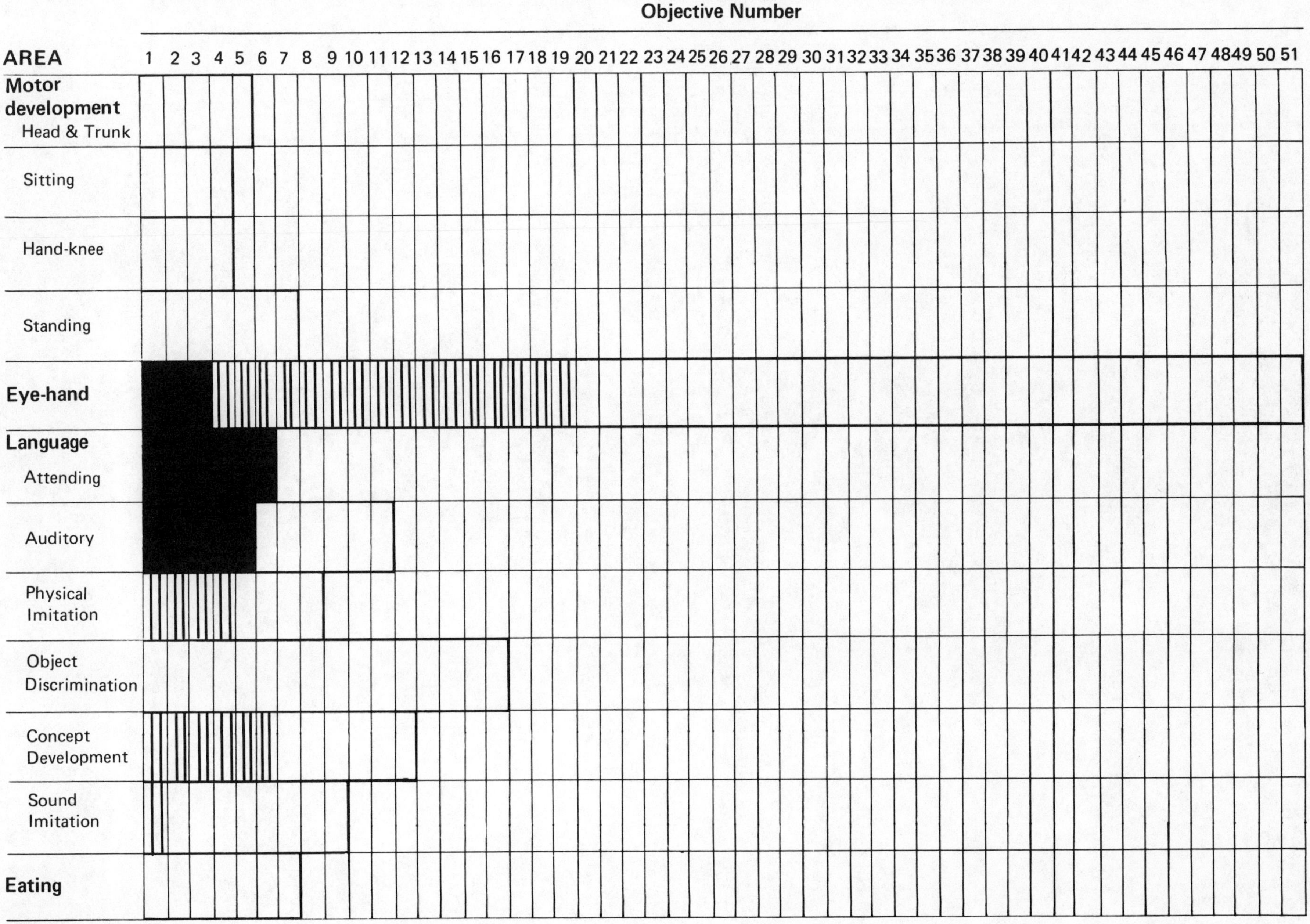

Objective Number
AREA
1 2 3 4 5 6 7 8 9 10 11 12 13 14 15 16 17 18 19 20 21 22 23 24 25 26 27 28 29 30 31 32 33 34 35 36 37 38 39 40 41 42 43 44 45 46 47 48 49 50 51
Motor development
Head & Trunk
Sitting
Hand-knee
Standing
Eye-hand
Language
Attending
Auditory
Physical Imitation
Object Discrimination
Concept Development
Sound Imitation
Eating

Baseline ■

Completed Objectives ▥

Comments:

STUDENT ASSESSMENT CHART

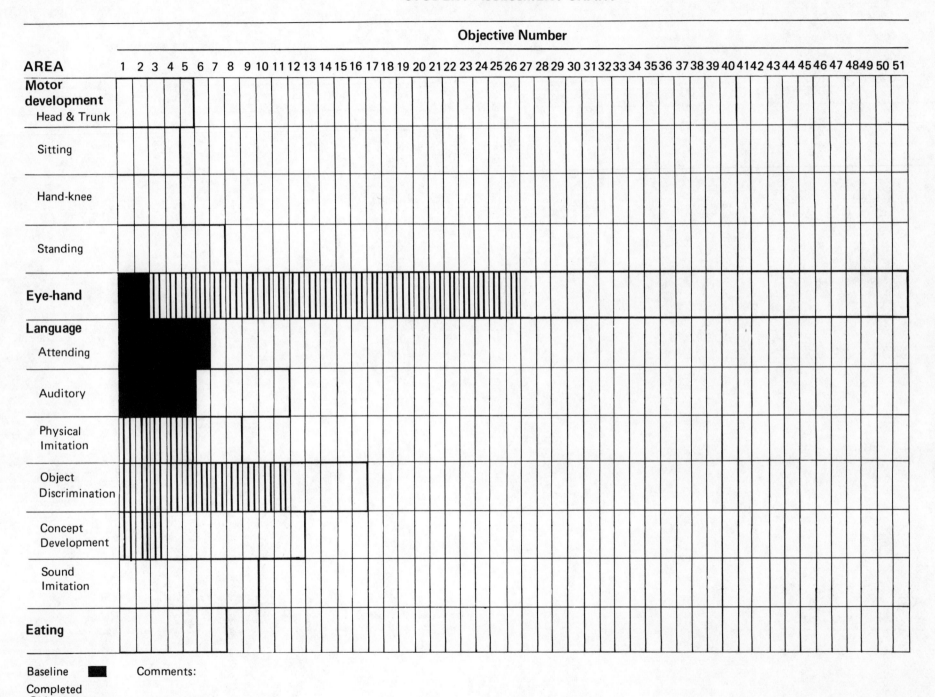

Objective Number

AREA — 1 2 3 4 5 6 7 8 9 10 11 12 13 14 15 16 17 18 19 20 21 22 23 24 25 26 27 28 29 30 31 32 33 34 35 36 37 38 39 40 41 42 43 44 45 46 47 48 49 50 51

Motor development
- Head & Trunk
- Sitting
- Hand-knee
- Standing

Eye-hand

Language
- Attending
- Auditory
- Physical Imitation
- Object Discrimination
- Concept Development
- Sound Imitation

Eating

Baseline ▮ Comments:

Completed Objectives ▥

429

STUDENT ASSESSMENT CHART

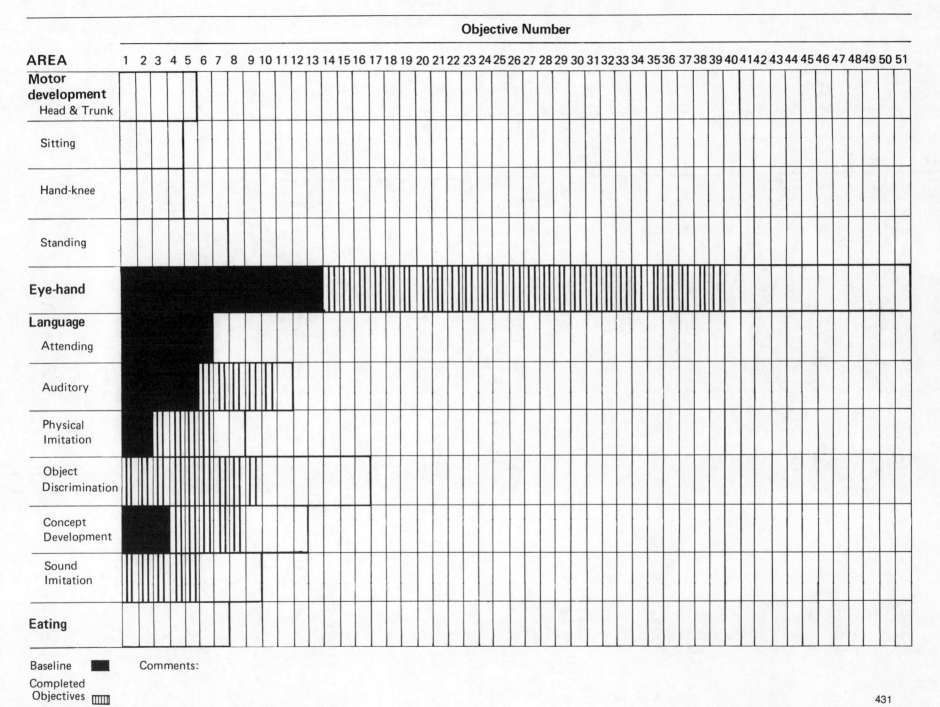

Objective Number

| AREA | 1 2 3 4 5 6 7 8 9 10 11 12 13 14 15 16 17 18 19 20 21 22 23 24 25 26 27 28 29 30 31 32 33 34 35 36 37 38 39 40 41 42 43 44 45 46 47 48 49 50 51 |

Motor development
Head & Trunk

Sitting

Hand-knee

Standing

Eye-hand

Language
Attending

Auditory

Physical Imitation

Object Discrimination

Concept Development

Sound Imitation

Eating

Baseline ■   Comments:

Completed Objectives ▥

431